Jonathan B. Piercy
The Power of Light; The Deception of Darkness

God Desires You

Dove Christian Publishers

Dedication

Ahmarée and Javid, my most precious and dearest earthly possessions. My sons, you have what it takes, and you know where to go to find the strength to successfully climb the rough side of life's mountain. I need you both to survive.

Table of Contents

Foreword

I have known Jonathan for a long time. Our fathers were very good friends, and as a boy, I watched them "holding court" for hours. As a young adult, Jonathan and my father became kindred spirits and engaged in many intellectual sparring matches. For much of this time, I was living in the USA, pursuing my professional boxing career. As a result, Jonathan and I didn't become close friends until about 16 years ago, when he ran as a candidate for the political party I supported in the Cayman Islands.

It isn't often we meet people we can relate to on a broad range of issues. As I became more acquainted with Jonathan, I realised he and I shared a deep love and commitment for our homeland, the beautiful Cayman Islands. We also find injustice abhorrent. We both have a deep love for the Bible and have had many conversations surrounding the love of God, country, justice and fairness, care and concern for our fellowman. Because we share many of the same fundamental beliefs, Jonathan and I have become brothers from another mother.

This book is about the love, mercy, goodness, and grace of God. It is a reminder to everyone that no matter where we may be in our lives, God is still present, eagerly awaiting our invitation to come into our lives so that He can transform us and bless us abundantly. This book is meant to motivate and enlighten readers about our true purpose in life. If we find our true purpose, God will use us in unbelievable ways, and He will prosper us.

I have been through some tough times, yet I can attest to God's goodness. Although I was much too young to understand as a young child, I now realise that God's hand has always been in my life, working on my behalf. As a young boy, I frequently prayed and spoke to God about my goals and aspirations. My dream, from about the age of two, was to become a professional boxer. Many people laughed at me and said I wasn't good enough. But our God is faithful.

When I was seven years old, I prayed and asked God to help me one day to be able to buy my own house, mortgage-free. Thirty years later, in the middle of the 2009 financial crisis, God answered that prayer. As for that boxing career, I have won eight titles, and I am still living my dream. God has parted many a Red Sea for me! If only you trust Him, He will do the same for you.

This book will encourage you if you are moving through life haphazardly, battling despair and hurt, questioning why you're experiencing such tough times, or why has life been so unkind. Jonathan intends to remind us of the good news of salvation, redemption, and forgiveness, as well as God's enduring love, mercy, and grace. You will find answers if you are searching for a greater understanding of the Creator of the universe and hoping to discover the real roadmap to life. Many of us have been discouraged by life's circumstances. We need to remember that no matter how big our mountains are, God is much bigger. He promises never to leave us or forsake us.

When you read this book, you will pick up on Jonathan's optimism and enthusiasm, that he comes from a position of great leisure and comfort. Not so! This book is inspired by Jonathan's personal testimony that God is true to His Word and will stick to us closer than a brother, even and especially during the hard times. God provides for the birds and the bees of the air, and so too will He provide for His children. As we all know, no matter the strength of our faith, when we face trying times, our faith is tested. Jonathan, ever the caring and compassionate man–while going through his struggles and challenges–reassures others who also struggle that God is still in control. He will always be the great "I AM."

I hope you will find Jonathan's words inspiring, empowering, and enlightening.

Charles E. Whittaker, Professional Boxer
Former USBA, NABO, WBA, IBO, NBA, WBC Champion,
and former number two ranked in the world by the IBF.

Acknowledgements

All praises to Yahuah (YHUH/God the Father) for setting a table before me in the presence of my enemies and anointing my head with oil. For allowing my enemies to stumble and fall. For keeping me in the palm of Your hand. You are the great I AM. Your mercies never cease! They are renewed every morning; great is Your faithfulness. Hallelujah in the highest! Eternal thanks for Your Son, Yahusha Ha'Mashiach (Jesus the Messiah), who died and rose again so I might have eternal life.

Thanks to Mummy and Daddy for your prayers over my life and for showing me the way.

Special thanks to the "Ravens" who, by God's divine love and guidance, fed me in every way imaginable during my most vulnerable times. You all know who you are. May God bless you abundantly from His riches in glory. Blessings eternal!

Introduction

A Most Sobering Dilemma

For God hath not given us the spirit of fear; but of power, and of love, and of a sound mind (2 Timothy 1:7).

Clinical depression affects millions of people throughout the world today. Within the Christian community, tens of thousands battle depression daily. It comes in many forms, and its impact varies widely. Some people suffer from major depression, while others face persistent depression. Many people struggle with bipolar disorder, seasonal depression, situational depression, or depressive psychosis. Most, if not all of us, will experience periods of anxiety and depression. This is perfectly normal. The uncertainty of life and the traumatic incidents of failure and loss, bring sudden, random, and sometimes permanent, changes that send many to ride on the turbulent, emotional rollercoaster of life. However, extended or continuous bouts of profound, deep sadness and anxiety, lasting for more than two weeks, affecting our ability to function as we normally would, can be a sign of clinical depression.

In addition to deep sadness, other common symptoms of clinical depression may include a general lack of interest in anything, feelings of hopelessness, guilt, fear, shame, and profound regret. An overpowering sense of worthlessness, meaninglessness, and brokenness. Clinical depression can cause profound changes in your sleep, sex drive, and appetite, difficulty in getting through normal activities, withdrawal from family and friends, and lack of mental focus, stamina, and energy. Emotions range from profound happiness to crippling fear and sadness.

Clinical depression pushes you into a very small box. It extinguishes all light and places you in a freezer with incapacitating, emotional cold, leaving you despondent. It removes all exits, trapping you. Clinical depression erases hope and blocks your ability to think critically about what needs to be done to loosen its death grip on your life. Instead, the black box gets darker, colder, smaller, and more suffocating. If left uninterrupted, it will lead you to its only final destination: A horrific dead end. There, you will find yourself questioning the reason for your existence and your purpose in life, which you feel at that moment is inconsequential. Ultimately, you may be left with an intense longing to end your life.

I can speak about this subject in graphic, sobering, authoritative, and deeply personal ways because, for many years, I was clinically depressed.

I know what it's like to not want to get out of bed. Wanting to keep the blackout shades, covering the bedroom windows, down. Not wanting even the smallest ray of sunlight to shine on the floor. Depressed from simply knowing the morning was breaking, I cursed the sunlight because it signalled another godforsaken day I had to face. For countless days, I didn't feel like taking a shower or coming out of my room to see or speak with anyone. Many days, had it not been for my dog, needing to go outdoors to do his business, I wouldn't have even ventured outside. I hated to hear my phone ring or receive a message from anyone. I just wanted to be left, the heck, alone.

I became one with the *physical* darkness. For a time, I found comfort and protection in it. I was able to disappear and vanish from anything that caused me grief, and I enjoyed the cocoon it provided. I could feel its grip fastening and interweaving itself into my life. I foolishly welcomed its presence. I was deeply depressed, which came from a place of feeling mostly unappreciated, demeaned, misunderstood, and unfairly treated.

These feelings grew exponentially because I liberally fed them with regret, doubt, shame, malice, hurt, rage, and revenge. Ostracising myself from people who cared for me, who tried to get into my personal space to assist me, added to my mental and spiritual decline. I became so disoriented. I couldn't identify friends from foes. I believed most wanted to get close to me simply to stick a dagger in my back, then criticise and admonish me for complaining about the pain while taking their precious time twisting it out. Some poured cold water on my dreams and aspirations. Others, I felt, chose not to see my many fruitless attempts to beat back the trials in my life and bravely move forward.

Feelings of worthlessness and meaninglessness preoccupied almost every thought. I washed daily and methodically in self-pity, incessantly reminding myself that no one loved me, that people are mostly selfish, and that the world is continually wicked and evil will eventually win. These self-deprecating thoughts were devoid of any optimism and, more importantly, hope. I convinced myself that I was walking alone–aimlessly in the world without a purpose or a plan and the best thing that could happen was for my life to end. No one knew just how far gone I was. I went to great lengths to mask and suppress these feelings. Writing this is the first time I have publicly revealed these thoughts and feelings.

Initially, I was unmolested by these beliefs and, to a large extent, welcomed the emotional metamorphosis. I felt justified in these feelings and content in playing the role of victim. Consequently, I felt the need to live in a cave where isolation was its walls and sorrow, its ceiling and floor. I became one with my (dark) environment, and the *spiritual* darkness started to shape me. What came next scared me.

I *literally* felt the pull of spiritual darkness. I sensed it consuming me, wiping out all thoughts of purpose and meaning in my life and replacing my last fleeting memories of hope with continual despair and failure. I remember feeling depressed during the days, but in the evenings, as the night crept into full bloom, I sensed a sliver of optimism about the promise of tomorrow and occasionally made general plans, a to-do list, so to speak. *Tomorrow, I will get up and go out. I will read and research tomorrow. I will go to a friend's house tomorrow. I'll reply to my emails and complete some work assignments.* For most people, some of these tasks are so minuscule they barely qualify as trivial accomplishments. Nevertheless, this was my proud and glorious depiction of optimism. Unfortunately, that optimism seldomly outlasted the night.

The darkness of depression overwhelmed me. It held me in its crushing grip. Not wanting to admit being depressed, I kept thinking I would eventually come out of it. I thought it was just some silly, melancholy feeling I could bring myself out from and shake off. I later came to realise that every attempt to overcome my depression in my own power ended in complete failure. The energy I exerted every time weakened me physically, psychologically and spiritually so that, eventually, I didn't have the energy to get up off the floor. For the first time, I realised I was way over my head. I needed supernatural help to overcome. This is when I began asking God to reach me because I couldn't even reach myself. I didn't know where I was, but I knew I was consumed in spiritual darkness. It felt like pure desolation, where demons were poised to consume me. I didn't know which way was up.

I couldn't find my true north. I did the only thing I thought worthwhile to do: "Yahusha (Jesus), save me!" I literally cried out to Him. *And it shall come to pass, that whosoever shall call on the name of the Lord shall be saved* (Acts 2:21).

That was the turning point of my life. I recognised I needed God's help. However, my transformation from darkness to light, out of depression, didn't happen overnight. As a matter of fact, I initially felt like my prayers hadn't even left my mind, let alone my room. However, as my desperation grew, my total faith and reliance on Him also grew. I earnestly pleaded with God to reach me supernaturally, telepathically, in some spiritual, indescribable way, through some hidden door that only He, divine Creator of the universe, could access.

Glory to God! He heard my prayers and reached me, precisely where I was and right on time. He has been leading me back to His tabernacle, His dwelling place, where His perfect love surrounds and protects me. It's been a gradual and sometimes painful journey back to the light, but I am so thankful to be alive. Having all of my faculties is a testament to the grace, mercy and loving-kindness of God. Hallelujah!

This book isn't about me. It's about God's infinite mercy, power, love and generosity toward us. He can reach us wherever we are. *If I ascend into heaven, You are there; If I make my bed in hell, behold, You are there* (Psalm 139:8 NKJV). The apostle Paul, who wrote most of the books contained in the New Testament Bible, asks:

> *Who shall separate us from the love of Christ? Shall tribulation, or distress, or persecution, or famine, or nakedness, or peril, or sword? As it is written, for thy sake we are killed all the day long; we are accounted as sheep for the slaughter. Nay, in all these things we are more than conquerors through Him that loved us. For I am persuaded, that neither death, nor life, nor angels, nor principalities, nor powers, nor things present, nor things to come, nor height, nor depth, nor any other creature, shall be able to separate us from the love of God, which is in Christ Jesus our Lord. (Romans 8:35–39)*

Fortunately, I was brought up in a home where God was central. From a very early age, I was taught many truths about my heavenly Father. The Bible was read to me from an early age and I was tasked with committing many verses to memory. Regrettably, not even my knowledge of the Bible could protect me from my depression. You see, I (intellectually) knew *of* Him, but I didn't *know* (experience) Him. *And ye shall seek me, and find me, when ye shall search for me with all your heart* (Jeremiah 29:13).

Many who are suffering today were not raised in a God-centred household. Many others believe there is a God, but don't know how to access Him. For a long time, I was one of these people. While in the midst of the darkness of depression, I didn't realise that without strong faith and a committed, personal relationship with my heavenly Father, I was quite literally fighting a losing battle. Many people today, are attempting to battle depression in their own strength. Many are fighting the symptoms of depression, like I was, without addressing the underlying cause. Approaching the situation from this angle makes the battle virtually impossible to win. Remember, the fruit of unbelief in God comes from the tree of deception. Specifically, from the branches of elaborate, multifarious, albeit organised, deliberate rebellion brought by naivety, apathy, and an unwillingness to search for and reconnect with our Creator. *The ox knoweth his owner, and the ass his master's crib: but Israel doth not know, my people doth not consider* (Isaiah 1:3).

Some may not believe in the riveting darkness of evil and sin, but that doesn't make it any less real. Some may not recognise evil when they first encounter it. We are told that "seeing is believing." We are sceptical about what we cannot see, smell, feel, or touch, i.e., prove. Others know and acknowledge these things exist because they have directly impacted their lives. For example, the senseless murders of their friends and loved ones, the sex trafficking of their teenage children or family members, drug and sex addiction that has decimated wholesome relationships, and lives cut short by unforeseen tragedy. These things should make it easy for people to accept that evil exists. Still, others have seen shadows or heard unexplained noises throughout their homes. Lights turning on and off without anyone tampering with the switch, or random items levitating. Others may sense an unseen, nefarious presence around them. Maybe some have experienced sudden and unexplained illnesses that cannot be diagnosed by a medical clinician or physician.

Those who have experienced such encounters may seek to investigate these phenomena, using philosophy or science, in an effort to explicate their existence and soften their frightful impact. Many people deny the existence of the supernatural, preferring to adhere to materialism. I will address this in greater detail in the chapter entitled, "Master of the Universe."

When people don't believe in something, they won't search for answers. Because they don't search, they will never find true enlightenment, ultimately losing out on knowledge. *But go and learn what this means: 'I desire mercy, not sacrifice.' For I have not come to call the righteous, but sinners"* (Matthew 9:13 NIV).

The Prince of Darkness, Satan, roams the earth looking to see whom he can destroy through naivety, unbelief and rebellion. *Be sober, be vigilant; because your adversary the devil, as a roaring lion, walketh about, seeking whom he may devour* (1 Peter 5:8).

The Power of Light; The Deception of Darkness is written for:

- Those who don't know who God is: *Hast thou not known? Hast thou not heard, that the everlasting God, the LORD, the Creator of the ends of the earth, fainteth not, neither is weary? there is no searching of his understanding. He giveth power to the faint; and to them that have no might he increaseth strength* (Isaiah 40:28–29). This is God saying, *Haven't you received the email? Haven't you seen the memo? I am the one and only God of heaven and earth.*
- Those who've never been introduced to His Word, the Bible: *For the word of God is alive and active. Sharper than any double-edged sword, it penetrates even to dividing soul and spirit, joints and marrow; it judges the thoughts and attitudes of the heart* (Hebrews 4:12 NIV).
- Those who don't know how to establish a relationship with Him: *If we confess our sins, he is faithful and just to forgive us our sins, and to cleanse us from all unrighteousness* (1 John 1:9).

All of these answers, promises, and more are found in the Bible. However, in the heat of battle, when we are being pursued and crushed by nefarious forces on all sides, we become obtuse and preoccupied with just surviving. The notion of reading the Bible or recalling Scripture remains far from us. Incredibly, in these darkest moments, God will sometimes reveal His plan and purpose for our lives. *"For I know the plans I have for you," declares the LORD, "plans to prosper you and not to harm you, plans to give you hope and a future"* (Jeremiah 29:11 NIV).

Unfortunately, without a powerful antidote to confront prolonged depression, doubt, hopelessness and crippling darkness, evil will lay waste to your mind. Perhaps the only thing preventing you from causing harm to yourself are the ad hoc flashbacks of people in your life whom you don't want to inadvertently hurt. Maybe those are your spouse, your children, your parents, your siblings or your friends. Conceivably, you don't want to leave your children behind in this cold and callous world without your guidance and protection.

Whatever it is that's holding you back from carrying out these dark and diabolical thoughts, I can tell you, unless it's divine and from a place of light, it's only a temporary stay to your ultimate, tragic demise. Unless you can tap into and unleash the great power of the Creator, and finally overcome the monster of dread, it will always recapture your soul. And make no mistake, this is what the entire battle between light and darkness, right and wrong, truth and error is all about. It's a battle for souls. But be encouraged and remember, *[you] can do all things through Christ which strengtheneth [you]* (Philippians 4:13).

Friend, hope arrives when we immediately call upon the name of the Lord and ask Him to save and liberate us. *Now the God of hope fill you with all joy and peace in believing, that ye may abound in hope, through the power of the Holy Ghost* (Romans 15:13).

Hope energises and sanitises the mind. It rids us of emotional clutter and negativity. It brightens and warms our lives as the sun brightens the skies and warms the atmosphere on a cold winter's day. Hope reminds us of who we are, and what we were created for. Our hope in God *is* the supernatural door through which the Holy Spirit enters to feed our minds and nourish our souls with the reassurance of God's steadfast love, mercy, goodness and faithfulness. These rays of hope enlarge our faith as we begin to walk, move, and have our being in the confidence that we have overcome our hellish existence and won the battle. *Then spake Jesus again unto them, saying, I am the light of the world: he that followeth me shall not walk in darkness, but shall have the light of life* (John 8:12).

When we exercise our faith, God, through the Holy Spirit, reaches us. We feel His presence as He compassionately and unambiguously reminds us that we are *His* children. You matter to God. *For God so loved the world, that he gave his only begotten Son, that whosoever believeth in him should not perish, but have everlasting life* (3:16). If you believe Him and hold on to His promises, you will experience a kind of love, a richness of life, and a sense of belonging and importance that you have never experienced before. His love will transform your reality, providing renewed hope and zeal for life, so that others around will see and acknowledge.

2020 Pandemic

Saying 2020 was an awful year would probably be the greatest understatement of the century. It was nothing short of a living nightmare, played out in a loop of horror. An inconceivable experience with a tidal wave of devastation, unlike anything encountered in the last hundred years. To state its impact more simply, 2020 was a total calamity. Most would agree, it's virtually impossible to understate just how horrific 2020 was. Aside from all the ordinary tragic events of a normal year, including but not limited to global warming and its devastating effects; poverty and famine; international war and strife; unreported genocide; untold crimes against humanity; crippling sanctions against countries–making it difficult for many to get access to food, clean water and medical care and the torment of sickness and death from common diseases. Unless you have been sleeping under a rock, you know I am speaking about the COVID (Coronavirus) pandemic.

The world reported hundreds of millions of cases of coronavirus. A high percentage of people recovered but, unfortunately, many lives were lost. Those who died from this horrendous virus included great-grandparents, grandparents, mothers, fathers, aunts, uncles, spouses, partners, sons, daughters, nieces, nephews, cousins, friends and co-workers. Due to the nature and severity of the contagion, entire countries were forced to shut down. Businesses, from small mum-and-pop establishments to high-street, gold-plated corporations and everything in between, were hit extremely hard.

World economies were reporting recessions with a real fear of a deep and lasting world depression. With every wave of the pandemic, countries like France and Italy had to repeatedly shut down and expand their national lockdown policies. The hardest-hit country in the world was the United States of America. Other countries hit hard by the pandemic included China, India, Brazil and Russia. It's now the middle of 2021, and the world is only now beginning to show signs of life. Major world markets are currently unravelling the devastation from the pandemic. Some countries are cautiously optimistic about the immediate future. They are walking a financial and socioeconomic tightrope, as they work to resuscitate their economies.

We are living in interesting and unprecedented times that shock our collective minds and create concern about the future. But we do not need to panic or let depression set in. I'm going to share a secret with you. These times were spoken about in the Bible. *And when ye shall hear of wars and rumours of wars, be ye not troubled: for such things must needs be but the end shall not be yet. For nation shall rise against nation, and kingdom against kingdom: and there shall be earthquakes in divers places, and there shall be famines and troubles: these are the beginnings of sorrows* (Mark 13:7–8).

There will be terrible times in the last days. People will be lovers of themselves, lovers of money, boastful, proud, abusive, disobedient to their parents, ungrateful, unholy, without love, unforgiving, slanderous, without self-control, brutal, not lovers of the good, treacherous, rash, conceited, lovers of pleasure rather than lovers of God—having a form of godliness but denying its power. Have nothing to do with such people. (2 Timothy 3:1–5 NIV)

As uncertain as the future seems right now, God's Word tells us these are just signs that the end is near. In the chapter entitled "Prayer without Faith," I share with you what He instructs us to do during these perilous times to ensure our victory. Rest assured, we need not worry. Instead, we need to speak with our Creator through sincere prayer and leave the battle to Him. The Bible states, ... *The prayer of a righteous person is powerful and effective* (James 5:16 NIV).

God's Word is true. Everything He says and everything He promises will come to pass. *So shall my word be that goeth forth out of my mouth: it shall not return unto me void, but it shall accomplish that which I please, and it shall prosper in the thing whereto I sent it* (Isaiah 55:11). *Not a word failed of any good thing which the LORD had spoken to the house of Israel. All came to pass* (Joshua 21:45 NKJV).

Besides providing us with solid instructions for life, the Word of God contains many promises. God promises to always be with us. *Be strong and of a good courage, fear not, nor be afraid of them: for the LORD thy God, he it is that doth go with thee; he will not fail thee, nor forsake thee* (Deuteronomy 31:6). If you hold on to these promises while trusting and believing that He is true to His Word, God will turn your night into day, your rain into sunshine, your sadness into gladness, your fear into hope and your despair, into a glorious testimony. Imagine what our testimonies could be, from overcoming great trials and tribulations.

You may have heard about the power of positive thinking. Countless books have been written on this subject. Many people have discussed and explored this phenomenon. Some are cynical about it, believing that positive thinking, producing beneficial outcomes, is a kind of New Age, spiritual, hocus-pocus philosophy. Nothing more than pie in the sky. They argue that if the power of positive thinking were true, why can't starving people around the world positively think about a "Happy Meal" and make it appear? How about the struggling, unemployed individual trying to make rent to avoid eviction? Should he think happy thoughts of finding his dream job and making six figures? Having unwavering faith, and putting in the requisite work equivalent to your faith, will eventually result in a favourable outcome. Even the many pitfalls and failures along the way will strengthen your resolve, keeping you focused on the goal. The truth is that faith without works *is* dead. It takes abundant faith to truly *keep* the faith.

You may be surprised to learn that the Bible encourages positive thinking. *Finally, brethren, whatsoever things are true, whatsoever things are honest, whatsoever things are just, whatsoever things are pure, whatsoever things are lovely, whatsoever things are of good report; if there be any virtue, and if there be any praise, think on these things* (Philippians 4:8). Just remember, nothing lasts forever. *Weeping may endure for a night, but joy cometh in the morning* (Psalm 30:5). If your goals are in line with God's plan and purpose for your life, and if you have the tenacity to persevere and the audacity to hope, no matter the difficulty and struggles along the way, you *will* succeed. Throughout our darkest moments, God is with us–to fight our battles. To protect us and encourage us. To let us know that we are His children and He will never leave us. Our part is to simply believe and follow Him.

The Unseen Battle

A behind-the-scenes battle is occurring daily in each of our lives. This battle is not the conventional sort. It cannot be seen in the physical realm, but the stakes are high. *Put on the full armor of God, so that you can take your stand against the devil's schemes. For our struggle is not against flesh and blood, but against the rulers, against the authorities, against the powers of this dark world and against the spiritual forces of evil in the heavenly realms. Therefore put on the full armor of God, so that when the day of evil comes, you may be able to stand your ground, and after you have done everything, to stand* (Ephesians 6:11–13 NIV).

Although we cannot see what's happening, we can certainly feel the effects of the battle. We often sense the battle amid circumstances in our lives or through random thoughts or feelings. Have you ever become overwhelmed with a feeling of anxiety or depression, or became consumed with dark and evil thoughts, for no apparent reason? Have you ever helped someone through an act of kindness and then questioned why you did what you did? After praying about something, have you experienced a feeling of defeat, depleted hope and crushed faith? This is not a coincidence; this is an attack. The battle *is* raging. When you feel this, simply say, "I rebuke you, Satan," and believe your words have the power to overcome.

Over time, you will discover transformational light that only God can provide. You will begin to experience a more fulfilling life through a different set of circumstances. You will discover the incredible power of the living light that only God can supply. You will come to understand that darkness and despair are deceptions created in the laboratory of Hell by its Chief Scientist. These forces have been unleashed upon the entire world, and we are being tested daily.

This book is for *you* if you've ever asked, "Why me? Why am I going through this trial and tribulation?" You feel like you're the only one fighting hard to get ahead. All of your efforts seem to be in vain, while everyone else seems to have an easy, uncomplicated life. If you have ever felt depressed, hopeless and ashamed or experienced a life plagued with regret, wishing you could turn back the hands of time and relive certain moments, this book is for you. Lamenting about past choices is, quite frankly, futile. It only leads to wallowing in regret. Besides, you know this isn't how life works. We cannot turn back the hands of time.

The good news, though, is that through God, we can redeem our lives and begin anew. *And we know that all things work together for good to them that love God, to them who are the called according to his purpose* (Romans 8:28).

If you love God and sincerely allow Him to guide your life, you will experience the rebirth of your life. This book explores what it means to have faith in God, as well as the incredible power you have access to through the exercising of that faith.

O LORD, you have searched me and known me! You know when I sit down and when I rise up; you discern my thoughts from afar. You search out my path and my lying down and are acquainted with all my ways. Even before a word is on my tongue, behold, O LORD, you know it altogether. You hem me in, behind and before, and lay your hand upon me. Such knowledge is too wonderful for me; it is high; I cannot attain it. Where shall I go from your Spirit? Or where shall I flee from your presence? If I ascend to heaven, you are there! If I make my bed in Sheol [abode of the dead], you are there! If I take the wings of the morning and dwell in the uttermost parts of the sea, even there your hand shall lead me, and your right hand shall hold me. If I say, "Surely the darkness shall cover me, and the light about me be night," even the darkness is not dark to you; the night is bright as the day, for darkness is as light with you. For you formed my inward parts; you knitted me together in my mother's womb. I praise you, for I am fearfully and wonderfully made. Wonderful are your works; my soul knows it very well. My frame was not hidden from you, when I was being made in secret, intricately woven in the depths of the earth. Your eyes saw my unformed substance; in your book were written, every one of them, the days that were formed for me, when as yet there was none of them. How precious to me are your thoughts, O God! How vast is the sum of them! If I would count them, they are more than the sand. I awake, and I am still with you. (Psalm 139:1–18 ESV)

Let us, therefore, embark on a journey together to discover the power of light and expose the deception of darkness.

Chapter 1
Master of the Universe

It is the glory of God to conceal a thing: but the honour of kings is to search out a matter (Proverbs 25:2).

I am Alpha and Omega, the beginning and the ending, saith the Lord, which is, and which was, and which is to come, the Almighty (Revelation 1:8).

Many people believe the world emerged out of chaos and that everything that has ever existed owes its existence to randomness, confusion, or some sort of galactic, astronomical event that took place billions of years ago. Through natural selection, luck and the passage of time, everything has perfectly evolved, and all can be explained using complex mathematic models and theoretical physics. Does this theory sound logical to you? Consider momentarily, when nature is keenly observed and thoroughly examined. It is the impeccable embodiment of laws of physics, order and intelligence, operating in perfect symbiosis. Unfortunately, as we know all too well, nature is negatively impacted and disrupted when this co-operation and interdependence is impeded. The theory of spontaneous, chaotic creation requires far more *faith* than it takes to believe in an intelligent Creator who, by thoughts and words, called everything into being.

The heavens declare the glory of God; the skies proclaim the work of his hands. Day after day they pour forth speech; night after night they reveal knowledge. They have no speech, they use no words; no sound is heard from them. Yet their voice goes out into all the earth, their words to the ends of the world.

1

In the heavens, God has pitched a tent for the sun. It is like a bridegroom coming out of his chamber, like a champion rejoicing to run his course. It rises at one end of the heavens and makes its circuit to the other; nothing is deprived of its warmth. (Psalm 19:1–6 NIV)

Imagine trying to create a soup bowl by throwing a glob of clay into a kiln without meticulously shaping or designing it in line with your vision. You fire up the kiln with no consideration for the appropriate temperature or length of time the clay should remain in the oven. Do you believe that when this exercise is completed, you will have a functional, aesthetically pleasing soup bowl? Instead, you've created a colossal "hot mess" fit only for the trash heap. If, for a brief moment, you choose to fully embrace evolution and Big Bang theories, you must dismiss logic. Let me state here that there is a difference between randomness and chaos.

Of course, some will point to the second law of thermodynamics (SLT) (once something exists, it can only get worse unless it's influenced by an outside force) to argue against evolution. Notwithstanding, this argument doesn't explain the beginning of matter and energy. Our universe is a closed, isolated system, which means it cannot be influenced by anything outside the universe. Isolated systems move toward greater disorder. Therefore, if we follow this law, it suggests that eventually, everything in nature collapses, with chaos ensuing.

What we see, however, is nature and the universe still holding their own. The planets are still on their axes; the North Star remains in the northern sky. The seasons of the year come around in an orderly fashion, year after year. The cycle of the moon is on a 28-day rotation (27.32 days, to be more exact). The earth's gravitational pull hasn't changed significantly over time. Human beings still look and behave like human beings: two arms and two legs attached to the torso. A pair of ears and eyes, a nose and mouth, all located on the face. We still put our pants on, one leg at a time. Fish still have all the features that define them as fish.

Nevertheless, outside of nature, we see SLT on full display. If we look at ancient ruins of cities, historical sites, or even the condition of an early-model vehicle that hasn't been well maintained and isn't influenced by an outside force (e.g., human beings), we will see SLT at work. All have broken down because of an increase in entropy, which is the measure of molecular disorder. These human creations break down because they are isolated and, for the most part, have been left alone.

How about the answer to the question: Where did all matter and energy originate from? *Through faith we understand that the worlds were framed by the word of God, so that things which are seen were not made of things which do appear* (Hebrews 11:3).

Before delving any deeper, it's imperative to first prove whether God's Word is true. How can I continue to cite Scripture, if there is doubt about its authoritative legitimacy? The litmus test, I first used, when trying to make this determination, was to investigate the accuracy of the predictions found throughout the Bible.

Son of man, because that Tyrus hath said against Jerusalem, Aha, she is broken that was the gates of the people: she is turned unto me: I shall be replenished, now she is laid waste: Therefore thus saith the Lord GOD; Behold, I am against thee, O Tyrus, and will cause many nations to come up against thee, as the sea causeth his waves to come up. And they shall destroy the walls of Tyrus, and break down her towers: I will also scrape her dust from her, and make her like the top of a rock. It shall be a place for the spreading of nets in the midst of the sea: for I have spoken it, saith the Lord GOD: and it shall become a spoil to the nations. And her daughters which are in the field shall be slain by the sword; and they shall know that I am the LORD. For thus saith the Lord GOD; Behold, I will bring upon Tyrus Nebuchadrezzar king of Babylon, a king of kings, from the north, with horses, and with chariots, and with horsemen, and companies, and much people. He shall slay with the sword thy daughters in the field: and he shall make a fort against thee, and cast a mount against thee, and lift up the buckler against thee. And he shall set engines of war against thy walls, and with his axes he shall break down thy towers. By reason of the abundance of his horses their dust shall cover thee: thy walls shall shake at the noise of the horsemen, and of the wheels, and of the chariots, when he shall enter into thy gates, as men enter into a city wherein is made a breach. With the hoofs of his horses shall he tread down all thy streets: he shall slay thy people by the sword, and thy strong garrisons shall go down to the ground. And they shall make a spoil of thy riches, and make a prey of thy merchandise: and they shall break down thy walls, and destroy thy pleasant houses: and they shall lay thy stones and thy timber and thy dust in the midst of the water. And I will cause the noise of thy songs to cease; and the sound of thy harps shall be no more heard (Ezekiel 26:2-13).

Some 200 years after this prediction was made, in 332 BC, Alexander the Great conquered the fortified island of Tyre. What makes this prediction fascinating is that at the time of Ezekiel, Tyre was the capital of Phoenicia, but the island fortress had not been built. Yet, we see that Ezekiel predicted her "walls" would be destroyed. Not only was the island captured by Alexander's army, precisely as foretold, but Alexander had them scrape away everything, leaving bare rock, just as was predicted by Ezekiel.

Micah 5:2 says, *But thou, Bethlehem Ephratah, though thou be little among the thousands of Judah, yet out of thee shall he come forth unto me that is to be ruler in Israel; whose goings forth have been from of old, from everlasting.* This prophecy was made by the prophet Micah approximately 700 years before Jesus Christ was born. As predicted, He was born in Bethlehem.

Who hath believed our report? And to whom is the arm of the LORD revealed? For he shall grow up before him as a tender plant, and as a root out of a dry ground: he hath no form nor comeliness; and when we shall see him, there is no beauty that we should desire him. He is despised and rejected of men; a man of sorrows, and acquainted with grief: and we hid as it were our faces from him; he was despised, and we esteemed him not. Surely he hath borne our griefs, and carried our sorrows: yet we did esteem him stricken, smitten of God, and afflicted. But he was wounded for our transgressions, he was bruised for our iniquities: the chastisement of our peace was upon him; and with his stripes we are healed. All we like sheep have gone astray; we have turned every one to his own way; and the LORD hath laid on him the iniquity of us all. He was oppressed, and he was afflicted, yet he opened not his mouth: he is brought as a lamb to the slaughter, and as a sheep before her shearers is dumb, so he openeth not his mouth. He was taken from prison and from judgment: and who shall declare his generation? for he was cut off out of the land of the living: for the transgression of my people was he stricken. And he made his grave with the wicked, and with the rich in his death; because he had done no violence, neither was any deceit in his mouth. Yet it pleased the LORD to bruise him; he hath put him to grief: when thou shalt make his soul an offering for sin, he shall see his seed, he shall prolong his days, and the pleasure of the LORD shall prosper in his hand. He shall see of the travail of his soul, and shall be satisfied: by his knowledge shall my righteous servant justify many; for he shall bear their iniquities. Therefore will I divide him a portion with the great, and he shall divide the spoil with the strong; because he hath poured out his soul unto death: and he was numbered with the transgressors; and he bare the sin of many, and made intercession for the transgressors (Isaiah 53).

The prophet Isaiah lived approximately 700 years before Jesus. Here, he predicts Jesus's birth and states Jesus would have no special physical features. He would not be seen as someone of high esteem and didn't come from nobility. Jesus took on an ordinary existence and was born into an ordinary family. Isaiah spoke of how contemptuous the Messiah would be treated by the very people (Jews) He called His own. Isaiah prophesied of how the Jews would ultimately reject Jesus and have Him put to death. The Jews would despise and reject Him as the Son of God. They would take Him before Pontius Pilate and falsely accuse Him. At His inquiry, Jesus would say nothing in His own defence. He would be like a sheep to the slaughter–objecting to nothing–giving His life willingly to be crucified. After His crucifixion, Jesus is buried among the wicked (sinful) but in a rich man's tomb. These events were all foretold by the prophet some 700 years before the birth of Jesus.

And Joshua adjured them at that time, saying, Cursed be the man before the LORD, that riseth up and buildeth this city Jericho: he shall lay the foundation thereof in his firstborn, and in his youngest son shall he set up the gates of it (Joshua 6:26). Joshua declared this curse over Jericho, approximately 525 years before the city was rebuilt. Just as he had predicted, Jericho would be rebuilt by one man. However, the man's eldest son died when the reconstruction began, and his youngest son died when the work reached completion. 1 Kings tells the story: *In his days did Hiel the Bethelite build Jericho: he laid the foundation thereof in Abiram his firstborn, and set up the gates thereof in his youngest son Segub, according to the word of the LORD, which he spake by Joshua the son of Nun* (16:34).

Finally, some 500 – 1000 years before crucifixion was even invented by the Romans, the prophet Zechariah and Israel's second king, David, described Jesus's death in words that flawlessly illustrated this reprehensible mode of capital punishment. Both writers assert that His body would be pierced, but none of His bones broken. These prophecies can be read in Zechariah 12:10 and Psalm 22, 34:20. Here is what's really intriguing about these prophecies: it was customary for the legs of the crucified to be broken before disposing of the body. Equally noteworthy, the Romans occasionally broke the legs of their condemned to limit the use of the thigh muscles during execution. This aided suffocation and hastened death.

Centuries later, the New Testament writers confirm the following: Jesus of Nazareth died on a Roman cross; His death was surprisingly quick (even Pilate was surprised at how quickly He gave up the ghost); His unusually quick demise eliminated the need for the usual breaking of bones; A spear was instead thrust into His side to prove that He was indeed, dead. I could go on, but you see the point.

Hundreds of prophecies and predictions contained in the Bible have come true with shocking accuracy. Other predictions, though, have yet to be fulfilled but are seemingly set to take place in the coming years. Read Daniel chapter two to discover the incredible accuracy of the rise and fall of every kingdom since ancient Babylon to present. Not even Michel de Nostredame (Nostradamus) has been as pinpoint accurate in his revelations as Daniel was regarding future events.

The Bible *is* the Word of God. It doesn't contain mythological stories and scenarios, found in other texts, that speak of other (false) gods. Many of the gods spoken about in these texts are introduced as gods of war, wrath, vengeance, death and so on.

In addition to the Bible being prophetically accurate, it was written by around 40 authors over a period of about 1,500 years. During this entire period, not a single passage in the Bible has been contradicted by other passages. The themes throughout the entire Bible text are consistent. What other text can claim such a feat? This unanimity of thought and purpose is exclusive in the world's literary history.

People from different times, different places, different ages, different educational and cultural backgrounds, all wrote portions of the Bible. Whether they were kings and rulers, physicians or prophets, Roman citizens hired as jackals to persecute and kill the earliest believers of Jesus, or lowly fishermen, they all contributed to what we know today as the Bible.

Yet when you read the Bible, its message is clear, concise, and flows as though it was written by a single author. This is because the source of the message came from a singular place:

- *The Spirit of the LORD spake by me, and his word was in my tongue* (2 Samuel 23:2).
- *Whom shall he teach knowledge? and whom shall he make to understand doctrine? them that are weaned from the milk, and drawn from the breasts. For precept must be upon precept, precept upon precept; line upon line, line upon line; here a little, and there a little: For with stammering lips and another tongue will he speak to this people* (Isaiah 28:9-11).
- *Then the LORD put forth his hand, and touched my mouth. And the LORD said unto me, Behold, I have put my words in thy mouth* (Jeremiah 1:9).
- *Knowing this first, that no prophecy of the scripture is of any private interpretation. For the prophecy came not in old time by the will of man: but holy men of God spake as they were moved by the Holy Ghost* (2 Peter 1:20–21).
- *All Scripture is breathed out by God and profitable for teaching, for reproof, for correction, and for training in righteousness* (2 Timothy 3:16 ESV).

Many other verses in the Bible plainly state that the Bible is the inspired Word of God. This is precisely why the Bible truth is alive and active (Hebrews 4:12).

The most encouraging and, indeed, fascinating discovery you'll learn about the Bible is that its overarching principle is love!

- *Whoever does not love does not know God, because God is love. This is how God showed his love among us: He sent his one and only Son into the world that we might live through him. This is love: not that we loved God, but that he loved us and*

> *sent his Son as an atoning sacrifice for our sins. Dear friends, since God so loved us, we also ought to love one another. No one has ever seen God; but if we love one another, God lives in us and his love is made complete in us* (1 John 4:8–12 NIV).

- *Finally, brethren, farewell. Be perfect, be of good comfort, be of one mind, live in peace; and the God of love and peace shall be with you* (2 Corinthians 13:11).
- *But thou, O Lord, art a God full of compassion, and gracious, long suffering, and plenteous in mercy and truth* (Psalm 86:15).

The essence of God, the order of His ways and the manifestation of His creation are all rooted in His love. If we love Him, we are instructed to keep His commandments (John 14:15). The Bible tells us, *For the wages of sin is death; but the gift of God [salvation through His son, as spoken of in 1 John 4:8–9] is eternal life, through Jesus Christ the Lord* (Romans 6:23). If we call on the name of the Lord, we will be saved (10:13). He saves us because He loves us. His love saves and covers. *Herein is love, not that we loved God, but that he loved us, and sent his Son to be the propitiation [atonement] for our sins. Beloved, if God so loved us, we ought also to love one another. No man hath seen God at any time. If we love one another, God dwelleth in us, and his love is perfected in us* (1 John 4:10-12). His *way* is love; it leads to *truth* and *is* eternal *life*. We discover these very same redeeming qualities in His Son. *Jesus saith unto him, I am the way, the truth, and the life: no man cometh unto the Father, but by me* (John 14:6). We are allowed to come to Him, through prayer, with our requests because His love grants us access. We are assured that He listens to the prayers of His children and will grant our requests if they are in accordance with His will for our lives.

> *We know that God does not listen to sinners. He listens to the godly person who does his will (9:31 NIV). And this is the confidence that we have in him, that, if we ask any thing according to his will, he heareth us: And if we know that he hear us, whatsoever we ask, we know that we have the petitions that we desired of him (1 John 5:14–15). Then you will call on me and come and pray to me, and I will listen to you. You will seek me and find me when you seek me with all your heart (Jeremiah 29:12–13 NIV).*

God also says in His Word that perfect love casts out fear. *There is no fear in love. But perfect love drives out fear, because fear has to do with punishment. The one who fears is not made perfect in love* (1 John 4:18 NIV). We don't have to fear or be anxious about the future. Revelation 20 gives us a glimpse into what will happen in the final days of Earth's existence. It tells us that Jesus, the Son of God, will return to gather and take to Heaven those who have loved Him and kept His commandments. 1 Thessalonians confirms this: *For the Lord himself shall descend from heaven with a shout, with the voice of the archangel, and with the trump of God: and the dead in Christ shall rise first: Then we which are alive and remain shall be caught up together with them in the clouds, to meet the Lord in the air: and so shall we ever be with the Lord* (4:16–17).

What a spectacular and glorious event! This is a promise you can believe because hundreds of other promises in the Bible have been fulfilled exactly as foretold. Inconceivable power, deep indescribable feelings of affection, protection and possession are wrapped up in His love. For example, the love I have for my children knows no bounds. It is this love for them that compels me to hug and kiss them and tell them I love them. Beyond that, my love for them induces me to support, encourage, protect, and claim them as my own while also providing sage advice. This love desires to see them succeed in all areas of their lives.

If we consider the love and affection we have for our parents, spouses, children, grandchildren, siblings, friends, etc., just imagine how much more love our heavenly Father has for us. When we come to fully understand and appreciate all that He has done to guarantee our salvation and keep us protected from the flaming arrows of the devil, we should *want* to obey Him. We should be excited to learn more about Him and His love toward us. Out of love, not obligation or fear, we should want to follow and serve Him.

Finally, I believe the Bible to be accurate, trustworthy, and true because of the results it has yielded. Of course, we cannot overlook the fact that many wars have been fought over religion and the Bible. However, this was never the desire of God. Many lies have been manufactured and many crimes committed in the name of the Bible. Even the devil will cite Scripture, though he twists it for his own purposes (see Matthew 4:1–11). Nevertheless, the Bible has many principles that, when followed and practised as they were intended, yield remarkable results. Many, including myself, can attest to this. Your life, believe it or not, is a living testament to the power, protection, and saving mercy of the living God. Your life could always be worse, your circumstances more dismal.

If it wasn't for God's love and mercy, the entire world would be consumed by death and destruction. Total desolation would be the imagery, annihilation our reality (Ezra 9:13-14).

He hath not dealt with us after our sins; nor rewarded us according to our iniquities (Psalm 103:10). *The thief comes only to steal and kill and destroy; I have come that they may have life, and have it to the full* (John 10:10 NIV). *But because of his great love for us, God, who is rich in mercy, made us alive with Christ even when we were dead in transgressions—it is by grace you have been saved* (Ephesians 2:4–5 NIV).

The Bible is a practical text. Anyone who reads it in search of truth and with a mind to discover God will agree. It reveals God's plan for us and how to achieve true and meaningful purpose in our lives.

For these and other reasons, I have come to the conclusion that the Bible *is* true, trustworthy, and can be relied upon for wisdom and understanding. It can be used as a guide to living a fulfilling and truly enterprising life. God's Word is specific, honest, powerful, and insightful. Everything contained in His Word points back to Him and what He has done and will continue to do for us. Therefore, one should most assuredly expect that everything in creation would also point to the existence, power, intelligence, glory, and majesty of God. So then, to answer the question once more of where did all matter and energy come from, let's again see what the Bible has to say. *For in him all things were created: things in heaven and on earth, visible and invisible, whether thrones or powers or rulers or authorities; all things have been created through him and for him. He is before all things, and in him all things hold together* (Colossians 1:16–17 NIV).

God's creation demonstrates His preciseness. *The heavens declare the glory of God; and the firmament sheweth his handywork* (Psalm 19:1). *But ask now the beasts, and they shall teach thee; and the fowls of the air, and they shall tell thee: Or speak to the earth, and it shall teach thee: and the fishes of the sea shall declare unto thee. Who knoweth not in all these that the hand of the LORD hath wrought this?*

(Job 12:7–9). As these Bible verses affirm, God created everything, including the matter, energy, order and intelligence found in creation.

If we consider our planet and understand what is required to support and sustain life on it, we would investigate deeper and develop a keener understanding of who God is and believe without reservation that He is the Master of the universe. Earth can support life because of its perfect conditions *for* life. Indeed, no other planets in our solar system can accommodate life. Let's consider the following:

- Earth is located at the right distance from our sun so that temperatures are conducive to life. No other planets in our solar system can claim this.
- We have the right atmospheric pressure for liquid water at our surface.
- We have the right ingredients, the right balance of heavy elements and organic molecules for life to exist.
- We have the right amount of water so that our world has both oceans and continents.[i]

It is fascinating to learn that other planets in our solar system have similarities to Earth, meaning some aspects of Earth are found on every planet. Yet, life cannot be sustained on any other planet because *all* features are required, in the right balance, to support life. The most notable feature required to sustain life is maintaining an exact distance from the sun. If Earth's orbit moved closer to the sun, we'd all burn. If it moved farther away, we'd all freeze.

Then there is π (pronounced pie). No number is quite as remarkable as pi, which is defined as the ratio of the circumference of a circle to its diameter. Pi is an irrational number; its exact value is inherently unknowable. Computer scientists have calculated billions of digits of pi, starting with 3.14159265358979323..., but because no identifiable pattern emerges in the succession of its digits, we could continue calculating the next digit and the next and the next for millennia, and we'd still have no idea which digit might emerge next. The digits of pi continue their meaningless procession to infinity. In nature, pi appears everywhere that there's a circle. The pupil of an eye, the sun, the concentric rings that travel outward from splashes in ponds, the girth of a tree trunk, the spiral of the DNA double helix, and so on. Pi also appears in the physics that describe waves, such as ripples of light and sound. It even enters into the equation that defines how precisely we can know the state of the universe, known as Heisenberg's uncertainty principle.[ii]

Another unique ratio that can be used to describe the proportions of everything from nature's smallest building blocks, such as atoms, to the most advanced patterns in the universe, like the unimaginably large celestial bodies, is called the golden ratio. Nature relies on this innate proportion to maintain balance. Mathematicians, scientists and naturalists have known about the golden ratio for centuries. It's derived from the Fibonacci sequence, named after its Italian founder, Leonardo Fibonacci (c.1170 – c.1250). In the sequence, each number is the sum of the two preceding numbers (1, 1, 2, 3, 5, 8, 13, etc.). So, after 1, the next number is 1+1=2, the next is 1+2=3, the next is 2+3=5 and so on. The ratio applies to honeybees, for example. If you divide the female bees by the male bees in any given hive, you will get 1.618. Sunflowers, which have opposing spirals of seeds, have a 1.618 ratio between the diameters of each rotation. This same ratio can be seen in relationships between different components throughout nature. Try measuring from your shoulder to your fingertips and then divide this number by the length from your elbow to your fingertips. Or measure from your head to your feet and divide that by the length from your belly button to your feet. Are the results the same? Somewhere in the area of 1.618? The golden ratio is seemingly unavoidable.[iii]

Using our solar system and these two ratios, I've demonstrated that an intelligent, great and powerful someone created everything in nature. The universe functions intelligently and orderly. Look at the size of the sun in our solar system. Consider the nuclear power it possesses. Yet because of the precise distance our planet is from the sun and the protective atmosphere, safe rays reach the Earth's surface. We even derive essential vitamin D from it. Without the sun, life is unsustainable. Regrettably, because of our destructive impact on Earth's atmosphere, the ozone layer has been damaged, letting in harmful UV rays.

Consider how the planets orbit the sun. They do so in an orderly fashion and don't collide into one another, or drift outside their orbits, or off their axes. There is no disorganised randomness or haphazardness found in creation. The oceans ebb and flow and follow a regular pattern, and even when serious storm systems emerge, the waters do not cover the entire Earth. *Should you not fear me?"*

declares the LORD. "Should you not tremble in my presence? I made the sand a boundary for the sea, an everlasting barrier it cannot cross. The waves may roll, but they cannot prevail; they may roar, but they cannot cross it (Jeremiah 5:22 NIV). Reefs and mangroves are designed to protect the shoreline and are strategically placed on the outskirts of tiny islands located in some of the deepest waters found on the planet. The master designer of the universe is God, whose intricate design and careful planning defy randomness.

For something to be designed, there must be a designer. For something to be organised, there must be an organiser. If the universe and our planet show signs of intelligent design, then the Creator must be intelligent. Has the world ever missed a winter or a spring? Every seed produces after its kind. Orange seeds produce orange trees and bear oranges. The same goes for apples, peaches, pears, mangoes, etc. You don't plant an apple seed and expect to harvest peaches. That's intelligent design. When you consider the diversity of nature, the number of species of fish, birds and land animals, you are forced to appreciate nature's unique diversity and brilliance. When you examine the petals of various species of flowers and see how intricately woven, delicately designed and incredibly colourful they are, it should lend insight into the world's complex and complete design. Creation is lavishly detailed and in full splendour; it shows meticulous design and careful planning.

If we look at the design of humans, it is exceedingly challenging to believe that we were not designed and created by an intelligent Creator. Every person has a unique personality, fingerprint, voice wave pattern, iris and DNA code. Even identical twins are unique in several ways and tend not to be totally *identical*.

And just how powerful is God, the Master of the universe? According to the Bible, God spoke everything into existence (Genesis 1).

In the beginning was the Word, and the Word was with God, and the Word was God. He was with God in the beginning. Through him all things were made; without him nothing was made that has been made. In him was life, and that life was the light of all mankind (John 1:1–4 NIV). *By the word of the LORD the heavens were made, their starry host by the breath of his mouth* (Psalm 33:6 NIV).

Isn't this amazing? God is so powerful that He spoke creation into existence. And not just creation, but all the intelligence that comes along with creation was uploaded simply by God speaking it into being. That is our God!

In discussing this topic with others, I often ask: *What is there, outside of nature, that human beings use every day that wasn't created by us or wasn't created using our intelligence?* Everything we use to cover and fashion our bodies was created by human intelligence, as well as our homes, furnishings, appliances, medicines, motor vehicles, roads and highways, factories, smartphones, tablets and other technological devices, currency, credit cards, and so much more. So, if we created everything we use outside of nature, why would we assume that nature, along with the life force of everything, including ourselves, wasn't created by the divine Creator?

Read all about creation in Genesis chapters 1 and 2. We did not evolve from monkeys, fish or slime. We were created by God. In His image and likeness (Genesis 1:27). Charles Darwin, known to many as the father of the theory of evolution, once said after examining the human eye that it was "absurd" to propose that the human eye evolved through spontaneous mutation and natural selection.[iv]

Equally fascinating to note is that the human eye hasn't "evolved" to X-ray vision. It doesn't naturally block harmful light emitted from computer screens or televisions, even though many of us have been using these devices for decades. We also don't have night vision, like nocturnal creatures, even though we've been hunting in the dark for millennia. Our DNA hasn't evolved and passed on any "new and improved" design to our offspring. Darwin was also quoted as saying, "In my most extreme fluctuations, I have never been an atheist in the sense of denying the existence of a God. I think that generally (and more and more so as I grow older) but not always, that an agnostic would be the most correct description of my state of mind."[v]

Unfortunately, the falsehoods of evolution being taught as truth have separated us from our Creator and His love. This separation, along with secular, "high" academic science and philosophical ideology, has caused many people to question the purpose of their lives. It has interrupted our hard-coded, divine relationship with the Master of the universe, and as a result, we have drifted farther from Him. However, He has never drifted from you, and if you call on Him, He will immediately save you. *The LORD your God is with you, the Mighty Warrior who saves. He will take great delight in you; in his love he will no longer rebuke you, but will rejoice over you with singing* (Zephaniah 3:17 NIV). Once again, we see that His love for us *is* the redeeming quality. It's the greatest force within God.

We must also acknowledge that evolution cannot support a moral ethic. Evolution suggests we are nothing more than enlarged protein molecules, a random combination of genes and chromosomes. It submits that we are, through millions of years of evolution, just a more intelligent form of the animal species. If this were true, it supplies no basis for a moral ethic. Without a moral ethic, civilisation would be in chaos and disarray. What would be right or wrong? Who determines what is right from wrong? The basic laws governing humanity would not have been established, let alone maintained. To believe we are simply an accident, not created for any purpose or to accomplish anything amazing, goes against the essence of what it means to have a sophisticated global community where *everyone* plays a part. It also goes against the order of nature.

We have set up systems to rule, guide and protect our way of life. The moral ethic we have constructed, as an overarching guidance system to promote laws, order and civility, is nothing we humans have fashioned on our own. Rather, they are founded upon God's Law.

I am the LORD thy God, which have brought thee out of the land of Egypt, out of the house of bondage. Thou shalt have no other gods before me. Thou shalt not make unto thee any graven image, or any likeness of any thing that is in heaven above, or that is in the earth beneath, or that is in the water under the earth. Thou shalt not bow down thyself to them, nor serve them: for I the LORD thy God am a jealous God, visiting the iniquity of the fathers upon the children unto the third and fourth generation of them that hate me; And shewing mercy unto thousands of them that love me, and keep my commandments. Thou shalt not take the name of the LORD thy God in vain; for the LORD will not hold him guiltless that taketh his name in vain. Remember the sabbath day, to keep it holy. Six days shalt thou labour, and do all thy work: But the seventh day is the sabbath of the LORD thy God: in it thou shalt not do any work, thou, nor thy son, nor thy daughter, thy manservant, nor thy maidservant, nor thy cattle, nor thy stranger that is within thy gates: For in six days the LORD made heaven and earth, the sea, and all that in them is, and rested the seventh day: wherefore the LORD blessed the sabbath day, and hallowed it. Honour thy father and thy mother: that thy days may be long upon the land which the LORD thy God giveth thee. Thou shalt not kill. Thou shalt not commit adultery. Thou shalt not steal. Thou shalt not bear false witness against thy neighbour. Thou shalt not covet thy neighbour's house, thou shalt not covet thy neighbour's wife, nor his manservant, nor his maidservant, nor his ox, nor his ass, nor any thing that is thy neighbour's (Exodus 20:2–17).

Jesus said unto him, Thou shalt love the Lord thy God with all thy heart, and with all thy soul, and with all thy mind. This is the first great commandment. And the second is like unto it, Thou shalt love thy neighbour as thyself. On these two commandments hang all the law and the prophets (Matthew 22:37–40).

Our intelligence is not accidental. Our ability to see and recognise the need for social order and to communicate and build upon the knowledge of others is not incidental. These things are hard wired into us—to think critically, to record and to learn from history, to have dominion and rule over the entire world as human beings, to discover the laws of science and use them to benefit and advance civilisation. These abilities are not small and inconsequential. Rather, they are at the very core of our progress and further evidence that our wisdom and knowledge came from outside ourselves.

Within every person, there beats a hopeful heart and an inquisitive mind. No other species have shown this level of sophisticated intelligence. We cannot simply and dismissively say we, as a species, somehow evolved to this station in life. Even early archaeological discoveries show the quest for knowledge has been humanity's greatest pursuit from the earliest of times. This suggests we have an origin that simply cannot be defined or revealed through a theory of evolution.

Furthermore, evolution removes any possibility and hope for eternity. Instead, it encourages the notion that life ends in a dark, cold grave, and all memory of existence will eventually die, as though we never existed. It supports the view that we live only to die and that life is a recurring nightmare. Is this the extent of humanity's creative, philosophical mind? I suspect not. This grim and dismissive view of life is not in accordance with what the true and Living Word of God says.

Where is the wise person? Where is the teacher of the law? Where is the philosopher of this age? Has not God made foolish the wisdom of the world? For since in the wisdom of God the world through its wisdom did not know him, God was pleased through the foolishness of what was preached to save those who believe. Jews demand signs and Greeks look for wisdom, but we preach Christ crucified: a stumbling block to Jews and foolishness to Gentiles, but to those whom God has called, both Jews and Greeks, Christ the power of God and the wisdom of God. For the foolishness of God is wiser than human wisdom, and the weakness of God is stronger than human strength (1 Corinthians 1:20–25 NIV).

Where does knowledge come from? Does it just fall from the sky like a morning mist?

For the LORD giveth wisdom: out of his mouth cometh knowledge and understanding (Proverbs 2:6). *Daniel answered and said, Blessed be the name of God for ever and ever: for wisdom and might are his: And he changeth the times and the seasons: he removeth kings, and setteth up kings: he giveth wisdom unto the wise, and knowledge to them that know understanding: He revealeth the deep and secret things: he knoweth what is in the darkness, and the light dwelleth with him* (Daniel 2:20–22).

And God gave Solomon wisdom and understanding exceeding much, and largeness of heart, even as the sand that is on the sea shore. And Solomon's wisdom excelled the wisdom of all the children of the east country, and all the wisdom of Egypt. For he was wiser than all men; than Ethan the Ezrahite, and Heman, and Chalcol, and Darda, the sons of Mahol: and his fame was in all nations round about. And he spake three thousand proverbs: and his songs were a thousand and five. And he spake of trees, from the cedar tree that is in Lebanon even unto the hyssop that springeth out of the wall: he spake

*also of beasts, and of fowl, and of creeping things, and of fishes.
And there came of all people to hear the wisdom of Solomon,
from all kings of the earth, which had heard of his wisdom*
(1 Kings 4:29–34).

We discover from these texts that all wisdom and knowledge come
from the supreme Master of the universe.

Let's consider the book of Job, found in the Old Testament of
the Bible. *He spreads out the northern skies over empty space; he
suspends the earth over nothing* (Job 26:7 NIV). Sir Isaac Newton,
who lived thousands of years after Job, discovered the laws of gravity
and realised Earth was truly suspended "on nothing." How and where
would Job have found such insight to make such a declaration without
knowledge about the laws of gravity or the principles in action that
causes our planets to be suspended in space?

Our universe wasn't created out of thin air or out of chaos. Rather,
it was created by God (Genesis 1:1). As King David writes in Psalm
139:6, God's knowledge is too lofty, too sophisticated for us to
understand. We need to concern ourselves with knowing that He loves
us, cares for us, and wants us to live a life of meaning (see John 3:16;
1 John 1:9; Jeremiah 29:11). Why would God send His only begotten
Son from Heaven to be born into a sinful world, die on a cross to
purchase humanity from the clutches of sin and death, thereby giving
us a chance at salvation and eternity, if we didn't have any value to
Him? Why would God listen to our prayers and forgive us of our sins
if our lives are meaningless to Him?

More than half of the New Testament is about God's redeeming
love, mercy, grace, and willingness to save us. Evolution teaches the
opposite. It doesn't provide us with hope for the future. It doesn't give
us the answers to many of our probing questions about life. It only
raises more questions. Evolution is simply a human-made *theory*, void
of any optimism or promise. The Bible points to a Creator, but many
people choose to instead worship creation.

*For since the creation of the world God's invisible qualities –
his eternal power and divine nature – have been clearly seen,
being understood from what has been made, so that people
are without excuse. For although they knew God, they neither
glorified him as God nor gave thanks to him, but their thinking*

became futile and their foolish hearts were darkened. Although they claimed to be wise, they became fools and exchanged the glory of the immortal God for images made to look like a mortal human being and birds and animals and reptiles. Therefore God gave them over in the sinful desires of their hearts to sexual impurity for the degrading of their bodies with one another. They exchanged the truth about God for a lie, and worshiped and served created things rather than the Creator – who is forever praised. Amen (Romans 1:20–25 NIV).

He created this world for us.

Then God said, "Let us make mankind in our image, in our likeness, so that they may rule over the fish in the sea and the birds in the sky, over the livestock and all the wild animals, and over all the creatures that move along the ground." So God created mankind in his own image, in the image of God he created them; male and female he created them. God blessed them and said to them, "Be fruitful and increase in number; fill the earth and subdue it. Rule over the fish in the sea and the birds in the sky and over every living creature that moves on the ground." (Genesis 1:26–28 NIV)

He made us a little lower than the angels.

What is mankind that you are mindful of them, human beings that you care for them? You have made them a little lower than the angels and crowned them with glory and honor. You made them rulers over the works of your hands; you put everything under their feet all flocks and herds, and the animals of the wild, the birds in the sky, and the fish in the sea, all that swim the paths of the seas. LORD, our Lord, how majestic is your name in all the earth! (Psalm 8:4–9 NIV).

So here is the good news: God *does* exist! Science proves it, creation screams it, and if you believe He exists, and search for Him, you will discover Him! *Then you will call on me and come and pray to me, and I will listen to you. You will seek me and find me when you seek me with all your heart* (Jeremiah 29:12–13 NIV). Start the journey today! You will not be disappointed. The suffocation of anxiety and depression will start to lift and your life will come alive with new meaning and purpose.

Chapter 2
Name Above all Names

Behold, a virgin shall be with child, and shall bring forth a son, and they shall call his name Emmanuel, which being interpreted is, God with us (Matthew 1:23).

Imagine your mum telling you an incredible story that happened to her when she was about two months pregnant with you. The story goes something like this:

I just recently found out that I was pregnant and was absolutely elated, beside myself with joy. I couldn't stop thinking about the life growing inside me. I'd always dreamt of having a wonderful, caring husband and at least three beautiful children to bring warmth and fullness into our home.

One day as I was home, preparing dinner and feeling ecstatic about carrying you, my firstborn, my thoughts drifted. *Are you a boy or a girl? What sort of personality will you have? Will you look like your dad, or will you have my looks and personality? Will you be healthy and strong?* I immediately said a little prayer asking God to give me a healthy, beautiful baby full of life and joy.

Other than your dad (Thomas) and the doctor, no one else knew about the pregnancy. Your dad and I had decided not to say anything to anyone until the start of the second trimester. I wasn't showing at this point and had only started to experience mild morning sickness.

If it's a girl, I'll name her Sarah, my mum's middle name. I'd always liked the sound of that name. I did some research and discovered that the name *Sarah* means, "Princess." *What a fitting name for my firstborn child! Yes, she will be Mummy's little princess.* I couldn't help but smile at the thought. If it's a boy, I would surprise Thomas by naming the little guy after him. This would please him. You see, Thomas was named after his dad, who was named after his father. If the baby was a boy, he would be the fourth-generation male in the family to carry the name, Thomas Austin Smith. My smile widened at this wonderful possibility.

While in deep thought, thinking about the future, I felt a presence in the corner of the living room, just across from the kitchen. I immediately thought it was Thomas. *He's probably trying to sneak up and surprise me with a warm hug and kiss to announce his arrival home for the evening.* Strange, I never heard him coming in, but I was in deep thought, so it's not bizarre. As I turned around to face the presence, I was stunned to see a stranger standing in the corner. Panic set in. Awash with fear, I wanted to scream but was unable to speak. Then I noticed how smartly dressed he was. My anxiety dropped, but my curiosity piqued.

"Don't be afraid, Jane," he said. "I am not here to hurt you. I am here to congratulate you on your pregnancy."

I didn't know what to make of this stranger and his words. *Who is he? How does he know my name and that I'm pregnant?*

Before I could voice my questions, he continued, "I know everything about you Jane, and so does the man who sent me to give you this news." *What news? Which man? Has my husband sent this man to play a prank on me?*

"Jane, you're going to have a beautiful baby boy." Tears of joy filled my eyes when I heard this. "I'm here to let you know that when your baby boy is born, you are to name him Michael, which means 'Who is like God?' Your son is going to be great, and has been chosen for a very special purpose. He will bring honour to God and your entire family. You and your husband will be proud of him. God will guide Michael's steps along his life's journey and use him in a mighty way." He looked over my shoulder and pointed to the stove. "Jane, the pot of water on the stove is boiling over."

Straightaway, I hurried to the stove, turned the fire down, and lifted the pot cover to stop the boil-over. When I turned back, the stranger had disappeared! I couldn't believe what had happened. Had I been dreaming? I pinched myself. *Nope, it wasn't a dream! Who was that guy? Who sent him?* I was so distraught that I turned off the stove and went to bed.

When Tom arrived home, I was about to tell him about my

encounter. However, I was interrupted when the phone rang. Tom was being called back to the office. I tried to wait up for him but lost the battle to exhaustion.

Later that night, Tom returned home. I was tucked into bed and peacefully asleep. As he recounts, he quietly showered and slipped into bed beside me, being careful not to wake me. He, too, was exhausted–having worked a 14-hour day–and before long, drifted off to sleep.

While asleep, your dad dreamt. He was in an open, lush valley with flowers in full bloom, protected on both sides by steep mountains. At the mouth of the valley, he sat under a big oak tree and looked out over a river. All of a sudden, everything stilled. Even the raging river quietened. He heard footsteps approaching from behind the tree. He turned and saw a man who looked like his grandfather. Though he'd never met his grandfather because he was killed during the second World War, he recognised the gentleman from family photos. The guy was wearing brown hiking boots, a long pair of blue jeans, a white T-shirt, and a baseball cap.

"Hey Thomas," the guy said as he approached and casually leaned against the massive tree trunk.

How does my grandfather know my name? He tried to ask this question but his mouth was dry and his tongue so thick he couldn't speak.

"I can't stay long, son, but I wanted to congratulate you on soon becoming a father. I have important information for you, Tom. I have been sent to let you know that the baby Jane is carrying is a precious, healthy boy. When your baby boy is born, you are to name him Michael, which means, 'Who is like God?' Your son is going to be great and has been chosen for a very special purpose. He'll bring honour to God and your entire family. You and Jane will be very proud of him. God will guide Michael's steps along his life's journey and use him in a mighty way."

Tom struggled to speak. He wanted to ask his grandfather so many questions. He felt his arm becoming numb and briefly looked at it. Immediately, he awoke. His arm was numb and tingly because he had been lying on it.

The dream startled Thomas. He remained in bed, eyes fixed on the ceiling of the bedroom. He replayed the dream over and over in his mind. *What a strange dream! My grandfather came and spoke to me about our baby. He told me it's a boy? He's going to be healthy...*

well, that's good. We must name him Michael? I was kind of hoping if the baby was a boy, Jane would allow me to name him Thomas Austin, after me, my dad, and granddad. God is going to use him in a very special way. Wow, just wow!

The more he replayed the dream, the more overwhelmed he became with joy and happiness. *What kind of dream was this? A boy? Is this my subconscious working in overdrive and influencing my dreams?* Thomas glanced at the clock on the night table beside the bed: 3:44 a.m. Unable to contain himself any longer, he decided to wake me.

He turned on the bedside light and gently nudged me, softly calling my name.

I turned to him, groggy but trying to muster a slight smile. "This should be good," I muttered as I rubbed my eyes and checked the clock.

Tom immediately launched into his dream. "I just had a dream and my grandfather told me that we are going to have a boy…"

I sat straight up! No longer half-asleep, I focused on Tom, excitement growing. I was about to cut him off and tell him about the stranger I had encountered but, curious to hear about his dream, I contained my enthusiasm. I heard the parts of his dream that were similar to the message I had received earlier: we were going to have a baby boy…would be healthy and vibrant…must be named Michael… do great things and be used by God. *Oh My! This is unbelievable!*

I then share my story with Tom. We both came to the same conclusion: the man who visited me and the man who looked like his grandfather must've been angels. We were convinced the baby I was carrying would be special, and we agreed to follow the instruction of the angels and call our son Michael. We were both overjoyed and immediately thanked God.

Fast-forward to the present day. You are the child who was spoken of. You are Michael! You have heard this story told at least a hundred times and you have done some pretty amazing things with your life. You are now 34 years old and just recently got married. You are a specialist surgeon who has accomplished some pretty astonishing things in a very short time. Through a special charity, you have travelled around the world, providing much needed care to the poorest and most vulnerable while spreading the good news of God's love. You completely acknowledge that it's only because of God that these doors have been opened to you. The story of your birth only further attests to that.

You've been blessed not only to repair people's bodies, but also to lead them to the One who repairs broken souls. God has used you tremendously to bring the good news to remote places of the world.

Recently, something extraordinary happened. You performed surgery to fix a cleft palate on a two-year-old child, whose healing and recovery were nothing short of miraculous. As a token of their appreciation, the village conducted a special traditional ceremony and presented you with ceremonial gifts. During the formality, they *changed* your name. Your *new* name is Maroose, which in their native tongue means, "The gifted one." You certainly appreciate the gesture and know it's their way of bestowing their highest honour upon you. However, since this time, everyone from the village calls you Maroose rather than your proper, legal name. Even a few of the doctors and accompanying staff on the medical team have called you Maroose on occasion. It's all good. But your *original* name and *where* your parents got that name remains special.

A similar story is found in the Bible regarding Jesus's birth. An angel visited both Mary and Joseph to announce the coming Son. The Book of Luke in the New Testament, tells us about Mary's encounter.

In the sixth month of Elizabeth's pregnancy, God sent the angel Gabriel to Nazareth, a town in Galilee, to a virgin pledged to be married to a man named Joseph, a descendant of David. The virgin's name was Mary. The angel went to her and said, "Greetings, you who are highly favored! The Lord is with you." Mary was greatly troubled at his words and wondered what kind of greeting this might be. But the angel said to her, "Do not be afraid, Mary; you have found favor with God. You will conceive and give birth to a son, and you are to call him Jesus. He will be great and will be called the Son of the Most High. The Lord God will give him the throne of his father David, and he will reign over Jacob's descendants forever; his kingdom will never end." "How will this be," Mary asked the angel, "since I am a virgin?" The angel answered, "The Holy Spirit will come on you, and the power of the Most High will overshadow you. So the holy one to be born will be called the Son of God. Even Elizabeth your relative is going to have a child in her old age, and she who was said to be unable to conceive is in her sixth month. For no word from God will ever fail." "I am the Lord's

*servant," Mary answered. "May your word to me be fulfilled."
Then the angel left her* (Luke 1:26–38 NIV).

The story of the angel of the Lord visiting Joseph to inform him about the birth of Jesus can be found in the first book of the New Testament.

This is how the birth of Jesus the Messiah came about: His mother Mary was pledged to be married to Joseph, but before they came together, she was found to be pregnant through the Holy Spirit. Because Joseph her husband was faithful to the law, and yet did not want to expose her to public disgrace, he had in mind to divorce her quietly. But after he had considered this, an angel of the Lord appeared to him in a dream and said, "Joseph son of David, do not be afraid to take Mary home as your wife, because what is conceived in her is from the Holy Spirit. She will give birth to a son, and you are to give him the name Jesus, because he will save his people from their sins." All this took place to fulfill what the Lord had said through the prophet: "The virgin will conceive and give birth to a son, and they will call him Immanuel" (which means "God with us"). When Joseph woke up, he did what the angel of the Lord had commanded him and took Mary home as his wife. But he did not consummate their marriage until she gave birth to a son. And he gave him the name Jesus (Matthew 1:18–25 NIV).

Some years ago, I was speaking with a friend who, very matter-of-factly, informed me that the name *Jesus* was *not* the name of the Son of God. I was puzzled and equally disconcerted. I thought it was a ridiculous claim to make and I initially dismissed it entirely. I mean, how could someone make such a ridiculous assertion? The name *Jesus* is recorded over 1300 times in the NIV Bible. The title *Christ* which means *Messiah* (anointed one), or more precisely *Mashiah* in Hebrew, is mentioned over 500 times in the KJV Bible.

A few weeks later, while having another conversation with him, he brought it up again. This time, I pushed back a little more. The first thing he said to me was the name of the Son of God could not be *Jesus*, because the letter *J* was only introduced into modern language approximately 500 years ago. He encouraged me to do some research on my own and not be so dismissive about the topic.

26

I took his challenge and ran with it. The first thing I researched and discovered was that the letter *J* was not used until 1524, when Gian Giorgio Trissino, an Italian Renaissance grammarian known as the father of the letter *J*, made a clear distinction between the two sounds of *I* and *J*.[vi] I found this information fascinating and felt the need to investigate further.

The next thing I learnt was that the capitalised word, *LORD*, in the Hebrew Bible is a marker, signifying the replacement of God's true and original name. The Hebrew word was represented by four letters, *YHWH*, used for centuries before the birth of Christ. "It was a firm tradition never to pronounce that word."[vii]

What this means is, wherever you find the title *LORD*, or the name *JESUS*, in all caps in the Bible, these are *not* original words. These all-caps names replace the original words found in the earliest texts. According to the translators, these replacements are equivalent in meaning. We know, however, if the word *LORD* or *JESUS* replaces something of unequal equivalence, it materially changes the text. For example, Luke 2:21 says, *And when eight days were accomplished for the circumcising of the child, his name was called JESUS, which was so named of the angel before he was conceived in the womb.* When I went to Strong's Concordance (an index of every word in the King James Bible), it said: "'JESUS' is of Hebrew origin and the name is Jehoshua." This is misleading because *J* doesn't exist in the Greek or Hebrew alphabet and was only created in the sixteenth century. I found this discovery very unsettling.

Next, I took a look at Isaiah 42:8: *I am the LORD: that is my name: and my glory will I not give to another, neither my praise to graven images.* The original Hebrew word that *LORD* has replaced is *Yehôvâh* (יְהֹוִה) and pronounced "yeh-ho-vaw" (to hear the pronunciation, Google search, "how to pronounce Yehovah"). Regarding the use of *LORD* and *Lord*, Christian Courier states the following:

"LORD"

LORD (all caps or small caps) reflects the original term YHWH (found 6,823 times), while Lord (standard capitalisation) is the English rendition of the Hebrew Adonai (used some 300 times).

As suggested above, one of the names for God, as conveyed in Hebrew, was YHWH (four consonants). Because the Jews considered this title to be very sacred, they did not pronounce it.

Eventually, the scribes borrowed vowels from the name Adonai based upon a point system, which reflected the way the language was spoken. Vowels were thus inserted into the sacred four-letter name (called the tetragrammaton, "four letters").

The Hebrew term YHWH is believed to derive from the root HWY, meaning "to be." The name suggests that God simply is, i.e. He possesses an underived existence; He is the eternal "I AM" (cf. Exodus 3:14: especially see the footnote in the ASV; cf. also John 8:58).

Also, this name became a special designation which emphasised God's relationship to the nation of Israel.

"Yehovah," or YHWH dramatically depicts one of the prime attributes of the Creator, His eternal existence. In addition, it stresses His enduring presence with Israel in their redemptive history.

"Lord"

The other term, "Lord" (standard capitalisation), as indicated earlier, is from Adonai. This word literally means, "my Lord," and it derives from a root which suggests "sovereign, strength, power."

It is a word particularly emphasising the authority of the Deity. It expresses the relationship of the Creator to His creatures and the responsibility they have to the one who made them and who owns them (cf. Romans 9:21).[viii]

Of course, because of the all-encompassing greatness, glory and majesty of God, other names and titles have been bestowed upon Him, such as:

- El Shaddai (Lord God Almighty)
- El Elyon (The Most High God)
- El Olam (The Everlasting God)
- Elohim (the plural Hebrew word for *God* that captures both YHWH and Yahusha, as spoken of in the creation story of Genesis 1)

Note that "El" in Hebrew means God/gods. *God* is simply a title for a deity. Remember, God (Elohim) was first the God of the Jews (Exodus 19:3–6). However, after their constant disobedience and rejection of His Son (John 1:11), YHWH sought after the non-Jews (called Gentiles in the Bible) and extended His love, grace, and mercy toward them (Romans 11:17–24). "Gentile Christians," are sometimes referred to as "spiritual Jews." *For he is not a Jew, which is one*

28

outwardly; neither is that circumcision, which is outward in the flesh: But he is a Jew, which is one inwardly; and circumcision is that of the heart, in the spirit, and not in the letter; whose praise is not of men, but of God [2:28–29].

Throughout my research, I also discovered that *YHWH,* are the four letters that represent the "unutterable name of Yehovah." The early Jews had so much respect and adulation for YHWH that they called His name only during worship. This definitely gives us a bit of insight into the level of veneration and deference we should place on His most holy name. The name of God is of such reverence that the third commandment tells us how to use this most holy name: *You shall not misuse the name of the LORD your God, for the LORD will not hold anyone guiltless who misuses his name* (Exodus 20:7 NIV).

As I continued to research, I discovered there is only one Hebrew letter (ןvav) that represents both *U* and *W. W* is a relatively new letter that developed over time. It was formerly comprised of two *U's* or a "double U" and makes the "oo" sound in the name, *Yah-oo-ah* ("oo" sound, like "moon"). After this discovery, I felt convicted to accept the pronunciation "Yahuah (YHUH)."

Unlike Greek, Aramaic, the language spoken by the Jews during the time of Jesus, significantly influenced the Hebrew language. So, while the original name *JESUS* replaces may have been pronounced differently in the Hebrew tongue, the translation would have been exact. However, the New Testament was written in Greek, and according to Strong's Concordance, the name *Jesus* "is the Greek *form* of the Hebrew name Yahusha." What is clear is that *Jesus* is not the *transliteration* of Yahusha, which names and titles should be.

In my opinion, and in the opinion of a growing number of linguists and Bible scholars, the human invention of the name *Jesus* does not adequately convey the meaning or significance of the original Hebrew name. According to the stories regarding the announcement of Jesus's birth by the angels visiting Mary and Joseph, both announced a name. The angels said He was to be called *Yahusha,* not *Jesus.* This was a very special name given to Yahusha by Yahuah (YHUH) himself. Not only was the name provided, but the meaning of the name was also disclosed. Who is worthy to go against the Most High?

And being found in fashion as a man, he humbled himself, and became obedient unto death, even the death of the cross.

Wherefore God also hath highly exalted him, and given him a name which is above every name: That at the name of Jesus every knee should bow, of things in heaven, and things in earth, and things under the earth; And that every tongue should confess that Jesus Christ is Lord, to the glory of God the Father (Philippians 2:8–11).

Can human beings create a new name and construct a meaning out of thin air that is equal to the original meaning YHUH gave to His Son? This is like someone creating the word "Fritch" and declaring it's the *new* name of Yahusha and means, "God is salvation." Where does this authority come from? Who sanctions it? Does it have the same supernatural power to save? Who creates everything and bestows wisdom and knowledge upon us all? Can humans create a name that is a name above all names?

Interestingly enough, when I started my quest to discover the real name of God's Son, I learnt that the vast majority of Jews familiar with basic Hebrew know that the name of the Son of God isn't *Jesus*. Remember, the Hebrew alphabet has **_never_** included the letter *J*.

According to Strong's Concordance, the name of the Son of God is *Yehowshuwa* and is pronounced *yeh·ho·shü´·ah*. In English, it is spelled and pronounced *Yahusha*. Now we must ask, what does Yahusha mean?

According to Strong's Concordance, as well as other credible sources, Yahusha means, "Yah (YHUH) is Salvation." According to Wikipedia, "Yahshua is a proposed transliteration of the original Hebrew name of Jesus…considered by Christians and Messianic Jews to be the Messiah. The name means Yahuah (Yah) is salvation (Shua)."[ix]

According to CEPHER:

In the Masoretic text, you see the name Yahusha spelled in the Hebrew as yod (י) heh (ה) vav (ו) shin (ש) vav (ו) ayin (ע) or Yahushua. Therefore, the assumption is that Mosheh added not only YAH, the name of He who visited Mosheh at the burning bush but also added the vav to create "shua" as the ending syllable.

Strong's Hebrew Dictionary 7737 sets forth הָוֵשׁ "shua" as the word "shavah." Its usage within the KJV means to level, i.e. equalise; figuratively, to resemble, by implication, to adjust (i.e. counterbalance, be suitable, compose, place, yield, etc.), avail, behave, bring forth, compare, countervail (be, make) equal, lay, be (make, a) like, make plain, profit, reckon.

Therefore, the name YAHUSHA can be understood as YAH, which is the shortened name of the Father, HU (in the Hebrew (אוה)), which means 'he,' and finally 'shua,' which means makes level or equal. Therefore, YAHUSHA means in this analysis, YAH is He who makes equal. The term YAH is found in 45 verses in the Tanakh, including Shemot (Exodus) 15:2 YAH הי is my strength עז and song תרמז, and he is become my yeshua (salvation) העוּשי: he הז is my EL לא, and I will prepare him a habitation והנ; my father's בא ELOHIYM מיהלא, and I will exalt מוּר him.

YAHUSHA has a wonderful meaning. Strong's H3467 declares that עשי (yâsha') is used as a primitive root, meaning properly, to be open, wide or free, that is (by implication) to be safe, causatively to free or succor, to avenge, defend, deliver, help, preserve, rescue, to be safe, to bring or to have salvation, to save, or to be a Saviour, or to get victory. We have elected to publish the name YAHUSHA, in the first instance because it is the most accurate transliteration of the name given to the Messiah, as he was given the same name as Husha/Yahusha son of Nun, whom the English world has always called Joshua. However, the name YAHUSHA means I AM HE who avenges, defends, delivers, helps, preserves, rescues, saves, brings salvation, your Saviour, who brings you to victory.[x]

Equipped with this information, we now understand why YHUH named His Son Yahusha. The name Yahusha means, "Yahuah saves." Whenever we call upon the name of the Son, we are declaring that the Father (Yahuah) saves! With this new discovery, we can now more clearly understand the sad and most profound observation Yahusha made when he said in John 5:43: *I am come in my Father's name, and ye receive me not: if another shall come in his own name, him ye will receive.* Was He also, in part, prophesying of a time we would replace

His most scared name for a totally fabricated one?

Furnished with this new insight, we can now more fully comprehend what Yahusha said in 14:6–7: … *I am the way, the truth, and the life: no man cometh unto the Father, but by me. If ye had known me, ye should have known my Father also: and from henceforth ye know him, and have seen him.* YHUH is above everything and is first in the Godhead. *If the Son therefore shall make you free, ye shall be free indeed* (8:36). Yahusha is YHUH's Word, manifested in flesh. *And the Word was made flesh, and dwelt among us, (and we beheld his glory, the glory as of the only begotten of the Father,) full of grace and truth* (1:14). *But the hour cometh, and now is, when the true worshippers shall worship the Father in spirit and in truth: for the Father seeketh such to worship him. God is a Spirit: and they that worship him must worship him in spirit and in truth* (4:23–24).

The name *Jesus* was originally *Iēsous* in Greek (no letter *J* existed until the sixteenth century) and pronounced *ee-ay-sooce*. It was a name created to *replace* Yahusha. Interestingly enough, the letter *J* has also **_never_** been included in the Greek alphabet. *Jesus* is a proper noun. However, the name Yahusha is more than just a proper noun. It's a verb because it means "to save," denoting action. The name Yahusha is also an adjective. It fully embodies the attributes of the proper noun by pointing toward *who's* doing, "the saving." *Yah* isn't just a proper noun. It's the root source and pure essence of who Yahusha is. The Son (Yahusha) carries the Father's name (Yahuah) and *is* the total embodiment of His name. The son *is* YHUH's Word, in flesh, who saves (John 1:14).

> *In the past God spoke to our ancestors through the prophets at many times and in various ways, but in these last days he has spoken to us by his Son, whom he appointed heir of all things, and through whom also he made the universe. The Son is the radiance of God's glory and the exact representation of his being, sustaining all things by his powerful word. After he had provided purification for sins, he sat down at the right hand of the Majesty in heaven* (Hebrews 1:1-3 NIV).

After grasping what the name *Yahusha* unambiguously means, it is difficult for me to replace it with any other name. I've decided to prominently use His original name and I justify its use, based upon its divine meaning. If we can say *Jesus*, can't we just as easily say, *Yahusha*?

When YHUH instructed Moses to go to Egypt to petition for the freedom of the Israelites, Moses expressed to Him that the Israelites would want to know who sent him. YHUH said to Moses: *I AM THAT I AM: and he said, Thus shalt thou say unto the children of Israel, I AM hath sent me unto you* (Exodus 3:14). This is an extraordinarily powerful portrayal YHUH has given of Himself. He is saying that I, YHUH, exist because I exist. I am eternal. He is also stating, "I am sovereign; all powerful; can do whatever I want; create whatever I want and be whomever I choose to be." YHUH knew this description of himself was appropriate after searching the collective hearts of the enslaved Hebrews. He knew this was their aggregated view of the true and living God. This title encapsulated the unlimited, matchless power and greatness of a supreme potentate, who would come and deliver them out of the hand of the Egyptians.

Understand, YHUH doesn't force you to accept what He knows. Instead, He will meet you where your thinking and intelligence are. Whatever your imagination is of a powerful Creator, He accepts that as your initial knowledge of Him. Through your desire to learn more about Him, He will reveal to you the fullness of who He is, and your understanding of Him will develop. His love for you and your love for Him will increase your understanding of Him (Jeremiah 29:13). You will experience all this and so much more when you invite Elohim into your life.

When I was in desperate need of finding the Son of God, I called upon His name. At the height of my storm, feeling totally washed up, fed up and depressed–nearly to the point of delirium–I cried, "Yahusha, save me!" I'd recently discovered this was His true name, but didn't know much more than that. I felt something divine, however, convincing me that if I wanted Him to save me, which I desired desperately, I had to call Him by His *God-given* name. When I think about it now, how could I have asked Him to save my life and preserve my soul without using His God-given name? I was convinced, convicted even, that this was His name. For *me* this means no other name given to Him by humanity has any power to save. For me, just as I suspect for you, a name *has* to matter.

YHUH knew the name of His Son was of such great importance that He sent angels, in advance of His birth, to declare His name to His mother and her husband. Not only is the name significant because of what it means, it also provided the matchless power and supernatural covering to protect Yahusha and His followers (disciples) from great evil while he was on Earth.

I believe His original name *still* has supernatural power today, as it did then. It still has inexplicable, impenetrable, warrior-grade attributes, so to speak. *I will remain in the world no longer, but they are still in the world, and I am coming to you. Holy Father, protect them by the power of your name, the name you gave me, so that they may be one as we are one. While I was with them, I protected them and kept them safe by that name you gave me. None has been lost except the one doomed to destruction so that Scripture would be fulfilled* (John 17:11–12 NIV).

Demons recognised the name Yahusha. *And there was in their synagogue a man with an unclean spirit; and he cried out, Saying, Let us alone; what have we to do with thee, thou Jesus of Nazareth? art thou come to destroy us? I know thee who thou art, the Holy One of God* (Mark 1:23–24). Remember, this wasn't the name the demon uttered. As stated earlier, there is no letter *J* in the Aramaic (the language spoken by Yahusha and the people of that day) or Hebrew alphabet. There is also no *J* in the Greek alphabet (the original language of the New Testament). As previously mentioned, Hebrew is much closer to Aramaic than Greek. Also, Strong's Concordance acknowledges the name *Jesus* here replaces the original name, *Yahusha*.

Most Christian pastors and scholars of the Bible know that His name *wasn't* Jesus. Ask them; they will tell you. Unfortunately, most will tell you the name doesn't really matter. It's bewildering how although most of us don't speak Greek, we insist on calling Yahusha by a Latin name (a dead language) supposedly transliterated from Greek, spelt using a letter not contained in either the Hebrew or Greek alphabet, given to Him by someone other than His Father, YHUH (note John 5:43). Yahusha was Jewish, born in Bethlehem (located today in the West Bank in Palestine, south of Jerusalem). Yet oddly, we are not familiar with His Aramaic or Hebrew name.

Once I learnt of His true name, and more significantly the meaning of it, I deeply felt the need to use it. Yahusha is the most powerful name I've ever known. It's so powerful; the name *alone* saves! That's because the name literally means, "YHUH saves!" *For whosoever shall call upon the name of the Lord shall be saved* (Romans 10:13), now comes alive! Now I know why, for a lack of knowledge, we perish.

Yahusha wants us to call on Him immediately. With every flaw and problem and not wait until tomorrow. Let's not wait until we are swept away with lies and pretence. Let's not attempt to dress up our sins and cover our shame. *For he saith, I have heard thee in a time accepted, and in the day of salvation have I succoured [aided] thee: behold, now is the accepted time; behold, now is the day of salvation* (2 Corinthians 6:2). We cannot clean up our own messes, and we definitely cannot save ourselves. We all need Yahusha's saving. He saves us *now*! He is the *Saviour.* His name, given to Him by His Father, embodies this. One name—immediate deliverance!

His name identifies His lineage. It exalts His Father. Speaking and teaching in the synagogue from as early as 12, He astonished all who listened. He performed hundreds of miracles that demonstrated His Father's restorative love, mercy, and grace. Yet because of obstinate unbelief, many refused to recognise Him. Yahusha was profoundly disappointed by the unbelief of the religious leaders and followers of His day. This is why He responded to them in the manner He did when they asked Him, "Where is your Father?" *"Jesus answered, Ye neither know me, nor my Father: if ye had known me, ye should have known my Father also"* (John 8:19).

They had a particular image in mind of who the Messiah would be. He didn't meet their expectations. He broke from tradition. He didn't come from a prominent family. He didn't have earthly possessions. He kept as His friends (disciples), fishermen, and men of low stature. He did not fraternise with the rich and powerful.

The Pharisees and some of the teachers of the law who had come from Jerusalem gathered around Jesus and saw some of his disciples eating food with hands that were defiled, that is, unwashed. (The Pharisees and all the Jews do not eat unless they give their hands a ceremonial washing, holding to the tradition of the elders. When they come from the marketplace they do not eat unless they wash. And they observe many other traditions, such as the washing of cups, pitchers and kettles.) So the Pharisees and teachers of the law asked Jesus, "Why don't your disciples live according to the tradition of the elders instead of eating their food with defiled hands?" He replied,

"Isaiah was right when he prophesied about you hypocrites; as it is written: "These people honor me with their lips, but their hearts are far from me. They worship me in vain; their teachings are merely human rules.' You have let go of the commands of God and are holding on to human traditions." And he continued, "You have a fine way of setting aside the commands of God in order to observe your own traditions!" (Mark 7:1–9 NIV)

Let your walk take you on a journey to discover truth. Maybe you believe the name doesn't matter. If so, pray about it and ask Elohim to guide you. If your journey hasn't taken you here yet, then He will make an exception. *Therefore since we are God's offspring, we should not think that the divine being is like gold or silver or stone—an image made by human design and skill. In the past, God overlooked such ignorance, but now he commands all people everywhere to repent* (Acts 17:29–30 NIV). This verse is saying, when we don't know any better, Elohim will overlook our ignorance.

If you have discovered and accepted the truth but continue to do things that go against newly discovered truth, you will be held accountable for rejecting it over tradition, peer pressure, or even complacency. *My people are destroyed for a lack of knowledge: because thou hast rejected knowledge, I will also reject thee, that thou shalt be no priest to me: seeing thou hast forgotten the law of thy God, I will also forget thy children* (Hosea 4:6). This text implies that the people's ignorance was from rebellion and thus, intentional. They had the knowledge but rejected it. *Therefore my people are gone into captivity, because they have no knowledge: and their honourable men are famished, and their multitude dried up with thirst* (Isaiah 5:13). Because of their rejection, they were taken into captivity. Divine truths that should have been passed down throughout the ages were lost, causing even the most well intended to starve and thirst for knowledge. Friend, you need to discover truth for yourself. If and when you do, don't reject it. *And ye shall know the truth, and the truth shall make you free* (John 8:32).

A popular school of thought suggests that the name doesn't really matter. It supports a view that we can call Yahusha *Jesus* or any other name we find in the Bible. Consider a group of individuals deliberating over *your* original name, its origin, translation,

36

importance, significance, etc., to determine whether it should be used when speaking or referring to you. After a comprehensive discourse, it is concluded that all which has been contemplated and uncovered be ignored. They continue to call you by what they *prefer*, precipitously disregarding all the apropos facts uncovered in the aforementioned discourse. Exhibiting that behaviour would be rather dismissive and flagrantly disrespectful, don't you think?

Now, consider who we are discussing here. The man at the centre of our discourse gave His life so that we could gain eternal life. *And they sung a new song, saying, Thou art worthy to take the book, and to open the seals thereof: for thou wast slain, and hast redeemed us to God by thy blood out of every kindred, and tongue, and people, and nation* (Revelation 5:9).

Another way to look at this is to imagine meeting someone for the first time. You tell her your name is "Sally" but she dismisses that name entirely, and decides to call you *Sue* because you "look like a Sue." How inappropriate is that? Should we not discover for ourselves the name of the man "Who Saves?" *The name of the LORD is a strong tower: the righteous runneth into it, and is safe* (Proverbs 18:10). The original name that *LORD* replaces here, according to Strong's Concordance, is *Yahuah (YHUH)*. Remember what *Yahusha* means? It means, "YHUH saves." Just like today, names mattered greatly to the Jewish people.

The meaning of names was of great significance, not only to the one carrying the name but also to their families. The simple fact, which is easily proven from authoritative sources, is that Yahusha was born a Jew, and He had an Aramaic/ Hebrew name. There is no such name as *Jesus* in the Aramaic/Hebrew language, even today.

Recalling the meaning of the name Yahusha and its association with the name Yahuah definitely adds a profound and fascinating dimension to the following verse: *Jesus saith unto him, Have I been so long time with you, and yet hast thou not known me, Philip? He that hath seen me hath seen the Father; and how sayest thou then, Show us the Father?* (John 14:9).

Let us further contemplate the following verses, as we consider whether the *original* name of the Father and the Son truly matter:

- *And God [Elohim] said moreover unto Moses, Thus shalt thou say unto the children of Israel, the LORD [YHUH] God [Elohim] of your fathers, the God [Elohim]of Abraham, the*

37

God [Elohim] of Isaac, and the God [Elohim] of Jacob, hath sent me unto you: this is my name for ever, and this is my memorial unto all generations (Exodus 3:15).

- *And it was in the heart of David my father to build an house for the name of the LORD [YHUH] God [Elohim] of Israel. And the LORD [YHUH] said unto David my father, Whereas it was in thine heart to build an house unto my name, thou didst well that it was in thine heart* (1 Kings 8:17-18).

- *And they that know thy name will put their trust in thee: for thou, LORD [YHUH], hast not forsaken them that seek thee* (Psalm 9:10).

- *In thy name shall they rejoice all the day: and in thy righteousness shall they be exalted. For thou art the glory of their strength: and in thy favour our horn shall be exalted* (89:16-17).

- *Because he hath set his love upon me, therefore will I deliver him: I will set him on high, because he hath known my name. He shall call upon me, and I will answer him: I will be with him in trouble; I will deliver him, and honour him* (91:14-15).

- *I am the LORD [YHUH]: that is my name: and my glory will I not give to another, neither my praise to graven images. Sing unto the LORD [YHUH] a new song, and his praise from the end of the earth, ye that go down to the sea, and all that is therein; the isles, and the inhabitants thereof* (Isaiah 42:8,10).

- *I am the LORD [YHUH], and there is none else, there is no God [Elohim] beside me: I girded thee, though thou hast not known me: That they may know from the rising of the sun, and from the west, that there is none beside me. I am the LORD [YHUH], and there is none else. I form the light, and create darkness: I make peace, and create evil: I the LORD [YHUH] do all these things* (45:5-7).

- *Go ye therefore, and teach all nations, baptizing them in the name of the Father, and of the Son, and of the Holy Ghost* (Matthew 28:19).

- *Neither is there salvation in any other: for there is none other name under heaven given among men, whereby we must be saved* (Acts 4:12).

- *By the grace God has given me, I laid a foundation as a wise builder, and someone else is building on it. But each one should build with care. For no one can lay any foundation other than the one already laid, which is Jesus Christ [Yahusha Ha'Mashiach]* (1 Corinthians 3:10-11 NIV).

- *For there is one God and one mediator between God and mankind, the man Christ Jesus [Yahusha Ha'Mashiach], who gave himself as a ransom for all people. This has now been witnessed to at the proper time* (1 Timothy 2:5-6 NIV).

- *But God's firm foundation stands, bearing this seal: "The Lord knows those who are his," and, "Let everyone who names the name of the Lord depart from iniquity"* (2 Timothy 2:19 ESV).

Remember, the word "LORD" replaces YHUH's *true* name. Further note, neither the name *Jesus* nor the titles *Christ or Lord,* was the name or titles originally ascribed. Strong's Bible Concordance will support this claim. I encourage you to search this matter out for yourself using the Bible and the Bible Concordance.

When worshipping our Creator, how can He accept our worship once we discover His true name but mulishly insist on calling Him something else? *And they shall see his face; and his name shall be in their foreheads* (Revelation 22:4). What name do you suspect will be in our foreheads? His original name, given to us throughout the ages by Him? Or some other name, manufactured by men who saw no need to keep His true name, sacred and established, throughout all generations. *Therefore my people will know my name; therefore in that day they will know that it is I who foretold it. Yes, it is I"* (Isaiah 52:6 NIV).

The Hindu gods are called by their names, even by people who don't speak Hindi. No matter where we go in the world, Buddha is known and called by his name. The founder of Islam, the Prophet Muhammad, peace be upon him, is also called by his name, no matter what language is spoken by those who practice Islam or speak of him. Calling someone by their proper name is a basic sign of familiarity and respect. We do know that names and titles of people are never deemed translatable. So why then was the name *Jesus* deliberately introduced into the Holy Scriptures?

The apostle Paul, who wrote most of the books contained in the New Testament, knew Yahusha's disciple, Cephas (Peter). Peter was Jewish and would not have called his Master, Iēsous (the Greek name supposedly given to Yahusha during His time on Earth). Why then do so many Christian believers insist on being so cavalier when it comes to calling Yahuah (YHUH) and Yahusha out of their names? Christians believe that Elohim is the one and only Creator, who by His mouth the worlds were created (Genesis 1:1; Psalm 33:6-9).

Christians believe that praise is the ultimate form of worship. How can we praise His holy name if we insist on not using His *holy* name in the praise? If we want to praise and worship YHUH and His Son, Yahusha, we need to start by calling them by their correct holy names. What do you think?

A story in Genesis, the first book of the Bible, tells how YHUH requested two brothers to build an altar and give an atonement sacrifice to Him. One did just as YHUH had instructed, and his sacrifice was accepted. The other decided to disobey YHUH and placed upon his altar the first fruits from his harvest as an atonement sacrifice (he was a crop framer). YHUH rejected it. Atonement sacrifices had to be blood sacrifices, so animal sacrifices were required. The brother, whose sacrifice was rejected by YHUH, was so angry he killed his brother. He was jealous and felt YHUH preferred his brother over him.

The brothers I'm referring to are Cain and Abel (Genesis 4). This is an example of YHUH not accepting anything from us unless it's in accordance with His will. When we discover His name for ourselves and accept it as truth, He will expect us to use it going forward.

When we truly understand the greatness of the One who created us, who loves us with an indescribable love, who sent His only Son to die on Calvary (Luke 23:33) so that one day we could live in glory with Him, I believe out of love–not obligation, we should want to call Him by His holy name. Calling Him by His name constrains us to think acutely about His many qualities. Consequently, we develop a deeper love, a greater understanding and a prodigious reverence for Him. The Bible informs us that we will not be judged for what we do not genuinely know. We certainly know that truth and knowledge are not static. We must therefore be open to receiving the light of truth, whenever it appears.

As we discover truth, we need to put away old beliefs. That said, we should embrace new-to-us doctrine, only after sincere prayer and a thorough investigation for ourselves. Christians who don't know better will not be held accountable. That's grace and mercy, and it's abundantly provided to us through His love.

As stated earlier, the name Yahusha is a verb. It means, "YHUH saves." To save implies action. The specific action, effected through the Father's love, is the bestowing of salvation, comprised of grace and mercy, through the Son. *Who is a God like you, pardoning iniquity and passing over transgression for the remnant of his inheritance? He does not retain his anger forever, because he delights in steadfast love. He will again have compassion on us; he will tread our iniquities underfoot. You will cast all our sins into the depths of the sea* (Micah 7:18-19 ESV).

YHUH sent His only son to be the perfect atoning sacrifice for our sin. *He saw that there was no one, he was appalled that there was no one to intervene; so his own arm achieved salvation for him, and his own righteousness sustained him* (Isaiah 59:16 NIV). Through these verses, we get to understand more definitively why calling upon the name of Yahusha will save us (Romans 10:13). Yahusha's name literally means, "YHUH saves!" *Therefore he is able to save completely those who come to God through him, because he always lives to intercede for them* (Hebrews 7:25 NIV).

The name Yahusha is also an adjective, as it characterises the great power of YHUH. *The LORD thy God in the midst of thee is mighty; he will save, he will rejoice over thee with joy; he will rest in his love, he will joy over thee with singing* (Zephaniah 3:17).

The name Yahusha is the personification of the Christian redemption story. But before we get there, the perceptive mind will sense that His name suggests, we are in need of saving. This means we are in danger, but from what? *Be sober, be vigilant; because your adversary the devil, as a roaring lion, walketh about, seeking whom he may devour* (1 Peter 5:8). Yahusha came to destroy the works of the devil. *He that committeth sin is of the devil; for the devil sinneth from the beginning. For this purpose the Son of God was manifested, that he might destroy the works of the devil* (1 John 3:8).

We are in danger of losing our lives and souls for eternity because of sin. However, YHUH wants us to be with Him for eternity and live in a place that is the pure quintessence of love and life. That's why He sent His Son (John 3:16). If we allow the devil to lead us and we reject YHUH, we are in jeopardy of going to a place that is full of suffering, anguish, despair, and perpetual death.

In flaming fire taking vengeance on them that know not God, and that obey not the gospel of our Lord Jesus Christ: Who shall be punished with everlasting destruction from the presence of the Lord, and from the glory of his power (2 Thessalonians 1:8–9).

He that overcometh shall inherit all things; and I will be his God, and he shall be my son. But the fearful, and unbelieving, and the abominable, and murderers, and whoremongers, and sorcerers, and idolaters, and all liars, shall have their part in the lake which burneth with fire and brimstone: which is the second death (Revelation 21:7–8).

Finally, YHUH *is* love. Regrettably, if we don't truly know Him, we will never experience the pure richness of His love. Sin separates us from the love of YHUH. *But your iniquities have separated between you and your God, and your sins have hid his face from you, that he will not hear* (Isaiah 59:2). Salvation, through His Son, leads us to His way, His truth, and the everlasting life He promises. Once He has us in His love, nothing can separate us from Him (Romans 8:35–39). He doesn't want us to follow Him out of blind, sycophantic obligation. We shouldn't think we can gain access to Him by following a strict set of religious laws or rituals. He wants us to come to Him and develop a personal, intimate relationship with Him.

He will then place His law in our hearts, and we will willingly follow Him. *For this is the covenant that I will make with the house of Israel after those days, saith the Lord; I will put my laws into their mind, and write them in their hearts: and I will be to them a God, and they shall be to me a people* (Hebrews 8:10).

Without YHUH, we are powerless. Darkness will consume us, and we will feel lost. YHUH *is* salvation! *Behold, God is my salvation, I will trust and not be afraid; 'For YAH, the LORD, is my strength and song; He also has become my salvation.'"* (Isaiah 12:2 NKJV). *But Israel shall be saved by the LORD With an everlasting salvation; You shall not be ashamed or disgraced Forever and ever.* (45:17 NKJV). He sent Yahusha to save us! Did you know that at the eleventh hour, Yahusha suffered great anxiety when contemplating the final events soon to take place? He was, after all, clothed in humanity and therefore suspectable to all the vulnerabilities we as humans regularly face. He asked YHUH, if it was His will, to *remove this cup from [Him]* (Luke 22:42). It was YHUH's will, however, to send His only Son, Yahusha, to die for you and me. You see, friend, only a perfect, blameless sacrifice would be accepted by YHUH. Only Yahusha would do.

And he was withdrawn from them about a stone's cast, and kneeled down, and prayed, Saying, Father, if thou be willing, remove this cup from me: nevertheless not my will, but thine, be done. And there appeared an angel unto him from heaven, strengthening him. And being in an agony he prayed more earnestly: and his sweat was as it were great drops of blood falling down to the ground. (22:41-44)

Yahusha *is* the Saviour!

He reaches us whenever we cry out to Him. It doesn't matter where we are or what we're going through. Like a flash of light, supernaturally, Yahusha sends angels who move through space, time and dimensions to come to our rescue. Sometimes, they even reveal themselves to us. *Be not forgetful to entertain strangers: for thereby some have entertained angels unawares* (Hebrews 13:2). Yahusha can speak encouragement to our minds or place a stranger in our lives to come to our aid. You could be homeless, hungry, struggling with drug addiction, dealing with anxiety, suffering from depression, experiencing poor health or debilitating grief from the profound loss of a loved one. You may be going through certain situations because you're being attacked (remember the story of Job). However, you're not equipped to successfully overcome in your own strength.

But Yahusha *is* the Good Shepherd. He will protect His sheep from the preying wolf. *I am the good shepherd: the good shepherd giveth his life for the sheep* (John 10:11). If you call upon the name of Yahusha, He *will* save you. This *is* His purpose. This *is* His name. This *is* His mission.

Yahusha told His disciples that to be the greatest in heaven, you must serve. He will lovingly serve salvation to all those who believe. Here is the overarching story throughout the Bible: Yahuah (YHUH) is love, and His Son, Yahusha, saves us through the powerful love of His Father. *Greater love hath no man than this, that a man lay down his life for his friends* (15:13).

Believe this message today and live under the protection of our Saviour, Yahusha Ha'Mashiach (Yahusha, the Messiah).

Chapter 3
The Images of Darkness

Since the children have flesh and blood, he too shared in their humanity so that by his death he might break the power of him who holds the power of death—that is, the devil—and free those who all their lives were held in slavery by their fear of death. For surely it is not angels he helps, but Abraham's descendants (Hebrews 2:14–16 (NIV).

From an early age, most of us have understood and recognised opposites. The opposite of big is small. We know the opposite of up is down. The opposite of left is right. The opposite of north is south. We also know the opposite of day is night.

With time and countless experiences, we have learnt that life is filled with degrees of variance as well as opposites. Some days we feel over the moon, full of optimism and hope. Some days are so brilliant, we wish them never to end. Take, for example, a dream vacation. Everything seems to fit right into place. The weather is gorgeous on the morning of the trip. The flight was great and the hotel, tours, services, and entertainment are magnificent.

But then other times, our best-laid plans blow up in our faces. Perhaps you finally land your dream job with the Fortune 500 company you always wanted to work for. Everything is great until a few months in. You discover the job is much more stressful than you could've ever imagined. Your dream job has become a nightmare. Just like that, your plans for the future, your happiness and desire for self-fulfilment have been decimated. Happiness is gone. Anxiety, doubt, and regret have taken up residence in your mind.

How about your marriage that ended in disappointment or even in a nasty divorce? This surely wasn't what you had in mind. You recall the first time you laid eyes on your wife from across the room. Your heart skipped a beat. Your palms started to sweat as you walked nervously across the room to introduce yourself. You knew immediately she was the one. However, 13 years later, you feel nothing but disdain toward her. You think to yourself, *Hell hath no fury, like a woman's scorn.* Yes, life goes on but you are left carrying baggage full of pain, regret, and deep sorrow. Most of the wounds, you may admit, are self-inflicted. Even so, the pain and regret are still very palpable and have become a constant torment to your soul.

These life events illustrate how we all encounter good and bad in our lives. Many of us believe we can learn from the bad experiences while being grateful for the good ones. Indeed, we can learn from our mistakes, becoming better, wiser, and more resilient individuals. Or, we can become bitter and allow these discomforting incidents to consume our lives. Somewhere in between these two options, many of us try to function while balancing our lives. Most of us have heard about yin and yang, a concept originating in ancient Chinese philosophy. Here, opposite forces are seen as interconnected and counterbalancing. It is commonly represented by the yin-yang symbol, a circle made up of black and white swirls, each containing a spot of the other.[xi] Many of us see some merit in this concept.

The same is true regarding our emotions. Many days we feel as though a battle is raging within us. We can choose to do good and become a force for good, or we can decide to do bad for selfish reasons. The latter will cause hurt and frustration in the lives of others and eventually cause hurt in our own lives. When we lie and cheat or do something we know we shouldn't, and our actions are discovered, it hurts the people we do these things to. The irony is that the people we hurt the most are usually those we claim to love the most. This devastates us emotionally.

Most of us lie to hide painful, frustrating, or inconvenient truths. We know our actions were wrong and, if discovered, would hurt our friends and family; so out of an abundance of care, we foolishly lie to cloak the problematic truth. For example, many husbands and wives engage in extramarital affairs. They then lie to cover the affair, or avoid telling the truth to save their spouse from unimaginable pain and embarrassment. How about employees who regularly cheat their employers by claiming to work the contractual number of hours but not putting in the agreed time. They then lie to protect their employers from feeling cheated and to protect themselves from disciplinary action. In the end, all these deceptive behaviours are usually discovered.

We may ask, "Why did I do this?" or "What was I thinking?" We wish we could go back and make different choices. Of course, this is impossible, and we soon learn how consequences follow actions. Eventually, we decide to move on and hopefully not repeat the same mistakes. Unfortunately, most of us find ourselves trapped, repeating the same mistakes. How many of us have a 0 for 6 losing streak in relationships? How about 0 for 3 in marriage? Or, 0 for 3 in DUIs? Perhaps it's 0 for 5 in career choices? I could go on, but you see the point.

Every time we get caught out and life punches us in the gut, we sincerely affirm learning our lesson and promise to never make the same daft mistake again. Nonetheless, our life's batting average tells a much different story. Many of us carry incredibly dismal failure rates because we are trying to overcome our susceptibilities in our own strength. We are trying to figure out life using the same intelligence that generated these miserable outcomes.

For God, who commanded the light to shine out of darkness, hath shined in our hearts, to give the light of the knowledge of the glory of God in the face of Jesus Christ. But we have this treasure in earthen vessels, that the excellency of the power may be of God, and not of us. We are troubled on every side, yet not distressed; we are perplexed, but not in despair; Persecuted, but not forsaken; cast down, but not destroyed; Always bearing about in the body the dying of the Lord Jesus, that the life also of Jesus might be made manifest in our body (2 Corinthians 4:6–10).

We are vessels. Vessels are designed to carry things. What we carry will determine what is poured into our lives, the lives of others, and the world around us. If we carry the Spirit of Elohim (the Holy Spirit), our lives will reflect this. *And the disciples were filled with joy, and with the Holy Ghost* (Acts 13:52). If we carry the spirit of the evil one, our lives will also reflect that. *But an evil spirit from the LORD came on Saul as he was sitting in his house with his spear in his hand. While David was playing the lyre, Saul tried to pin him to the wall with his spear, but David eluded him as Saul drove the spear into the wall.*

That night David made good his escape (1 Samuel 19:9-10 NIV). One thing to remember: we cannot *not* carry a spirit.

As vessels, we will always carry a spirit within us. Therefore, we need to invite the Holy Spirit into our lives, or we will be occupied, without consent, by forces of evil. The Holy Spirit is not intrusive. It doesn't invite itself into our lives. Rather, we must invite it into our minds to occupy our vessels. *Behold, I stand at the door, and knock: if any man hear my voice, and open the door, I will come in to him, and will sup with him, and he with me* (Revelation 3:20).

When an impure spirit comes out of a person, it goes through arid places seeking rest and does not find it. Then it says, "'I will return to the house I left.'" When it arrives, it finds the house swept clean and put in order. Then it goes and takes seven other spirits more wicked than itself, and they go in and live there. And the final condition of that person is worse than the first (Luke 11:24–26 NIV).

These verses in Luke vividly highlight what takes place in the spirit world regarding the behaviour of demonic forces. They explain why we keep repeating the same mistakes over and over. Why, when we relapse into self-destructive behaviour, it worsens over time. They clarify why it's always more difficult to pull away after every relapse. For those who have experienced this first-hand, you know what these verses describe is accurate and true.

You have probably, at one time or another, asked Elohim (the plural Hebrew word for *God* that captures both YHUH and Yahusha, as spoken of in the creation story of Genesis 1. Also see John 1:18; John 14:8-9) to get you out of a toxic relationship. Maybe you asked for help to overcome drug and sex addiction, gambling, lying, stealing, or other detrimental situations. For a moment, you saw and took the way of escape He made for you. You begin to live without these issues plaguing your life. Then one day you find yourself missing that toxic person, that vicious addiction, or fruitless behaviour, and before you know it, you're right back to those old, susceptible habits. But now you're in deeper. Your life is worse than before. Had you "swept and cleaned" your house (mind), welcomed and kept the Holy Spirit in your life, allowing it to fully occupy and infiltrate your soul, the demons wouldn't have been able to re-enter. *Submit yourselves therefore to God. Resist the devil, and he will flee from you* (James 4:7).

We need to understand that we cannot continue to do the same thing over and over and expect a different result. Many of our defeats come from a lack of knowledge through rebellion (Hosea 4:6). We know what we should do. Nevertheless, because of habit, peer pressure, fear, convenience, or pleasure, we ignore and wholly reject what we must do for what we want to do. It's like being stuck on a merry-go-round. We dance to a malevolent tune we know we should hate but have grown to enjoy. What terrifically rebellious souls we have become.

Why is this? *For since by man came death, by man came also the resurrection of the dead. For as in Adam all die, even so in Christ shall all be made alive* (1 Corinthians 15:21-22). *Let no man say when he is tempted, I am tempted of God: for God cannot be tempted with evil, neither tempteth he any man: But every man is tempted, when he is drawn away of his own lust, and enticed. Then when lust hath conceived, it bringeth forth sin: and sin, when it is finished, bringeth forth death* (James 1:13-15).

Sin has done a number to the entire world. Humanity is powerless against sin. Only through the redemptive power of YHUH can we overcome sin. When we invite the Holy Spirt into our lives, we begin to move in the Holy Spirit, and the power of Elohim is made manifest.

The law was without power because it was made weak by our sinful selves. But God did what the law could not do: He sent his own Son to earth with the same human life that everyone else uses for sin. God sent him to be an offering to pay for sin. So God used a human life to destroy sin. He did this so that we could be right just as the law said we must be. Now we don't live following our sinful selves. We live following the Spirit. People who live following their sinful selves think only about what they want. But those who live following the Spirit are thinking about what the Spirit wants them to do. If your thinking is controlled by your sinful self, there is spiritual death. But if your thinking is controlled by the Spirit, there is life and peace. Why is this true? Because anyone whose thinking is controlled by their sinful self is against God. They refuse to obey God's law. And really they are not able to obey it. Those who are ruled by their sinful selves cannot please God. But you are not ruled by your sinful selves. You are ruled by the Spirit, if that Spirit of God really lives in you. But whoever does not have the Spirit of Christ does not belong to Christ. Your body will always be dead because of sin. But if Christ is in you, then the Spirit gives you life, because Christ made you right with God. God raised Jesus from death. And if God's Spirit lives in you, he will also give life to your bodies that die. Yes, God is the one who raised Christ from death, and he will raise you to life through his Spirit living in you. So, my brothers and sisters, we must not be ruled by our sinful selves. We must not live the way our sinful selves want. If you use your lives to do what your sinful selves want, you will die spiritually. But if you use the Spirit's help to stop doing the wrong things you do with your body, you will have true life (Romans 8:3-13 ERV).

Sin, which is simply the disobedience of YHUH's Law, separates us from His salvation.

Whosoever committeth sin transgresseth also the law: for sin is the transgression of the law. And ye know that he was manifested to take away our sins; and in him is no sin. Whosoever abideth in him sinneth not: whosoever sinneth hath not seen him, neither known him. Little children, let no man deceive you: he that doeth righteousness is righteous, even as he is righteous. He that committeth sin is of the devil; for the devil sinneth from the beginning. For this purpose the Son of God was manifested, that he might destroy the works of the devil (1 John 3:4–8).

This separation causes us to live in spiritual darkness. *In whom the god of this world hath blinded the minds of them which believe not, lest the light of the glorious gospel of Christ, who is the image of God, should shine unto them* (2 Corinthians 4:4).

Spiritual darkness is simply the absence of YHUH's light. YHUH is light. 1 John 1:5 says, *This then is the message which we have heard of him, and declare unto you, that God is light, and in him is no darkness at all.* Likewise, Ezekiel 10:4 says, *Then the glory of the LORD went up from the cherub, and stood over the threshold of the house; and the house was filled with the cloud, and the court was full of the brightness of the LORD'S glory.*

YHUH is also love. *He that loveth not knoweth not God; for God is love.* (1 John 4:8). 4:18 NIV, says: *There is no fear in love. But perfect love drives out fear, because fear has to do with punishment. The one who fears is not made perfect in love.* Yes, friend, He's not only untainted light, but also untainted love. YHUH is *perfect* love and light. He drives away *all* fear. In Him, we are totally redeemed! We no longer have to fear punishment and condemnation from sin. The punishment of sin is torment, first emanating through feelings of failure, inadequacy and victimhood. Left unrestrained, it leads to total separation, destruction, and eternal death.

By now, you should have a good idea of who is behind anxiety, depression, fear, and failure. Let's see, however, whom the Bible identifies as being behind these forces.

- *And this is the condemnation, that light is come into the world, and men loved darkness rather than light, because their deeds were evil* (John 3:19).
- *For I know that good itself does not dwell in me, that is, in my sinful nature. For I have the desire to do what is good, but I cannot carry it out. For I do not do the good I want to do, but the evil I do not want to do—this I keep on doing* (Romans 7:18-19 NIV).
- *Be sober, be vigilant; because your adversary the devil, as a roaring lion, walketh about, seeking whom he may devour* (1 Peter 5:8).
- *The thief cometh not, but for to steal, and to kill, and to destroy: I am come that they might have life, and that they might have it more abundantly* (John 10:10).
- *For we wrestle not against flesh and blood, but against principalities, against powers, against the rulers of the darkness of this world, against spiritual wickedness in high places* (Ephesians 6:12).

These Bible verses make it absolutely clear that because of our sinful nature, we gravitate toward evil, which robs us of the light that comes from YHUH. Our minds become occupied with thoughts of darkness and confusion. These thoughts guarantee repeated failure and the erosion of self-worth. When confusion enters our minds, we no longer think sensibly but, instead, recklessly. This causes our minds to drift and stray farther. While roaming in confusion, the devil is there to devour us.

For though we walk in the flesh, we do not war after the flesh: (For the weapons of our warfare are not carnal, but mighty through God to the pulling down of strongholds;) Casting down imaginations, and every high thing that exalteth itself against the knowledge of God, and bringing into captivity every thought to the obedience of Christ; And having in a readiness to revenge all disobedience, when your obedience is fulfilled (2 Corinthians 10:3–6).

Satan's only goal is to distract us long enough to rob us of our light and joy and weaken our minds and hearts with doubt. He brings railing accusations before YHUH against us in an attempt to have our souls condemned and destroyed, thereby separating us from YHUH for eternity. However, we are never alone. By YHUH's mercy and grace, and the redemptive blood of the Lamb, we will overcome.

And I heard a loud voice saying in heaven, Now is come salvation, and strength, and the kingdom of our God, and the power of his Christ: for the accuser of our brethren is cast down, which accused them before our God day and night. And they overcame him by the blood of the Lamb, and by the word of their testimony; and they loved not their lives unto the death (Revelation 12:10–11).

The greatest indication of darkness controlling our lives is a lapse in judgment. But even before we get there, we start the downward spiral by questioning our most fundamental beliefs. We question the existence of Elohim. We question the purpose of our existence. We want to know why we are such losers and why we cannot seem to accomplish anything. We start to envy the success and happiness of others. We feel Elohim cannot exist because if He did, our lives wouldn't be in such turmoil. Many of us also fail to acknowledge the existence of the devil, of evil, or the susceptibility of our flesh.

We conveniently forget that we are all sinners and our sins have separated us from YHUH (Isaiah 59:2). As sinners, we deserve to be punished (Romans 6:23). We are not entitled to anything good. We conveniently forget that all good gifts come from YHUH (James 1:17). The same YHUH whose very existence we find ourselves questioning. We almost entirely disregard the power of YHUH's goodness toward us because we don't *feel* it.

Perhaps you don't feel His goodness because you don't possess an abundance of material things. Unfortunately, you have failed to acknowledge that you have life, health, and strength. You are of sound mind. You overlook the fact that you have all your needs and some of your wants. These are some of the blessings that the flesh cannot touch. Life is never perfect, but if you would stop with self-pity long enough to count your blessings, you would realise just how blessed and truly rich you are. That is YHUH's goodness on display!

Perhaps, you don't feel His mercy because of the unbearable loss of your child. This traumatic event could easily cause you to lose your faith in Elohim. That would be the natural reaction after experiencing something as horrific as this. Do you remember what Job declared after losing all of his children in one day along with his health and wealth? *Though he slay me, yet will I trust in him: but I will maintain mine own ways before him* (Job 13:15). Try to resist blaming Elohim or feeling abandoned by Him. Instead, pray for strength, faith, wisdom, and understanding. Of course, choosing this path is difficult; nevertheless, it isn't impossible.

You may discover that when dealing with immense tragedy and loss in this way, it brings you closer to Elohim. It opens doors of greater understanding and leads you to recommitting it all to Him, trusting Him uncompromisingly. Sometimes during these severe storms of life, the radiance of His glory is more magnified and its warmth and protection more deeply felt. *But for you who revere my name, the sun of righteousness will rise with healing in its rays. And you will go out and frolic like well-fed calves* (Malachi 4:2 NIV).

Throughout this terrible ordeal, you may come to discover that death isn't a punishment but rather the vehicle that moves us along on the journey to eternity. *And as it is appointed unto men once to die, but after this the judgment: So Christ was once offered to bear the sins of many; and unto them that look for him shall he appear the second time without sin unto salvation* (Hebrews 9:27–28).

Losing a child can never be easy. By far, it must be the most dreadful experience of any parent. However, the sharpness of the pain will lessen when YHUH's healing balm (love) is applied. Where there is healing, there, too, is clarity.

Perhaps you don't feel His grace because your circumstances are grim and what happened to you was grossly unfair. Trust Him to use the situation to bring about something good in your life. Sometimes we need a nudge, or even a push, to get us moving toward what YHUH has for us. Sometimes, He uses uncomfortable situations to ignite our faith and get us moving. All things work together for good to those who love YHUH (Romans 8:28). Remember, *Seek ye first the kingdom of God, and his righteousness; and all these things shall be added unto you* (Matthew 6:33).

Many of us don't know the success formula to life. It's Matthew 6:33! Too often, we view ourselves as victims and not victors. When we question the existence of YHUH and feel like we know what's best for our lives, we become self-absorbed. His light is snuffed out and darkness rolls in. Notice what happened when Lucifer became self-absorbed and felt equal to YHUH.

> *How art thou fallen from heaven, O Lucifer, son of the morning! how art thou cut down to the ground, which didst weaken the nations! For thou hast said in thine heart, I will ascend into heaven, I will exalt my throne above the stars of God: I will sit also upon the mount of the congregation, in the sides of the north: I will ascend above the heights of the clouds; I will be like the most High. Yet thou shalt be brought down to hell, to the sides of the pit* (Isaiah 14:12–15).

How quickly does light leave and darkness fill the space? The moment you doubt the power and existence of YHUH and feel a rush of self-importance (ego), the light in your life dims. The moment these thoughts enter your consciousness and you allow them to put down roots in the garden of your mind, your spirit begins to wither and dwindle from the lack of wisdom and knowledge that comes from the light of truth. The longer you entertain these dubious thoughts, the dimmer your light becomes. Remember those beautiful, red, long-stem roses you purchased for, or received from, that special someone on Valentine's Day? As beautiful and vibrant as those roses were, they were dead from the moment they were cut away from the bush. YHUH cannot entertain darkness, not even for a second. *And he said unto them, I beheld Satan as lightning fall from heaven* (Luke 10:18).

Maybe you don't immediately falter and fail. It may appear as though you are succeeding for a while, thinking your success is of your own doing and not YHUH's. You may even admonish yourself for foolishly believing in someone or something you couldn't see. You might trick yourself into believing you're making it because your balance sheet shows growth. The house and neighbourhood you live in reaffirm that you've made it. The car you drive, the clothes and jewellery you wear, assert that you're on top of the world. Your friends and family applaud your success. You're doing what it takes to build generational wealth for your family. You feel as though you have "arrived." You are living it up, having fun. Banging out and flossing! Living a life of opulence and excess.

However, when the party is over, all the lights and music turned off and all your friends have left, you will remove the mask of vanity and ego. Vast emptiness and personal, painful failures will once again flood the spaces of your mind. All your misdirected thoughts, fantasies, and earthly possessions come into sharp focus to soothe your mind and stroke your ego. But nothing can lessen the feeling of meaninglessness.

Once again images of darkness re-emerge. Self-doubt, pity, sadness, emptiness, loss, fear, regret, and more sweep across your consciousness. These feelings quickly lead you back to the hollow throne of depression and anxiety. King Solomon says in Psalm 127:1–2, *Unless the LORD builds the house, the builders labor in vain. Unless the LORD watches over the city, the guards stand watch in vain. In vain you rise early and stay up late, toiling for food to eat—for he grants sleep to those he loves* (NIV).

The following is what the sons of Korah say about those who foolishly believe that Elohim isn't in the mix. They (the ungodly) allow hubris to misguide them into believing they can preserve their wealth and prominence forever. Pay keen attention to how they describe the life of the unbeliever holding on to things and the futility of it all.

Hear this, all peoples! Give ear, all inhabitants of the world, both low and high, rich and poor together! My mouth shall speak wisdom; the meditation of my heart shall be understanding. I will incline my ear to a proverb; I will solve my riddle to the music of the lyre. Why should I fear in times of trouble, when the iniquity of those who cheat me surrounds me, those who trust in their wealth and boast of the abundance of their riches? Truly no man can ransom another, or give to God the price of his life, for the ransom of their life is costly and can never suffice, that he should live on forever and never see the pit. For he sees that even the wise die; the fool and the stupid alike must perish and leave their wealth to others. Their graves are their homes forever, their dwelling places to all generations, though they called lands by their own names. Man in his pomp will not remain; he is like the beasts that perish. This is the path of those who have foolish confidence; yet after them people approve of their boasts. Selah. Like sheep they are appointed for Sheol [abode of the dead]; death shall be their shepherd and the upright shall rule over them in the morning. Their form shall be consumed in Sheol, with no place to dwell. But God will ransom my soul from the power of Sheol, for he will receive me. Selah. Be not afraid when a man becomes rich, when the glory of his house increases. For when he dies he will carry nothing away; his glory will not go down after him. For though, while he lives, he counts himself blessed—and though you get praise when you do well for yourself—his soul will go to the generation of his fathers, who will never again see light. Man in his pomp yet without understanding is like the beasts that perish (Psalm 49 ESV).

The darkness, which comes from separation of YHUH's love through our sin, spooks us and foggy our minds with indecisiveness and confusion. Instead of seeking guidance from Elohim, we rely on our own strength and knowledge. Our adversary knows that for as long as we try to fight him in our own strength, he will be victorious (Ephesians 6:12). We are naive to believe that in our own strength, we could overcome the forces of evil.

Do you know who Satan is?

Son of man, take up a lament concerning the king of Tyre and say to him: "This is what the Sovereign LORD says: 'You were the seal of perfection, full of wisdom and perfect in beauty. You were in Eden, the garden of God; every precious stone adorned you: carnelian, chrysolite and emerald, topaz, onyx and jasper, lapis lazuli, turquoise and beryl. Your settings and mountings were made of gold; on the day you were created they were prepared. You were anointed as a guardian cherub, for so I ordained you. You were on the holy mount of God; you walked among the fiery stones. You were blameless in your ways from the day you were created till wickedness was found in you.

56

Through your widespread trade you were filled with violence, and you sinned. So I drove you in disgrace from the mount of God, and I expelled you, guardian cherub, from among the fiery stones. Your heart became proud on account of your beauty, and you corrupted your wisdom because of your splendor. So I threw you to the earth; I made a spectacle of you before kings. By your many sins and dishonest trade, you have desecrated your sanctuaries. So I made a fire come out from you, and it consumed you, and I reduced you to ashes on the ground in the sight of all who were watching. All the nations who knew you are appalled at you; you have come to a horrible end and will be no more'." (Ezekiel 28:12–19 NIV)

How could you ever expect to win against such an incredible, powerful angelic being without putting on the *whole* armour of YHUH?

Put on the whole armour of God, that ye may be able to stand against the wiles of the devil. For we wrestle not against flesh and blood, but against principalities, against powers, against the rulers of the darkness of this world, against spiritual wickedness in high places. Wherefore take unto you the whole armour of God, that ye may be able to withstand in the evil day, and having done all, to stand. Stand therefore, having your loins girt about with truth, and having on the breastplate of righteousness; And your feet shod with the preparation of the gospel of peace; Above all, taking the shield of faith, wherewith ye shall be able to quench all the fiery darts of the wicked. And take the helmet of salvation, and the sword of the Spirit, which is the word of God: Praying always with all prayer and supplication in the Spirit, and watching thereunto with all perseverance and supplication for all saints (Ephesians 6:11–18).

Also remember that the devil's soldiers were once angels of the heavenly host. *For if God spared not the angels that sinned, but cast them down to hell, and delivered them into chains of darkness, to be reserved unto judgment* (2 Peter 2:4). *And his tail drew the third part of the stars of heaven, and did cast them to the earth* (Revelation 12:4). I don't know what a third translates to in terms of real numbers, but the Bible says the number of the angels are "innumerable" (Hebrews 12:22).

The circumstances of our lives that shape our experiences each day have everything to do with the battle taking place in the spiritual world. We stand to be victorious whenever we battle through the Holy Spirit.

For those who are led by the Spirit of God are the children of God. The Spirit you received does not make you slaves, so that you live in fear again; rather, the Spirit you received brought about your adoption to sonship. And by him we cry, "Abba, Father." The Spirit himself testifies with our spirit that we are God's children. Now if we are children, then we are heirs— heirs of God and co-heirs with Christ, if indeed we share in his sufferings in order that we may also share in his glory (Romans 8:14-17 NIV).

Did you know that when we worship YHUH, demons flee? When we praise and worship YHUH, it's a war against the forces of evil. When we sincerely praise YHUH, we overcome!

And he said, Hearken ye, all Judah, and ye inhabitants of Jerusalem, and thou king Jehoshaphat, Thus saith the LORD unto you, Be not afraid nor dismayed by reason of this great multitude; for the battle is not yours, but God's. To morrow go ye down against them: behold, they come up by the cliff of Ziz; and ye shall find them at the end of the brook, before the wilderness of Jeruel. Ye shall not need to fight in this battle: set yourselves, stand ye still, and see the salvation of the LORD with you, O Judah and Jerusalem: fear not, nor be dismayed; to morrow go out against them: for the LORD will be with you. And Jehoshaphat bowed his head with his face to the ground: and all Judah and the inhabitants of Jerusalem fell before the LORD, worshipping the LORD. And the Levites, of the children of the Kohathites, and of the children of the Korhites, stood up to praise the LORD God of Israel with a loud voice on high. And they rose early in the morning, and went forth into the wilderness of Tekoa: and as they went forth, Jehoshaphat stood and said, Hear me, O Judah, and ye inhabitants of Jerusalem; Believe in the LORD your God, so shall ye be established;

believe his prophets, so shall ye prosper. And when he had consulted with the people, he appointed singers unto the LORD, and that should praise the beauty of holiness, as they went out before the army, and to say, Praise the LORD; for his mercy endureth for ever. And when they began to sing and to praise, the LORD set ambushments against the children of Ammon, Moab, and mount Seir, which were come against Judah; and they were smitten. For the children of Ammon and Moab stood up against the inhabitants of mount Seir, utterly to slay and destroy them and when they had made an end of the inhabitants of Seir, every one helped to destroy another. And when Judah came toward the watch tower in the wilderness, they looked unto the multitude, and, behold, they were dead bodies fallen to the earth, and none escaped (2 Chronicles 20:15–24).

Due to our limited, mental faculties and spiritual fallibilities, we become bewildered. Relying on our *own* intelligence, we try to answer our own questions. How insane is that? This flicker of self-endowed knowledge provides only enough light to create images from the shadows. The dim glint of our wild and vain imaginations dazzle us. Images of danger show up in our minds, and fear and distress set in. We question everything, just as a lost soldier would, without the benefit of a commanding officer. Without a compass or the benefit of a guiding star, we question what direction to advance in.

Without Yahusha as our commanding officer, these questions lead to more doubt and increased frustration. Frustration to confusion, confusion to anxiety, anxiety to desperation. Desperation will make us grab hold of anything. A drowning person would hold on to a boulder in a frantic attempt to save themself.

The images of darkness include mental torment, fear, despair and worry. Worry unquestionably affects our physical and mental state. It's the constant feeling of uncertainty that stirs the mind crazy. It stops us from thinking rationally. Every bit of advice (even conflicting advice) we receive, we attempt to apply to our lives. Every self-help book that's recommended, we read. In the process, we lose discernment.

So what do we do? Number one is to recognise the enemy. *Delivering thee from the people, and from the Gentiles, unto whom now I send thee, To open their eyes, and to turn them from darkness to light, and from the power of Satan unto God, that they may receive forgiveness of sins, and inheritance among them which are sanctified by faith that is in me* (Acts 26:17–18). *Lest Satan should get an advantage of us: for we are not ignorant of his devices* (2 Corinthians 2:11). The enemy is Satan. We need to put on the armour of YHUH as instructed in Ephesians 6:11–18. Notice what the shield, helmet, and sword represent. Also notice the role that prayer plays, recognising that the prayer of a righteous person is powerful and effective (James 5:16).

When we pray, we should praise the Most High, recalling His many promises to bless us and keep us. We ought to also acknowledge that He is YHUH and He cannot change (Malachi 3:6). Neither can He fail.

> *Lift up your eyes to the heavens, and look upon the earth beneath: for the heavens shall vanish away like smoke, and the earth shall wax old like a garment, and they that dwell therein shall die in like manner: but my salvation shall be forever, and my righteousness shall not be abolished* (Isaiah 51:6). *It is of the LORD'S mercies that we are not consumed, because his compassions fail not. They are new every morning: great is thy faithfulness* (Lamentations 3:22–23).

When we believe and rely on the power of Elohim, something supernatural occurs. Mental clutter begins to abate. Clarity and focus enter the mind and a sense of hope emerges. Light enters and darkness (which is the absence of light) vanishes like smoke in a strong breeze. *The people that walked in darkness have seen a great light: they that dwell in the land of the shadow of death, upon them hath the light shined* (Isaiah 9:2). *For we preach not ourselves, but Christ Jesus the Lord; and ourselves your servants for Jesus' sake. For God, who commanded the light to shine out of darkness, hath shined in our hearts, to give the light of the knowledge of the glory of God in the face of Jesus Christ* (2 Corinthians 4:5–6).

2 Timothy 2:25–26, tells us, *Opponents [those who resist the urging of the Holy Spirit] must be gently instructed, in the hope that God will grant them repentance leading them to a knowledge of the truth, and that they will come to their senses and escape from the trap of the devil, who has taken them captive to do his will* (NIV). We overcome darkness by simply accepting and allowing light to enter our hearts and minds. In John 8:12, Yahusha Ha'Mashiach (Yahusha

the Messiah) says, *I am the light of the world: he that followeth me shall not walk in darkness, but shall have the light of life.*

The Bible tells you exactly who you are. *But ye are a chosen generation, a royal priesthood, an holy nation, a peculiar people; that ye should shew forth the praises of him who hath called you out of darkness into his marvellous light: Which in time past were not a people, but are now the people of God: which had not obtained mercy, but now have obtained mercy* (1 Peter 2:9–10). Unfortunately, oftentimes throughout our lives, when we feel down and out, crushed, and exhausted, we lose sight of who we are and how important we are to our Creator.

> *But now thus saith the LORD that created thee, O Jacob, and he that formed thee, O Israel, Fear not: for I have redeemed thee, I have called thee by thy name; thou art mine. When thou passest through the waters, I will be with thee; and through the rivers, they shall not overflow thee: when thou walkest through the fire, thou shalt not be burned; neither shall the flame kindle upon thee* (Isaiah 43:1–2). *For we are his workmanship, created in Christ Jesus unto good works, which God hath before ordained that we should walk in them* (Ephesians 2:10).

The devil's plan is to make us feel vulnerable and worthless. When we feel this way, we welcome him into our minds, and he ruins our lives. He hates us and wants to destroy us. Isn't it amazing how the devil reaches us through our thoughts? *Keep thy heart [mind] with all diligence; for out of it are the issues of life* (Proverbs 4:23). These disrupting thoughts are usually centred around trying to find clarity and meaning. However, because we reject truth (light) for the pleasures (darkness) of this world and to satisfy the desires of our hearts, we go down the wrong path. *The heart is deceitful above all things and beyond cure. Who can understand it? "I the LORD search the heart and examine the mind, to reward each person according to their conduct, according to what their deeds deserve."* (Jeremiah 17:9-10 NIV).

Even Yahusha was tempted in a similar way by Satan (Matthew 4:1–11). The devil is incomprehensibly deceptive. *And no marvel; for Satan himself is transformed into an angel of light* (2 Corinthians 11:14).

The Law of YHUH and the keeping of His Law will guard our minds from the forces of darkness. Yes, His Law has preserving and guiding power. Remember, even Yahusha quoted the Law of His Father when being tempted by Satan in the wilderness. Please note, I am not speaking about being saved by the Law. We know, however, that Satan is the father of wickedness (lawlessness) and is the antithesis of YHUH. Therefore, if the Most High is about establishing Law and Order, then Satan has to be about breaking YHUH's Law and causing disorder. This will be discussed in greater detail in my next book.

In John 8:44, Yahusha lets us know that Satan is a liar and a murderer from the beginning. When we doubt or question YHUH's purpose and plan for our lives, we take our eyes off of Him and, before long, we are doing things we shouldn't even be thinking about. It's incredible how much we question the existence and power of YHUH when we lose sight of Him and seek after other things for insight and wisdom. This is a trap. This behaviour is yet another way we invite the devil into our lives. When he enters, he brings all hell with him.

Some people who claim to be Christians and believers are sometimes so deceived that they even seek the insight of spiritual mediums, who consult with the dead. These individuals point to Bible verses to justify their behaviour. This is how dark and demonic lost Christians can become when the light of truth is no longer within them. *Woe unto them that call evil good, and good evil; that put darkness for light, and light for darkness; that put bitter for sweet, and sweet for bitter* (Isaiah 5:20). The Bible explicitly teaches us not to engage in this behaviour.

> *Regard not them that have familiar spirits, neither seek after wizards, to be defiled by them: I am the LORD your God* (Leviticus 19:31). *When someone tells you to consult mediums and spiritists, who whisper and mutter, should not a people inquire of their God? Why consult the dead on behalf of the living? Consult God's instruction and the testimony of warning. If anyone does not speak according to this word, they have no light of dawn* (Isaiah 8: 19–20 NIV).

Some of us dress our children up for Halloween and place them before the altar of Satan, all in the name of good fun. *Abstain from all appearance of evil* (1 Thessalonians 5:22). How many have "played" a Ouija board for fun? *Ye cannot drink the cup of the Lord, and the cup of devils: ye cannot be partakers of the Lord's table and of the table of devils. Do we provoke the Lord to jealousy? are we stronger than he?* (1 Corinthians 10:21-22). Spiritual darkness has led many astray.

Some of our beliefs concerning the dead have become corrupted. Some believe that their deceased loved ones have gone to Heaven and have become their guardian angels. Where in YHUH's Word is this taught? *But I fear, lest by any means, as the serpent beguiled Eve through his subtilty, so your minds should be corrupted from the simplicity that is in Christ* (2 Corinthians 11:3). Darkness leads us to seek the futility of the dark. We follow its teachings and principles there. *Let him not deceive himself by trusting what is worthless, for he will get nothing in return* (Job 15:31 NIV). In the end, these deceptions lead to destruction. *There is a way which seemeth right unto a man, but the end thereof are the ways of death* (Proverbs 14:12). You may be asking, where are my deceased loved ones?

- *For to him that is joined to all the living there is hope: for a living dog is better than a dead lion. For the living know that they shall die: but the dead know not any thing, neither have they any more a reward; for the memory of them is forgotten. Also their love, and their hatred, and their envy, is now perished; neither have they any more a portion for ever in any thing that is done under the sun* (Ecclesiastes 9:4-6).
- *Whatever your hand finds to do, do it with all your might, for in the realm of the dead, where you are going, there is neither working nor planning nor knowledge nor wisdom* (9:10 NIV).
- *Then shall the dust return to the earth as it was: and the spirit shall return unto God who gave it* (12:7)
- *No one has ever gone into heaven except the one who came from heaven—the Son of Man* (John 3:13 NIV).
- *But a man dies and is laid low; he breathes his last and is no more. As the water of a lake dries up or a riverbed becomes parched and dry, so he lies down and does not rise; till the heavens are no more, people will not awake or be roused from their sleep* (Job 14:10-12 NIV).

The remains of the deceased are where they were laid to rest, and their spirit (breath) has gone back to God. The texts above are clear: the dead have no knowledge of what's happening after they've passed.

Once we acknowledge there is a battle raging and call upon the name of Yahusha, we will immediately be saved. Never forget, His name means, "YHUH saves!" Yahusha will guide us out of darkness and into pure light (1 John 1:5). *Thy word is a lamp unto my feet, and a light unto my path* (Psalm 119:105). Do not entertain the devil. Don't debate him. When we try to justify certain actions or behaviour that, in our conscience, we know isn't right, we're holding court with Satan. When we play devil's advocate, we're entertaining him. *Yet Michael the archangel, when contending with the devil he disputed about the body of Moses, durst not bring against him a railing accusation, but said, The Lord rebuke thee* (Jude 1:9). The devil doesn't need you to be his advocate. In fact, he is the *accuser* of the brethren!

The images of darkness cannot hold you if you pledge your allegiance to Yahusha. The Holy Spirit will transform you. *And be not conformed to this world: but be ye transformed by the renewing of your mind, that ye may prove what is that good, and acceptable, and perfect, will of God* (Romans 12:2). YHUH *is* salvation! *It is because of him that you are in Christ Jesus, who has become for us wisdom from God—that is, our righteousness, holiness and redemption* (1 Corinthians 1:30 NIV). When you are transformed, the rapacious hunger for the things of this world, seeded in your heart, subsides and is replaced with the fruit of the Holy Spirit.

Now the works of the flesh are manifest, which are these; Adultery, fornication, uncleanness, lasciviousness, Idolatry, witchcraft, hatred, variance, emulations, wrath, strife, seditions, heresies, envyings, murders, drunkenness, revellings, and such like: of the which I tell you before, as I have also told you in time past, that they which do such things shall not inherit the kingdom of God. But the fruit of the Spirit is love, joy, peace, longsuffering, gentleness, goodness, faith, meekness, temperance: against such there is no law (Galatians 5:19–23).

We should be aware that some people practice a form of godliness. A faith of piousness while exchanging truth for error and trying to make wrong right.

But mark this: There will be terrible times in the last days. People will be lovers of themselves, lovers of money, boastful, proud, abusive, disobedient to their parents, ungrateful, unholy, without love, unforgiving, slanderous, without self-control, brutal, not lovers of the good, treacherous, rash, conceited, lovers of pleasure rather than lovers of God — having a form of godliness but denying its power. Have nothing to do with such people. They are the kind who worm their way into homes and gain control over gullible women, who are loaded down with sins and are swayed by all kinds of evil desires, always learning but never able to come to a knowledge of the truth (2 Timothy 3:1–7 NIV).

This behaviour is extremely dangerous to the body of Yahusha. *They claim to know God, but by their actions they deny him. They are detestable, disobedient and unfit for doing anything good* (Titus 1:16 NIV). Instead of speaking truth to power, many believers today prefer to say nothing at all in the face of evil. Unfortunately, many so-called leaders of faith reason that by speaking the truth, they will face backlash; cancel culture can be ruthless. But we can never cancel truth and righteousness. *"And if in a truthful, just and righteous way you swear, 'As surely as the LORD lives,' then the nations will invoke blessings by him and in him they will boast"* (Jeremiah 4:2 NIV).

Regrettably, these individuals could've been vessels of light. Instead, for whatever reason, they chose to hide their lights under a bushel (measuring bowl), failing to accomplish the great work commissioned by YHUH. *You are the light of the world. A town built on a hill cannot be hidden. Neither do people light a lamp and put it under a bowl. Instead they put it on its stand, and it gives light to everyone in the house. In the same way, let your light shine before others, that they may see your good deeds and glorify your Father in heaven* (Matthew 5:14–16 NIV).

We need to be cognisant that a half-truth is a full lie. When Satan deceives us, his greatest and most powerful lies are sprinkled with generous amounts of truth. False beliefs and doctrine can erode our relationship with Elohim, and, before long, we may find ourselves right back where we started. Regular Bible study, while seeking the Holy Spirit to lead us into *all* truth, will keep deception at bay. Remember, salvation is an individual quest. The discovery of truth is the personification of growth and real freedom in Elohim.

Notice how Jude 1:12-13 describe these imposters. *These people are blemishes at your love feasts, eating with you without the slightest qualm— shepherds who feed only themselves. They are clouds without rain, blown along by the wind; autumn trees, without fruit and uprooted —twice dead. They are wild waves of the sea, foaming up their shame; wandering stars, for whom blackest darkness has been reserved forever* (NIV).

Only the truth can set us free from the bondage of sin (John 8:32). Today, more than ever, the world needs to hear from truth-tellers. Disappointingly, many know the truth but out of fear, cultural norms, convenience, or in keeping with political correctness, they refuse to spread the truth of YHUH, which could free millions of people from the bonds of sin. YHUH will severely punish all those who give preference to sin. *Just as Jannes and Jambres opposed Moses, so also these teachers oppose the truth. They are men of depraved minds, who, as far as the faith is concerned, are rejected. But they will not get very far because, as in the case of those men, their folly will be clear to everyone* (2 Timothy 3:8–9 NIV). Haven't we seen this prophetic warning unfold? Indeed, many of us have seen popular, charismatic Christian leaders publicly fall from grace, sometimes experiencing cringing, painful humiliation. YHUH's Word *is* true.

YHUH cannot accept sin for righteousness. He cannot do the desperately needed supernatural work in us if we refuse to start over on *His* new path. We have to leave the baggage of sin behind and take up His yoke. *Come to me, all you who are weary and burdened, and I will give you rest. Take my yoke upon you and learn from me, for I am gentle and humble in heart, and you will find rest for your souls* (Matthew 11:28–29 NIV). YHUH *is* the God of Glory. When He becomes Lord over your life, you win the battle and overcome the forces of evil.

> *The LORD is thy keeper: the LORD is thy shade upon thy right hand. The sun shall not smite thee by day, nor the moon by night. The LORD shall preserve thee from all evil: he shall preserve thy soul. The LORD shall preserve thy going out and thy coming in from this time forth, and even for evermore* (Psalm 121:5-8).

A battle is raging over your soul. The devil would like to claim you for himself and see you destroyed along with him and his angels. But YHUH is full of goodness. He wants to see another outcome for your life. *Do I take any pleasure in the death of the wicked? declares the*

66

Sovereign LORD. Rather, am I not pleased when they turn from their ways and live? But if a wicked person turns away from the wickedness they have committed and does what is just and right, they will save their life (Ezekiel 18:23,27 NIV).

And the great dragon was cast out, that old serpent, called the Devil, and Satan, which deceiveth the whole world: he was cast out into the earth, and his angels were cast out with him. And I heard a loud voice saying in heaven, Now is come salvation, and strength, and the kingdom of our God, and the power of his Christ: for the accuser of our brethren is cast down, which accused them before our God day and night. And they overcame him by the blood of the Lamb, and by the word of their testimony; and they loved not their lives unto the death. Therefore rejoice, ye heavens, and ye that dwell in them. Woe to the inhabiters of the earth and of the sea! for the devil is come down unto you, having great wrath, because he knoweth that he hath but a short time (Revelation 12:9–12).

YHUH has glorious plans for you. He wants you to spend eternity with Him in paradise. *For the Lord himself shall descend from heaven with a shout, with the voice of the archangel, and with the trump of God: and the dead in Christ shall rise first: Then we which are alive and remain shall be caught up together with them in the clouds, to meet the Lord in the air: and so shall we ever be with the Lord* (1 Thessalonians 4:16–17).

Blessed be the name of Yahuah and His Son Yahusha, forever and ever. Hallelujah!

Chapter 4
Living in the Light:
The Rays of Hope

When I was a child, I talked like a child, I thought like a child,
I reasoned like a child. When I became a man, I put the ways
of childhood behind me. For now we see only a reflection as in
a mirror; then we shall see face to face. Now I know in part;
then I shall know fully, even as I am fully known. And now these
three remain: faith, hope and love. But the greatest of these is
love (1 Corinthians 13:11–13 NIV).

According to the dictionary, light is the natural agent that stimulates
sight and makes things visible. Light is also a source of illumination.
Throughout the Bible, Elohim (the plural Hebrew word for *God* that
captures both YHUH and Yahusha, as spoken of in the creation story
of Genesis 1. Also see John 1:18; John 14:8-9) is described many times
as the Creator of all things, the giver of life, love, mercy, and grace, the
source of all wisdom and knowledge, all-powerful and all-knowing.
He promises to guide us from darkness into His marvellous light. *The*
people which sat in darkness saw great light; and to them which sat
in the region and shadow of death light is sprung up (Matthew 4:16).

When I was a child, I witnessed my parents praying earnestly for
their household. They prayed with such great sincerity and unwavering
belief that I was certain their prayers were being heard and answered.
As a matter of fact, the strength and veracity of their prayers convinced
me that our entire household was protected and covered by the love,
mercy, and grace of Elohim. I *knew* He had heard their prayers and
would honour their supplications.

I grew up in a working, middle-class home in the Cayman Islands.
Contrary to popular belief, most of the citizens and residents of

the Cayman Islands are not rich. We don't all work in the financial services industry. My dad worked for the only utility company on the island. Throughout his career there, he held different non-managerial positions. Ninety-five percent of the time he was the only breadwinner of our household–Mum, my five siblings and me. On his single income, he built a house for us and purchased acreage across the islands for investment and farming purposes. Daddy also ensured that all of his children were properly clothed and fed, received a solid education, but more importantly, demonstrated, by example, the importance of having a personal relationship with our heavenly Father.

Like many men from his era, my dad showed very little emotion and shared almost no information about the battles he regularly fought to ensure we had all we needed. My father was a student of the Bible and was always reading and studying YHUH's Word. The more I consider just how difficult it must have been for him as the sole provider for our family, the more I realise just how richly blessed we were and where all of our blessings ultimately came from.

To this day, I cannot comprehend how my dad was able to do so much with so little. We never went without. I recall going away on summer vacations to the U.S., and all of us children having spending money. Until I had the opportunity and great privilege of becoming a parent, I had no real appreciation for just how difficult it must've been for him to be a faithful and constant provider.

As it relates to me, I wasn't the only provider for my children. My children's mums have always worked and, together, we have provided for our children. Even with two incomes, it hasn't always been easy being a constant provider. I can only imagine the prayers and strength of my parent's faith when they beseeched the throne of Elohim with their humble requests for provision and protection. Elohim is *always* faithful.

Almost two decades ago, my brother was involved in a serious car accident on his way home after a night out. He lost control of the vehicle he was driving. The vehicle flipped and he was knocked unconscious. Fortunately, his friends, who were driving ahead of him, noticed he was no longer behind them and turned back to look for him. When they came upon the scene of the accident, they immediately sprang into action, pulling him out of the vehicle through the driver's side window. As soon as they moved my half-conscious brother away from the wrecked vehicle, it exploded. The flames shot up over 30 feet high and the vehicle burnt for over 20 minutes.

My brother, as you can imagine, was deeply moved and overcome by emotion immediately following the accident. He went to his friend's house and called our mum, who was off-island visiting family in the United States. It was around 3 a.m. when he spoke with Mum. The first thing he asked her was, "Mummy, did you pray for me tonight?" Her response was the usual, praise Elohim, "I pray for you all, every night!"

My brother wasn't left unscathed. He didn't realise it at the time, but after experiencing excruciating pain in the hours following the ordeal and being persuaded by our mum to go to the hospital and get checked out, it was discovered he had suffered a broken back. Later that morning, when my sister and I visited the scene of the accident, we noticed the rocks beneath and around the vehicle had disintegrated to powder from the heat of the explosion. There was a tree, about 15 feet from the explosion, that later died as a result of the fire. Although dead, it remained in place for several years on the shoreline and reminded me every time I passed by that had it not been for Elohim's mercy, my brother would have died that night, at that spot.

Because my brother was unconscious, he wouldn't have had the presence of mind to escape the fire and would have burnt to death. Today, he is walking and has full mobility. That is the power of Elohim. YHUH saves! The prayer of a righteous person is powerful and effective (James 5:16). Hallelujah!

My other siblings and I have also walked away from serious car accidents and other calamities that could have ended much differently. For sure, the presence of the Holy Spirit has kept my family protected. Even during my ordeal of being attacked by demonic forces, my mother and others stood in the gap and offered intercessory prayer on my behalf. I was too weak, too broken at the time to pray for myself. Those who prayed for me never lost hope. They always believed and stood on the promises of the Most High contained in the living Word of Truth. I am living proof that YHUH's Word is true. He cannot fail. He is always present, and if it is His will, He will deliver us from danger and destruction.

When we trust and believe YHUH's promises for our lives, we live a life of faith. We journey in the light of truth, and the rays emanating from His light are filled with hope. *And hope does not put us to shame, because God's love has been poured out into our hearts through the Holy Spirit, who has been given to us* (Romans 5:5 NIV). We may ask, "What is hope?" Hope is expectation, the deep desire to see something transpire. *For in this hope we were saved. But hope that is seen is no hope at all. Who hopes for what they already have? But if we hope for what we do not yet have, we wait for it patiently* (8:24–25 NIV).

Faith is what we practice when there is no guarantee that our desires or expectations will manifest. Remember without *true* faith, there can be no *real* hope. Faith is holding on to something with strong and absolute conviction, *hoping* for the materialisation of your desire, without any tangible guarantees. Frequently what we hope for is the opposite of what is more likely to occur. *Now faith is the substance of things hoped for, the evidence of things not seen* (Hebrews 11:1). Faith is unrelenting belief.

Hope and faith are not reserved for Christians or religious believers alone. Most of us have exercised a measure of hope and faith throughout our lives. Have you ever studied for an exam, prepared for a job interview, or watched your favourite team play with the belief that everything would work out in accordance with your desires? That's you exercising hope and faith. Someone who gambles on a sporting event is also exercising a measure of faith. What he or she is gambling on specifically (the spread) is hope.

The reality though, is that life isn't a gamble. It is also not a movie. There are no second chances or do-overs. The outcomes are permanent. The pain and disappointments are real and sometimes lasting. Joy and happiness, for those who live a "default" type of existence, are sporadic, fleeting moments. However, there's another way that provides a personal guide and a roadmap to living in the light of knowledge and the hope of a better tomorrow. *And I will bring the blind by a way that they knew not; I will lead them in paths that they have not known: I will make darkness light before them, and crooked things straight. These things will I do unto them, and not forsake them* (Isaiah 42:16).

When we study and meditate on the Word of YHUH, we discover His love, power, wisdom, knowledge and countless promises. Consequently, our confidence in Him builds. When we read about His faithfulness, graciousness, and mercy toward us, hope springs within us. Our prayers, praise, and worship will reflect an attitude of gratitude, thankfulness, immovable faith, and endless hope in the promises of YHUH and the power of the redeeming blood of His Son, Yahusha.

When we feed our spirits on these verses and pause to reflect on our lives and how by His grace we have made it thus far, we will no longer feel vulnerable and weak, but blessed and highly favoured. We will live in the light of truth, wisdom, knowledge, and understanding. We will absorb the warm rays of hope emanating from the one true light giver. Here are some verses for you to meditate on:

- *For whom the Lord loveth he chasteneth, and scourgeth every son whom he receiveth* (Hebrews 12:6).
- *For God so loved the world, that he gave his only begotten Son, that whosoever believeth in him should not perish, but have everlasting life* (John 3:16).
- *Whoever does not love does not know God, because God is love. This is how God showed his love among us: He sent his one and only Son into the world that we might live through him. This is love: not that we loved God, but that he loved us and sent His Son as an atoning sacrifice for our sins. Dear friends, since God so loved us, we also ought to love one another. No one has ever seen God; but if we love one another, God lives in us and his love is made complete in us* (1 John 4:8–12 NIV).
- *There is no fear in love. But perfect love drives out fear, because fear has to do with punishment. The one who fears is not made perfect in love* (v.18 NIV).
- *The eyes of your understanding being enlightened; that ye may know what is the hope of his calling, and what the riches of the glory of his inheritance in the saints, And what is the exceeding greatness of his power to us-ward who believe, according to the working of his mighty power, Which he wrought in Christ, when he raised him from the dead, and set him at his own right hand in the heavenly places* (Ephesians 1:18–20).
- *To open their eyes, and to turn them from darkness to light, and from the power of Satan unto God, that they may receive forgiveness of sins, and inheritance among them which are sanctified by faith that is in me* (Acts 26:18).
- *May the God of hope fill you with all joy and peace as you trust in him, so that you may overflow with hope by the power of the Holy Spirit* (Romans 15:13 NIV).
- *Hast thou not known? hast thou not heard, that the everlasting God, the LORD, the Creator of the ends of the earth, fainteth not, neither is weary? there is no searching of his*

understanding. He giveth power to the faint; and to them that have no might he increaseth strength (Isaiah 40:28–29).

- *God hath spoken once; twice have I heard this; that power belongeth unto God* (Psalm 62:11).
- *Indeed these are the mere edges of His ways, And how small a whisper we hear of Him! But the thunder of His power who can understand?* (Job 26:14 NKJV).
- *He hath made the earth by his power, he hath established the world by his wisdom, and hath stretched out the heavens by his discretion* (Jeremiah 10:12).
- *Thus saith the LORD; Cursed be the man that trusteth in man, and maketh flesh his arm, and whose heart departeth from the LORD. For he shall be like the heath in the desert, and shall not see when good cometh; but shall inhabit the parched places in the wilderness, in a salt land and not inhabited. Blessed is the man that trusteth in the LORD, and whose hope the LORD is. For he shall be as a tree planted by the waters, and that spreadeth out her roots by the river, and shall not see when heat cometh, but her leaf shall be green; and shall not be careful in the year of drought, neither shall cease from yielding fruit* (17:5-8).
- *For in him all things were created: things in heaven and on earth, visible and invisible, whether thrones or powers or rulers or authorities; all things have been created through him and for him. He is before all things, and in him all things hold together* (Colossians 1:16–17 NIV).
- *Wherein in time past ye walked according to the course of this world, according to the prince of the power of the air, the spirit that now worketh in the children of disobedience: Among whom also we all had our conversation in times past in the lusts of our flesh, fulfilling the desires of the flesh and of the mind; and were by nature the children of wrath, even as others. But God, who is rich in mercy, for his great love wherewith he loved us, even when we were dead in sins, hath quickened us together with Christ, (by grace ye are saved;) And hath raised us up together, and made us sit together in heavenly places in Christ Jesus* (Ephesians 2:2–6).
- *And he said unto me, My grace is sufficient for thee: for my strength is made perfect in weakness. Most gladly therefore*

will I rather glory in my infirmities, that the power of Christ may rest upon me (2 Corinthians 12:9).

- *For the LORD giveth wisdom: out of his mouth cometh knowledge and understanding* (Proverbs 2:6).

- *If any of you lack wisdom, let him ask of God, that giveth to all men liberally, and upbraideth not: and it shall be given him* (James 1:5).

- *So shall the knowledge of wisdom be unto thy soul: when thou hast found it, then there shall be a reward, and thy expectation shall not be cut off* (Proverbs 24:14).

- *You have searched me, LORD, and you know me. You know when I sit and when I rise; you perceive my thoughts from afar. You discern my going out and my lying down; you are familiar with all my ways. Before a word is on my tongue you, LORD, know it completely. You hem me in behind and before, and you lay your hand upon me. Such knowledge is too wonderful for me, too lofty for me to attain. Where can I go from your Spirit? Where can I flee from your presence? If I go up to the heavens, you are there; if I make my bed in the depths, you are there* (Psalm 139:1–8 NIV).

- *Daniel answered and said, Blessed be the name of God for ever and ever: for wisdom and might are his: And he changeth the times and the seasons: he removeth kings, and setteth up kings, he giveth wisdom unto the wise, and knowledge to them that know understanding: He revealeth the deep and secret things: he knoweth what is in the darkness, and the light dwelleth with him* (Daniel 2:20–22).

The Bible contains thousands of verses that speak about the love, power, wisdom, and knowledge of YHUH. When I reflect on the verses above and contemplate my life, I can tell you that I am the quintessential, living example of YHUH's love, grace, mercy, and faithfulness. When I contemplate where I was just a short while ago, and where I'm at today, it's a miraculous testament to His steadfast love, mercy, grace, and power over my life. The outpouring of His wisdom and knowledge in my life, guiding my steps and lighting my path, has brought me to where I am. This is what living in the light is all about. What He did for me, He can and will do for you. All you need to do is believe that He is who He says He is. *I am Alpha and Omega, the beginning and the end, the first and the last. Blessed are they that do his commandments, that they may have right to the tree of life, and may enter in through the gates into the city. For without are dogs, and sorcerers, and whoremongers, and murderers, and idolaters, and whosoever loveth and maketh a lie* (Revelation 22:13–15). He will then prove Himself to you.

> *And ye shall seek me, and find me, when ye shall search for me with all your heart* (Jeremiah 29:13). *Bring the full tithe into the storehouse, that there may be food in my house. And thereby put me to the test, says the LORD of hosts, if I will not open the windows of heaven for you and pour down for you a blessing until there is no more need. I will rebuke the devourer for you, so that it will not destroy the fruits of your soil, and your vine in the field shall not fail to bear, says the LORD of hosts* (Malachi 3:10–11 ESV).

Let go, and let YHUH work in your life. He will do amazing things when you fully trust and believe in Him. *But they that wait upon the LORD shall renew their strength; they shall mount up with wings as eagles; they shall run, and not be weary; and they shall walk, and not faint* (Isaiah 40:31). When you see His glorious work in your life, you will never doubt Him again. *Instead of your shame you will receive a double portion, and instead of disgrace you will rejoice in your inheritance. And so you will inherit a double portion in your land, and everlasting joy will be yours* (61:7 NIV). You'll strive to walk daily under His shadow, protection, and care. Your personal relationship, built on a foundation of unwavering faith, will strengthen you from day to day.

Some people believe they've been wronged by YHUH. They ask themselves hard questions, such as: *Why did He allow me to lose my loved ones to COVID-19 (or some other sickness or disease)? Why did I lose my business as a result of the ravaging pandemic and/or my entire retirement fund to a bad investment?*

The hard answer is that life is unfair. Life is cruel and the devil is here to lie, kill, and destroy (John 10:10). In this life, we'll be tested. Satan is the Prince of Darkness.

> *In whom the god of this world hath blinded the minds of them which believe not, lest the light of the glorious gospel of Christ,*

who is the image of God, should shine unto them (2 Corinthians 4:4). *Wherein in time past ye walked according to the course of this world, according to the prince of the power of the air, the spirit that now worketh in the children of disobedience* (Ephesians 2:2). *I will not say much more to you, for the prince of this world is coming. He has no hold over me, but he comes so that the world may learn that I love the Father and do exactly what my Father has commanded me. "Come now; let us leave* (John 14:30–31 NIV).

We will be tormented, challenged and even suffer for periods of time throughout our lives. We live in a world ruled by the devil. He hates us because of the love YHUH has for us. *We know that anyone born of God does not continue to sin; the One who was born of God keeps them safe, and the evil one cannot harm them. We know that we are children of God, and that the whole world is under the control of the evil one* (1 John 5:18–19 NIV). Satan thought that because of our sinful (fallen) state, YHUH would have damned our souls as He did his, but He didn't. Instead, He sent His one and only Son to die on Calvary and redeem us from our debt to sin (John 3:16). Because of YHUH's redeeming love for us, Satan hates us. Because we are His, Satan wants to destroy us. *I will say to the north, Give up; and to the south, Keep not back: bring my sons from far, and my daughters from the ends of the earth; Even every one that is called by my name: for I have created him for my glory, I have formed him; yea, I have made him* (Isaiah 43:6-7).

The devil is roaming the Earth, saturating humanity with wickedness and bringing death, torment, and destruction to our lives. But Elohim is here to protect and strengthen us. *But the Lord is faithful, and he will strengthen you and protect you from the evil one* (2 Thessalonians 3:3 NIV). He is here to guide us through the valley of the shadow of death without fear. *Yea, though I walk through the valley of the shadow of death, I will fear no evil: for thou art with me; thy rod and thy staff they comfort me* (Psalm 23:4).

We rejoice because we know that, through Yahusha, we've already won the battle and are victorious. *For whatsoever is born of God overcometh the world: and this is the victory that overcometh the world, even our faith* (1 John 5:4). When we have Yahusha as our protector and deliverer, death no longer has its grip of despair, punishment, and finality over us. *O death, where is thy sting? O grave, where is thy victory? The sting of death is sin; and the strength of sin is the law. But thanks be to God, which giveth us the victory through our Lord Jesus Christ* (1 Corinthians 15:55–57).

Salvation to the unknowing unbeliever is a mystery. The concept of salvation wasn't even fully understood by the prophets of the Old Testament. They did not fully understand the prophecies they foretold. They didn't fully understand how it would all play out or what would cause certain things to be set in motion for their prophecies to be fulfilled. This is another example of how YHUH used His people, under the inspiration of the Holy Spirit, to write the Scriptures contained in the Bible today. It also explains why there aren't any contradictions in the Bible. Everything in the Bible comes from the same spring of inspiration.

What the prophets knew was that Yahusha would come and be the sacrificial Lamb for the world. Nevertheless, they did not know every minute detail. Even the angels didn't fully understand YHUH's plan of salvation for us, a fallen, rebellious and sinful creation.

Concerning this salvation, the prophets, who spoke of the grace that was to come to you, searched intently and with the greatest care, trying to find out the time and circumstances to which the Spirit of Christ in them was pointing when he predicted the sufferings of the Messiah and the glories that would follow. It was revealed to them that they were not serving themselves but you, when they spoke of the things that have now been told you by those who have preached the gospel to you by the Holy Spirit sent from heaven. Even angels long to look into these things (1 Peter 1:10–12 NIV).

The angels do not understand every facet of salvation. They have looked into the matter, intriguingly investigating it. I cannot help but imagine how the heavenly host must contemplate YHUH's mercy, grace, and love toward us. One-third of the angels sinned and were cut off from His redemption. Yet, YHUH is slow to anger and patient with us. He sent His Son to redeem us and sends His angels to minister to us and protect us.

And, behold, the angel of the Lord came upon him, and a light shined in the prison: and he smote Peter on the side, and raised him up, saying, Arise up quickly. And his chains fell off from his hands. And the angel said unto him, Gird thyself, and bind on thy sandals. And so he did. And he saith unto him, Cast thy garment about thee, and follow me. And he went out, and followed him; and wist not that it was true which was done by the angel; but thought he saw a vision. When they were past the first and the second ward, they came unto the iron gate that leadeth unto the city; which opened to them of his own accord: and they went out, and passed on through one street; and forthwith the angel departed from him. And when Peter was come to himself, he said, Now I know of a surety, that the LORD hath sent his angel, and hath delivered me out of the hand of Herod, and from all the expectation of the people of the Jews (Acts 12:7–11).

I imagine the angels observing us and immediately recognising how much we resemble our heavenly Father. Yet, our sin and rebellion have made us so carnal, so mortal, so fallen. Perhaps they cannot fully comprehend sin and rebellion, although they know what the effects of sin are. Surely, they must observe how blind and imperfect we are. Still, every now and then, they glimpse His glory in us. Sin and rebellion have really done a number on us. Much of the time we're spiritually deficient, timid and lost. Undoubtedly, we are always in need of the covering of Yahusha's blood and the saving love, grace and mercy, of YHUH. We know those who die in Yahusha are assured life forevermore.

Brothers and sisters, we do not want you to be uninformed about those who sleep in death, so that you do not grieve like the rest of mankind, who have no hope. For we believe that Jesus died and rose again, and so we believe that God will bring with Jesus those who have fallen asleep in him. According to the Lord's word, we tell you that we who are still alive, who are left until the coming of the Lord, will certainly not precede those who have fallen asleep. For the Lord himself will come down from heaven, with a loud command, with the voice of the archangel and with the trumpet call of God, and the dead in Christ will rise first. After that, we who are still alive and are left will be caught up together with them in the clouds to meet the Lord in the air. And so we will be with the Lord forever. Therefore encourage one another with these words (1 Thessalonians 4:13–18 NIV).

Satan tried to prevent this (our salvation) from happening. Had Yahusha yielded to temptation, His sacrifice would not have been acceptable to YHUH. However, because Yahusha walked in perfect obedience to His Father's will, He didn't sin and consequently was the perfect atoning sacrifice.

Then I saw in the right hand of him who sat on the throne a scroll with writing on both sides and sealed with seven seals. And I saw a mighty angel proclaiming in a loud voice, "Who is worthy to break the seals and open the scroll?" But no one in heaven or on earth or under the earth could open the scroll or even look inside it. I wept and wept because no one was found who was worthy to open the scroll or look inside. Then one of the elders said to me, "Do not weep! See, the Lion of the tribe of Judah, the Root of David, has triumphed. He is able to open the scroll and its seven seals." (Revelation 5:1–5 NIV).

Because of Yahusha's sinless life on Earth, His subsequent death and resurrection, we have the hope of obtaining eternal life.

Do not let your hearts be troubled. You believe in God; believe also in me. My Father's house has many rooms; if that were not so, would I have told you that I am going there to prepare a place for you? And if I go and prepare a place for you, I will come back and take you to be with me that you also may be where I am. You know the way to the place where I am going (John 14:1–4 NIV). *Therefore we are buried with him by baptism into death: that like as Christ was raised up from the dead by the glory of the Father, even so we also should walk in newness of life. For if we have been planted together in the likeness of his death, we shall be also in the likeness of his resurrection* (Romans 6:4–5).

Remember Proverbs 25:2: *It is the glory of God to conceal a matter; to search out a matter is the glory of kings* (NIV). Only

YHUH knows everything. His infinite love, mercy, and grace aren't fully understood, but they are His gifts to us.

Seek ye the LORD while he may be found, call ye upon him while he is near: Let the wicked forsake his way, and the unrighteous man his thoughts: and let him return unto the LORD, and he will have mercy upon him and to our God, for he will abundantly pardon. For my thoughts are not your thoughts, neither are your ways my ways, saith the LORD. For as the heavens are higher than the earth, so are my ways higher than your ways, and my thoughts than your thoughts (Isaiah 55:6–9).

Because of YHUH's love, we are more than conquerors, and nothing can separate us from Him (Romans 8:35–39). We know if we continue to follow Elohim and place all of our trust and reliance in Him, He will restore us and place His Spirit within us. *Now unto him [YHUH] that is able to do exceeding abundantly above all that we ask or think, according to the power [Holy Spirit] that worketh in us* (Ephesians 3:20).

We know death is just a part of life. *For the wages of sin is death; but the gift of God is eternal life through Jesus Christ our Lord* (Romans 6:23). *Wash me throughly from mine iniquity, and cleanse me from my sin. For I acknowledge my transgressions: and my sin is ever before me. Against thee, thee only, have I sinned, and done this evil in thy sight: that thou mightest be justified when thou speakest, and be clear when thou judgest* (Psalm 51:2–4).

So here are the rays of hope! We have the knowledge that when we or our loved ones die in Him, we will see each other again. Death and separation are not forever. The grave isn't the end to our existence. If we pursue YHUH, we may die once, but we'll live again and this time, it will be for eternity. *And if the Spirit of him who raised Jesus from the dead is living in you, he who raised Christ from the dead will also give life to your mortal bodies because of his Spirit who lives in you.* (Romans 8:11 NIV).

Remember, one reason we believe the promises contained in the Bible is because of the many predictions that have come to pass. We see, based on our own life experiences, that the Bible's depictions of a life operating in darkness are accurate. I can personally attest that living in the light is also as gratifying and precise, as described in the pages of the Bible. *And the peace of God, which passeth all understanding, shall keep your hearts and minds through Christ Jesus* (Philippians 4:7).

Living in the light gives you a peaceful confidence and lasting assurance that you are remarkable and here for a purpose. You will no longer be tossed to and fro by the storms of life. Living in the light and basking in the rays of hope changes your perspective and mindset. You will worry less and pray more. You will search for and find riches that are beyond the reach of this carnal world, like joy, peace, love, patience, knowledge, wisdom, and understanding. You will praise and worship YHUH more and see His work on display in your life, daily. You'll stop feeling like a powerless victim and become a powerful victor. You will prepare your heart for Heaven, intentionally fixing your eyes on the giver of life and the source of your salvation.

Can you imagine living in a perfect place under sinless conditions? Imagine an existence where there is no sickness, death, pain, or sorrow. *And God shall wipe away all tears from their eyes; and there shall be no more death, neither sorrow, nor crying, neither shall there be any more pain: for the former things are passed away* (Revelation 21:4).

When you live in His light, you will praise and worship under the rays of hope during periods of joy and happiness, giving YHUH thanks for His mercy and loving kindness toward you. Of course, you're never immune or totally ring-fenced from experiencing the pandemonium of life. Being a Christian or a believer in the Most High doesn't mean that life will no longer have its challenges. You will still be tempted and tested by pride, ego, compulsion, vice, betrayal, doubt, slander, pain, depression, failure, grief, sickness, death, etc. Nevertheless, you will overcome, not just get over, if you remain under the shadow (love) of the Almighty.

Life has sharp peaks and deep valleys. But the Master is always there to smooth the rough edges and support us along the steep gradients, while guiding and protecting us.

During times of difficulty, you will praise Him for giving you a spirit of faith and perseverance. You know you'll be victorious over your trials, because YHUH is your God. He cannot fail. *And the LORD shall make thee the head, and not the tail; and thou shalt be above only, and thou shalt not be beneath; if that thou hearken unto the commandments of the LORD thy God, which I command thee this day, to observe and to do them* (Deuteronomy 28:13). The spirit of anxiety, depression, fear, low self-esteem, addiction, etc., cannot overcome you when you are in the presence of YHUH's light. These things are spiritual, emotional, and psychological pestilences. They cannot thrive in an environment where the presence of YHUH's light, love, and truth abounds and sanitises.

These plagues can only survive in the toxic environment of darkness, punishment, sin, uncertainty, fear, and despair. *But ye are a chosen generation, a royal priesthood, an holy nation, a peculiar people; that ye should shew forth the praises of him who hath called you out of darkness into his marvellous light* (1 Peter 2:9).

You and I live with the blessed hope that YHUH's love, mercy, and grace will cover and carry us through our troubles and our moments of weakness. His grace *is* sufficient, and nothing can separate us from His love, if we follow Him unconditionally. There is great *hope* in this knowledge! Our salvation is *guaranteed* if we follow Him. Our victory is certain in Yahusha Ha'Mashiach! There is an end to darkness, naivety, and lack of understanding when we allow YHUH's truth to illuminate our lives and light our paths.

Remember, I stated earlier, you and I are vessels. If you carry the Holy Spirit within you, He will dwell in you and you will be His holy temple. *And when he was demanded of the Pharisees, when the kingdom of God should come, he answered them and said, The kingdom of God cometh not with observation: Neither shall they say, Lo here! or, lo there! for behold, the kingdom of God is within you* (Luke 17:20–21). Just imagine the fullness of life you will experience through the indwelling of the Holy Spirit.

God that made the world and all things therein, seeing that he is Lord of heaven and earth, dwelleth not in temples made with hands; Neither is worshipped with men's hands, as though he needed anything, seeing he giveth to all life, and breath, and all things; And hath made of one blood all nations of men for to dwell on all the face of the earth, and hath determined the times before appointed, and the bounds of their habitation; That they should seek the Lord, if haply they might feel after him, and find him, though he be not far from every one of us: For in him we live, and move, and have our being; as certain also of your own poets have said, For we are also his offspring (Acts 17:24–28).

He that dwelleth in the secret place of the most High shall abide under the shadow of the Almighty. I will say of the LORD, He is my refuge and my fortress: my God; in him will I trust. Surely he shall deliver thee from the snare of the fowler, and from the noisome pestilence. He shall cover thee with his feathers, and under his wings shalt thou trust: his truth shall be thy shield and buckler. Thou shalt not be afraid for the terror by night; nor for the arrow that flieth by day; Nor for the pestilence that walketh in darkness; nor for the destruction that wasteth at noonday. A thousand shall fall at thy side, and ten thousand at thy right hand; but it shall not come nigh thee. Only with thine eyes shalt thou behold and see the reward of the wicked. Because thou hast made the LORD, which is my refuge, even the most High, thy habitation; There shall no evil befall thee, neither shall any plague come nigh thy dwelling. For he shall give his angels charge over thee, to keep thee in all thy ways. They shall bear thee up in their hands, lest thou dash thy foot against a stone. Thou shalt tread upon the lion and adder: the young lion and the dragon shalt thou trample under feet. Because he hath set his love upon me, therefore will I deliver him: I will set him on high because he hath known my name. He shall call upon me, and I will answer him: I will be with him in trouble; I will deliver him, and honour him. With long life will I satisfy him, and shew him my salvation (Psalm 91).

Remain under the shadow of YHUH. Under the banner of His love!

May the light of His truth and the rays of its glorious hope lift you to His throne of grace. When you live in this environment, *nothing* can separate you from His perfect, redeeming, steadfast love.

Chapter 5
Prayer Without Faith

Therefore I say unto you, What things soever ye desire, when ye pray, believe that ye receive them, and ye shall have them (Mark 11:24).

And all things, whatsoever ye shall ask in prayer, believing, ye shall receive (Matthew 21:22).

As I stated in the introduction, I suffered from depression for years. Depression consumed me. It took over my mind and occupied my thoughts. *How long wilt thou forget me, O LORD? for ever? how long wilt thou hide thy face from me? How long shall I take counsel in my soul, having sorrow in my heart daily? how long shall mine enemy be exalted over me? Consider and hear me, O LORD my God: lighten mine eyes, lest I sleep the sleep of death;* (Psalm 13:1–3). Just as a wild weed aggressively spreads throughout a garden and competes for every inch of space, choking the good plants and depleting the soil of essential nutrients, so too, does depression spread, choking and killing the essential emotional and spiritual nutrients needed to produce calm, balanced, virtuous thoughts.

A hopeful and optimistic mind will cultivate a spirit of stability and calm. Through our unwavering obedience and faith, we will remain under the protection of the Most High and maintain a spirit of self-control. This isn't the case when we live a life that's unpleasing to Elohim (the plural Hebrew word for *God* that captures both YHUH and Yahusha, as spoken of in the creation story of Genesis 1. Also see John 1:18; John 14:8-9).

Living a life of rebellion almost entirely destroyed me. When I was at my lowest and had no more fight left in me, I cried out to Yahusha and He heard my cry. *In my distress I called upon the LORD, and cried unto my God: he heard my voice out of his temple, and my cry came before him, even into his ears* (Psalm 18:6). My cry was genuine. It was without ego, pretence, or arrogance. It was spontaneous and without formality. I didn't kneel with my eyes closed, hands clasped and head bowed. My prayer wasn't scripted or verbose. It was impulsive, full of desperation and urgency, bare and without shame. It was a profoundly truthful and distressing cry. This is why Yahusha came to my rescue.

> *And when thou prayest, thou shalt not be as the hypocrites are: for they love to pray standing in the synagogues and in the corners of the streets, that they may be seen of men. Verily I say unto you, They have their reward. But thou, when thou prayest, enter into thy closet, and when thou hast shut thy door, pray to thy Father which is in secret; and thy Father which seeth in secret shall reward thee openly. But when ye pray, use not vain repetitions, as the heathen do: for they think that they shall be heard for their much speaking. Be not ye therefore like unto them: for your Father knoweth what things ye have need of, before ye ask him* (Matthew 6:5–8).

My prayer was deeply personal, full of contrition, and genuine. I felt its release from my soul and had the faith and confidence that *this* prayer would be heard by Elohim. *Let us therefore come boldly unto the throne of grace, that we may obtain mercy, and find grace to help in time of need* (Hebrews 4:16). At that moment, my belief in Him was strong because it was all I had left to rely upon. Everything I had relied on previously to sustain me was gone. I was praying for my life. I was praying for my very soul. I knew that only He could find and deliver me out of the dark, slimy pit I was in.

> *I waited patiently for the LORD; he turned to me and heard my cry. He lifted me out of the slimy pit, out of the mud and mire; he set my feet on a rock and gave me a firm place to stand. He put a new song in my mouth, a hymn of praise to our God. Many will see and fear the LORD and put their trust in him. Blessed is the one who trusts in the LORD, who does not look to the proud, to those who turn aside to false gods* (Psalm 40:1–4 NIV).

This was my SOS to Elohim. Miraculously, after *this* prayer, my life started to change for the better. I felt a calm, reassuring Holy Spirit come over me and my mind began to declutter. I felt His instruction to let go and allow Him to lead. I did! Elohim led me away from the ambivalence, pain, depression, disappointment, regret, shame, mental chaos, and spiritual darkness. *Good and upright is the LORD: therefore will he teach sinners in the way. The meek will he guide in judgment: and the meek will he teach his way. All the paths of the LORD are mercy and truth unto such as keep his covenant and his testimonies* (Psalm 25:8-10). My thoughts became increasingly clearer each day after I surrendered to Him. I began each morning by praying and reading the Bible and asking Him to guide and direct my steps.

There were times when I felt unsure, like I wasn't understanding what He wanted me to do. During these times I asked for signs, specific signals that only He, Creator God, could deliver. *I will instruct you and teach you in the way you should go; I will counsel you with my loving eye on you* (32:8 NIV). Many times, after receiving confirmation within my spirit, anxiety would cause me to hesitate. Yet, for my own good, I had to trust and believe. So I prayed to Elohim for greater faith, strength, and confidence in Him.

> *The LORD is my shepherd; I shall not want. He maketh me to lie down in green pastures: he leadeth me beside the still waters. He restoreth my soul: he leadeth me in the paths of righteousness for his name's sake. Yea, though I walk through the valley of the shadow of death, I will fear no evil: for thou art with me; thy rod and thy staff they comfort me. Thou preparest a table before me in the presence of mine enemies: thou anointest my head with oil; my cup runneth over. Surely goodness and mercy shall follow me all the days of my life: and I will dwell in the house of the LORD for ever* (Psalm 23).

I was being taught to walk by faith and not by sight (2 Corinthians 5:7). It was during this time I realised just how important faith was. For the first time, I realised why my prayers had primarily not been answered. I was *talking* to Elohim, but I wasn't *praying* to Him. Anyone can talk to Elohim. However, only those who have *faith* will be able to pray to Him. Prayers are audible or inaudible communications with our Creator that, *through faith,* present us boldly before His throne.

They are usually filled with requests for our wants and needs. If we're honest, many of us rush through our prayers as if we're putting together a Christmas wish list to give to Santa Claus. This is not the type of prayer Elohim is desirous of.

As a child, I was afraid to sit on Santa's lap, yet I was forced to do so. I wanted nothing to do with the man from the North Pole, but I certainly wanted to give him my Christmas wish list! This is how many of us feel about Elohim. Religious ceremonies, public events, and traditional customs *force* us to come to Him in prayer. These prayers aren't very effective.

When ye come to appear before me, who hath required this at your hand, to tread my courts? Bring no more vain oblations; incense is an abomination unto me; the new moons and sabbaths, the calling of assemblies, I cannot away with; it is iniquity, even the solemn meeting. Your new moons and your appointed feasts my soul hateth: they are a trouble unto me; I am weary to bear them. And when ye spread forth your hands, I will hide mine eyes from you: yea, when ye make many prayers, I will not hear: your hands are full of blood (Isaiah 1:12-15).

He doesn't hear prayers that lack faith, sincerity, humility, and repentance. *God is a Spirit: and they that worship him must worship him in spirit and in truth* (John 4:24). *Then shall ye call upon me, and ye shall go and pray unto me, and I will hearken unto you. And ye shall seek me, and find me, when ye shall search for me with all your heart* (Jeremiah 29:12–13). He wants us to faithfully seek Him with all sincerity and with a spirit of humbleness and contrition. *Let my prayer be set forth before thee as incense; and the lifting up of my hands as the evening sacrifice* (Psalm 141:2).

How can there be any truth in you when you pray insincerely or with doubt in your heart? You're not sure if Elohim is hearing you or listening to you. Because of your scepticism, He will not hear you or answer your prayers. The Bible tells us He doesn't hear the prayer of the unrighteous (John 9:31). Disobedience (sin) and unbelief separates us from Him and causes us to become unrighteous.

And Samuel said, Hath the LORD as great delight in burnt offerings and sacrifices, as in obeying the voice of the LORD?

Behold, to obey is better than sacrifice, and to hearken than the fat of rams. For rebellion is as the sin of witchcraft, and stubbornness is as iniquity and idolatry. Because thou hast rejected the word of the LORD, he hath also rejected thee from being king (1 Samuel 15:22-23). *See to it, brothers and sisters, that none of you has a sinful, unbelieving heart that turns away from the living God. But encourage one another daily, as long as it is called "Today," so that none of you may be hardened by sin's deceitfulness* (Hebrews 3:12-13 NIV).

When we prepare our hearts and minds to pray, we must believe that our prayers will be heard and received. When I cried out to Him, I *knew* He would hear my prayer. While it wasn't formal, I desperately desired to communicate with Him. I wanted Him to hear me. I needed Him to save me! I believed that He would hear and deliver me. My plea was sincere, genuine, but most importantly, I *believed* that everything I asked of Him, He would do. When preparing to pray, you must believe, in faith, that your prayers will reach the throne of Elohim. He will hear you! *And this is the confidence that we have in him, that, if we ask any thing according to his will, he heareth us: And if we know that he hear us, whatsoever we ask, we know that we have the petitions that we desired of him* (1 John 5:14–15).

Yahusha Ha'Mashiach's disciples asked Him one day, after He had finished praying to His Father, to teach them how to pray. He then spoke what we today refer to as the Lord's Prayer:

After this manner therefore pray ye: Our Father which art in heaven, Hallowed be thy name. Thy kingdom come, Thy will be done in earth, as it is in heaven. Give us this day our daily bread. And forgive us our debts, as we forgive our debtors. And lead us not into temptation but deliver us from evil: For thine is the kingdom, and the power, and the glory, for ever. Amen (Matthew 6:9–13).

When we analyse this prayer, we discover:

1. The location of YHUH. Additionally, we are to venerate His name (again we see the importance of His name), which is a form of glorification. *Our Father which art in heaven, hallowed be thy name.*

2. We pray for YHUH's Kingdom to come and dwell within us (see also Luke 17:21). Through the indwelling of the Holy Spirit, we ask for His will to be fulfilled, through us, in Earth as it is in Heaven. *Thy kingdom come, Thy will be done in earth, as it is in heaven.*

3. We pray for our daily needs to be supplied. *Give us this day our daily bread.*

4. *Forgive us our debts.* According to His Law, sin causes us to accrue debt in the form of punishment and, ultimately, total death (body and spirit). When He forgives us, we no longer die the eternal death, but will receive His gift of eternal life.

5. We pledge to forgive those who have wronged us. *As we forgive our debtors.*

6. We pray for guidance, safety, protection and deliverance. *And lead us not into temptation, but deliver us from evil.*

7. We acknowledge His supremacy, power and great majesty. *For thine is the kingdom, and the power, and the glory, for ever.*

Of course, this is the ultimate template. Out of urgency, we often drop the formalities and get straight to the point. Just remember, Elohim knows your heart and can see your sincerity. He will come to your aid and reward you for your earnestness and faithfulness.

What is faith? According to Hebrews 11:1, *Faith is the substance of things hoped for, the evidence of things not seen.* But what does this *really* mean? Faith is the elemental material, i.e., the strong, singular, bold, unrelenting belief needed to claim something significant and essential. Although not fully aware of the fastidious intricacies involved in the outcome (evidence of things not seen), we are wholly aware that the desired result *will* manifest and comprehensively impact our entire lives (limitless blessings). In faith, we believe that Yahusha was the son of YHUH. *And many other signs truly did Jesus in the presence of his disciples, which are not written in this book: But these are written, that ye might believe that Jesus is the Christ, the Son of God; and that believing ye might have life through his name* (John 20:30-31). He died on the cross for our sins, but YHUH rose Him up from the grave. *This man was handed over to you by God's deliberate plan and foreknowledge; and you, with the help of wicked men, put him to death by nailing him to the cross. But God raised him from the dead, freeing him from the agony of death, because it was impossible for death to keep its hold on him* (Acts 2:23-24 NIV). He is now in Heaven interceding for us. *Therefore he is able to save completely those who come to God through him, because he always lives to intercede for them* (Hebrews 7:25 NIV). By his stripes we are healed (Isaiah 53:5), no longer sick to sin, Hallelujah!

Faith is what we practice when we deeply yearn for something. We live with the hope of receiving what we long for. Even when everything tells us it will never happen and it's impossible, we remain faithful and live with the hope that one day, our desires will become a reality. Faith keeps us focused on the mission, the goal, the high calling. It holds everything together.

Until we all reach unity in the faith and in the knowledge of the Son of God and become mature, attaining to the whole measure of the fullness of Christ. Then we will no longer be infants, tossed back and forth by the waves, and blown here and there by every wind of teaching and by the cunning and craftiness of people in their deceitful scheming. Instead, speaking the truth in love, we will grow to become in every respect the mature body of him who is the head, that is, Christ. From him the whole body, joined and held together by every supporting ligament, grows and builds itself up in love, as each part does its work (Ephesians 4:13-16 NIV)

Strong unwavering faith is a spiritual and moral standard of excellence.

Faith is what that cancer patient exercises when earnestly asking Elohim for healing after receiving that grim prognosis from the oncologist. Faith is practised when someone requests to have their mortgage refinanced, even though they recently lost their job. It's the single mother beseeching Elohim to open a way for her to get all the groceries she needs with only $20 in her pocket. It is the university student entreating Elohim for understanding to a whole set of mathematical equations that are difficult to grasp. Faith is believing, even when everything tells you to stop hoping, stop wishing, stop believing and come to terms with your present circumstances.

When you refuse to accept reality as played out in the physical realm but instead, in faith, make your requests known, and believe that Elohim can make a way out of no way, He will come to your rescue

91

and show you just how great He is. The Elohim of the Bible is the same Elohim of today.

In only six days, He created the universe and made man in His image and likeness. He took the Israelites, His chosen people, out of Egyptian slavery, parted the Red Sea, and had them cross over on dry land. Elohim fed His chosen people in the wilderness for 40 years, caused manna to fall from heaven during this period and, eventually, led them to the Promised Land. He fought their battles for and with them. In one particular war, He made the sun stand still so they could see to defeat the enemy. In another situation, He blinded the eyes of their enemies. Several times, He allowed confusion and fear to control the minds of the Israelite enemies, causing them to fight and destroy themselves. Once, this particular event occurred while the Israelites praised and worshipped YHUH (2 Chronicles 20:15–24).

YHUH sent His Son into the world to save us from the consequences of sin, which are torment, destruction and eternal death. His Son, while on Earth, performed countless miracles, including healing the sick, casting demons out of people, feeding the poor, and raising the dead. He ultimately died on the cross of Calvary for you and me (Isaiah 53:5; John 19). He later rose from the dead.

For I delivered unto you first of all that which I also received, how that Christ died for our sins according to the scriptures; And that he was buried, and that he rose again the third day according to the scriptures: And that he was seen of Cephas, then of the twelve: After that, he was seen of above five hundred brethren at once; of whom the greater part remain unto this present, but some are fallen asleep. After that, he was seen of James; then of all the apostles. And last of all he was seen of me also, as of one born out of due time (1 Corinthians 15:3-8).

His resurrection defied the finality of death. *Knowing that Christ being raised from the dead dieth no more; death hath no more dominion over him. For in that he died, he died unto sin once: but in that he liveth, he liveth unto God* (Romans 6:9–10).

As a consequence, Yahusha has power over Hell and the grave and is now in Heaven petitioning His Father on our behalf. *I am he that liveth, and was dead; and, behold, I am alive for evermore, Amen; and have the keys of hell and of death* (Revelation 1:18). *Who shall lay any thing to the charge of God's elect? It is God that justifieth. Who is he that condemneth? It is Christ that died, yea rather, that is risen again, who is even at the right hand of God, who also maketh intercession for us* (Romans 8:33–34).

Tell me, what is too great for YHUH? What is impossible for YHUH? *For with God nothing shall be impossible* (Luke 1:37). We increase our faith by learning of YHUH and His greatness. Knowing that He is still on His throne and His mercies endure forever empowers us to ask and believe. If we ask with all sincerity and faith, He will hear us and He will answer us.

Now faith is the substance of things hoped for, the evidence of things not seen. For by it the elders obtained a good report. Through faith we understand that the worlds were framed by the word of God, so that things which are seen were not made of things which do appear. By faith Abel offered unto God a more excellent sacrifice than Cain, by which he obtained witness that he was righteous, God testifying of his gifts: and by it he being dead yet speaketh. By faith Enoch was translated that he should not see death; and was not found, because God had translated him: for before his translation he had this testimony, that he pleased God. But without faith it is impossible to please him: for he that cometh to God must believe that he is, and that he is a rewarder of them that diligently seek him. By faith Noah, being warned of God of things not seen as yet, moved with fear, prepared an ark to the saving of his house; by the which he condemned the world, and became heir of the righteousness which is by faith. By faith Abraham, when he was called to go out into a place which he should after receive for an inheritance, obeyed; and he went out, not knowing whither he went. By faith he sojourned in the land of promise, as in a strange country, dwelling in tabernacles with Isaac and Jacob, the heirs with him of the same promise: For he looked for a city which hath foundations, whose builder and maker is God. Through faith also Sara herself received strength to conceive seed, and was delivered of a child when she was past age, because she judged him faithful who had promised. Therefore sprang there even of one, and him as good as dead, so many as the stars of the sky in multitude, and as the sand which is by the sea shore innumerable. These all died in faith, not having received the promises, but having seen them afar off, and were persuaded of them, and embraced them, and confessed that they were strangers and pilgrims on the earth. For they that say such things declare plainly that they seek a country. And truly, if they had been mindful of that country from whence they came out, they might have had opportunity to have returned. But now they desire a better country, that is, an heavenly: wherefore God is not ashamed to be called their God: for he hath prepared for them a city. By faith Abraham, when he was tried, offered up Isaac: and he that had received the promises offered up his only begotten son, Of whom it was said, That in Isaac shall thy seed be called: Accounting that God was able to raise him up, even from the dead; from whence also he received him in a figure. By faith Isaac blessed Jacob and Esau concerning things to come. By faith Jacob, when he was a dying, blessed both the sons of Joseph; and worshipped, leaning upon the top of his staff. By faith Joseph, when he died, made mention of the departing of the children of Israel; and gave commandment concerning his bones. By faith Moses, when he was born, was hid three months of his parents, because they saw he was a proper child; and they were not afraid of the king's commandment. By faith Moses, when he was come to years, refused to be called the son of Pharaoh's daughter; choosing rather to suffer affliction with the people of God, than to enjoy the pleasures of sin for a season; Esteeming the reproach of Christ greater riches than the treasures in Egypt: for he had respect unto the recompence of the reward. By faith, he forsook Egypt, not fearing the wrath of the king: for he endured, as seeing him who is invisible. Through faith he kept the passover, and the sprinkling of blood, lest he that destroyed the firstborn should touch them. By faith they passed through the Red Sea as by dry land: which the Egyptians assaying to do were drowned. By faith the walls of Jericho fell down, after they were compassed about seven days. By faith the harlot Rahab perished not with them that believed not, when she had received the spies with peace. And what shall I more say? for the time would fail me to tell of Gedeon, and of Barak, and of Samson, and of Jephthae; of David also, and Samuel, and of the prophets: Who through faith subdued kingdoms, wrought righteousness, obtained promises, stopped the mouths of lions. Quenched the violence of fire, escaped the edge of the sword, out of weakness were made strong, waxed valiant in fight, turned to flight the armies of the aliens. Women received their dead raised to life again and others were tortured, not accepting deliverance; that they might obtain a better resurrection: And others had trial of cruel mockings and scourgings, yea, moreover of bonds and imprisonment: They were stoned, they were sawn asunder, were tempted, were slain with the sword: they wandered about in sheepskins and goatskins; being destitute, afflicted, tormented; (Of whom the world was not worthy:) they wandered in deserts, and in mountains, and in dens and caves of the earth. And these all, having obtained a good report through faith, received not the promise: God having provided some better thing for us, that they without us should not be made perfect (Hebrews 11).

Carefully contemplate the demonstrations and attestations of faith contained in this Hebrews chapter. It will strengthen your faith. *Consequently, faith comes from hearing the message, and the message is heard through the word about Christ* (Romans 10:17 NIV). Your faith cannot be blind or fickle. It should be strong and held together by deep conviction. Your personal experiences, through believing and trusting YHUH to make a way for you, along with these Bible accounts, will build and strengthen your faith and character. These stories, along with your personal experiences, will highlight and attest to how dependable YHUH is. How great and mighty He is. How *faithful* He is. Hallelujah!

This fuller understanding of Him will allow us to glimpse just how much we mean to Him and how much He loves us. This is our YHUH Eloah, of glory! Our deliverer and our strong tower (Proverbs 18:10). *God is our refuge and strength, a very present help in trouble* (Psalm 46:1). In Him, is our source of life (John 14:6), love (1 John 4:8), wisdom (*The LORD by wisdom hath founded the earth; by understanding hath he established the heavens* [Proverbs 3:19]), and knowledge (*That ye might walk worthy of the Lord unto all pleasing, being fruitful in every good work, and increasing in the knowledge of God* [Colossians 1:10]). His grace and mercy are never-ending (Lamentations 3:22–23) and His protection, certain (*The LORD shall preserve thee from all evil: he shall preserve thy soul* [Psalm 121:7]). He is all-powerful (omnipotent), all-knowing (omniscient), and ever present (omnipresent). Remember, *nothing* is impossible with YHUH!

If you call out to Yahusha in faith and unpretentiously, He *will* save you. Remember, His name means, "YHUH saves!"

> *The righteous cry, and the LORD heareth, and delivereth them out of all their troubles* (Psalm 34:17). *The LORD is nigh unto all them that call upon him, to all that call upon him in truth. He will fulfil the desire of them that fear him: he also will hear their cry, and will save them* (145:18–19).

Sometimes you may be so overwhelmed with ambivalence or so deep in your depression and despair that you cannot even coherently express yourself to Him. Even then, Elohim hears you and will deliver you. *Likewise the Spirit also helpeth our infirmities: for we know not what we should pray for as we ought: but the Spirit itself maketh intercession for us with groanings which cannot be uttered. And he that searcheth the hearts knoweth what is the mind of the Spirit because he maketh intercession for the saints according to the will of God* (Romans 8:26-27).

The love of YHUH is infinite and indescribable! He loves you and *will* save you *if* you call upon Him. *And I will bring the third part through the fire, and will refine them as silver is refined, and will try them as gold is tried: they shall call on my name, and I will hear them: I will say, It is my people: and they shall say, The LORD is my God* (Zechariah 13:9).

Prayer without the application of faith is powerless. It's like a soldier on the battlefield with his assault rifle but no ammunition. Prayer without faith is like trying to bake a cake in a cold oven. Having a *little* faith is like trying to bake a cake at 100 degrees instead of 375. You must have the appropriate faith for your prayer to be heard and effective.

The mixing of the cake ingredients should be considered your work or action. You cannot expect to pray for something without doing your part. *What doth it profit, my brethren, though a man say he hath faith, and have not works? can faith save him? If a brother or sister be naked, and destitute of daily food, And one of you say unto them, Depart in peace, be ye warmed and filled; notwithstanding ye give them not those things which are needful to the body; what doth it profit? Even so faith, if it hath not works, is dead, being alone* (James 2:14–17).

You must be fully committed to whatever you ask of Elohim. You can demonstrate this, by putting time and effort into whatever it is you're praying for. The Bible says in James 2:26, *For as the body without the spirit is dead, so faith without works is dead also.* Verse 18 says, *But someone will say, "You have faith; I have deeds." Show me your faith without deeds, and I will show you my faith by my deeds* (NIV). These scriptures highlight just how impossible it is to exhibit faith without exerting any effort to achieve our goals. Equally, steadfast faith will produce remarkable, unwavering effort.

Just ask any successful entrepreneur if they started their business with no effort, great scepticism, and crippling doubt. Of course not! Instead, most will tell you of the countless hours of hard work and effort they dedicated to create their dream. Many times, they became discouraged and were advised by friends and family to throw in the towel. Others will tell you how they leveraged all they had. There were times when some experienced unemployment, homelessness, hunger, ridicule, and rejection. Even so, they believed in their dreams and kept the faith. They persevered and weathered many storms, and today, they are successful beyond their wildest dreams.

Some people say they have faith and believe, yet they worry about everything. They are pessimistic, surrounded by doubt, running from one fire to the next and accomplishing little in terms of progress. These folks, unfortunately, insist on micromanaging every facet of life. These individuals are living by sight, not by faith. They believe if they don't show up to work in the morning, the entire operation will crash and burn. They become anxious when they go on vacation because they are unable to micromanage and oversee operations.

Others grow discouraged by the group Bible study or the street evangelism they are conducting because it's not going as planned. *I have planted, Apollos watered; but God gave the increase. So then neither is he that planteth any thing, neither he that watereth; but God that giveth the increase* (1 Corinthians 3:6-7). Perhaps, there are some who are in charge of the praise and worship choir at church. They choreograph and frame the worship so tightly that the congregation and choir members are anxious and distracted by their energy, missing the prodigious opportunity to receive the blessing that comes from *making a joyful noise unto the LORD* (Psalm 100:1). Yes, practice must be organised and the choir director should work assiduously toward achieving the highest level of excellence. However, after doing their level best, everyone should be satisfied with the effort and ask Elohim to do the rest.

I'm not making a case for mediocrity or accepting failure. I am saying, after we give our best, in faith, we must believe that Elohim will do the rest. Elohim's participation, His involvement in "baking the cake," is what will make the results all the more wonderful. *Do not be anxious about anything, but in every situation, by prayer and petition, with thanksgiving, present your requests to God. And the peace of God, which transcends all understanding, will guard your hearts and your minds in Christ Jesus* (Philippians 4:6–7 NIV).

When we lack faith, we displease Elohim. We lack faith because we don't believe, and unbelief is offensive to Him. This lack of belief comes from doubting the existence and power of Elohim. We need to have a clear understanding of who, "I AM" is. *But let him ask in faith, nothing wavering. For he that wavereth is like a wave of the sea driven with the wind and tossed. For let not that man think that he shall receive any thing of the Lord. A double minded man is unstable in all his ways* (James 1:6–8). *But without faith it is impossible to please him: for he that cometh to God must believe that he is, and that he is a rewarder of them that diligently seek him* (Hebrews 11:6). When we become intimately acquainted with Elohim, our faith will grow exponentially.

Faith is a precondition to becoming and remaining a believer in Elohim. Yet, faith isn't unique to the Christian walk. As mentioned previously, a true believer's faith is not blind and without substance. It comes after reading the Bible, the Word of YHUH, while considering, investigating, and recognising how faith is active in your life. This is what makes the believer's faith different, exceptional, and set apart. Without challenges, trials, tribulations, storms, and moments of defeat, how would your faith grow? How would you see Elohim operating in your life? Without trials, what would your testimony be? When would you ever feel the need to submit to His will? Would you ever feel the need to go to Him and seek out your salvation if you never felt the need to be saved?

For whom the Lord loveth he chasteneth, and scourgeth every son whom he receiveth. If ye endure chastening, God dealeth with you as with sons; for what son is he whom the father chasteneth not? (Hebrews 12:6–7). To chasten means to correct, reprimand, punish, and chastise with the intention of improving someone's behaviour. Sometimes we need to go through the paces of life to improve our character and strengthen our faith and belief. Other times, we find ourselves in bad situations because we fail to follow the Master's lead. Disobedience leads to disappointment. *Fools because of their transgression, and because of their iniquities, are afflicted. Their soul abhorreth all manner of meat; and they draw near unto the gates of death. Then they cry unto the LORD in their trouble, and he saveth them out of their distresses. He sent his word, and healed them, and delivered them from their destructions* (Psalm 107:17–20). Sometimes horrific situations occur, that will ultimately bring glory to YHUH (John 9:1-3). These situations can provide the greatest growth, in our faithful walk with Him.

Then said Martha unto Jesus, Lord, if thou hadst been here, my brother had not died. But I know, that even now, whatsoever thou wilt ask of God, God will give it thee. Jesus saith unto her, Thy brother shall rise again. Martha saith unto him, I know that he shall rise again in the resurrection at the last day. Jesus said unto her, I am the resurrection, and the life: he that believeth in me, though he were dead, yet shall he live: And whosoever liveth and believeth in me shall never die. Believest thou this? She saith unto him, Yea, Lord: I believe that thou art the Christ, the Son of God, which should come into the world. And when she had so said, she went her way, and called Mary her sister secretly, saying, The Master is come, and calleth for thee (John 11:21-28). *Jesus saith unto her [Martha], Said I not unto thee, that, if thou wouldest believe, thou shouldest see the glory of God? Then they took away the stone from the place where the dead was laid. And Jesus lifted up his eyes, and said, Father, I thank thee that thou hast heard me. And I knew that thou hearest me always: but because of the people which stand by I said it, that they may believe that thou hast sent me. And when he thus had spoken, he cried with a loud voice, Lazarus, come forth. And he that was dead came forth, bound hand and foot with graveclothes: and his face was bound about with a napkin. Jesus saith unto them, Loose him, and let him go. Then many of the Jews which came to Mary, and had seen the things which Jesus did, believed on him* (v.40-45).

Yahusha never questioned the power, intelligence, or capability of His Father. Moreover, everything He did, He did it through the power of His Father. *Then answered Jesus and said unto them, Verily, verily, I say unto you, The Son can do nothing of himself, but what he seeth the Father do: for what things soever he doeth, these also doeth the Son likewise. For the Father loveth the Son, and sheweth him all things that himself doeth: and he will shew him greater works than these, that ye may marvel* (John 5:19–20).

Because Yahusha's faith was unshakable, He was able to perform scores of astonishing miracles and overcome countless temptations. He knew His Father intimately and was very well acquainted with His great power and majesty. He recognised YHUH as the Most High, and He operated in lockstep with His will. Yahusha knew if He followed YHUH without deviation, He could ask His Father for anything and it would be given Him. His disciples, however, lacked that level of faith and communion. Consequently, they were unable to perform certain miracles.

> *And I brought him to thy disciples, and they could not cure him. Then Jesus answered and said, O faithless and perverse generation, how long shall I be with you? how long shall I suffer you? bring him hither to me. And Jesus rebuked the devil; and he departed out of him: and the child was cured from that very hour. Then came the disciples to Jesus apart, and said, Why could not we cast him out? And Jesus said unto them, Because of your unbelief: for verily I say unto you, If ye have faith as a grain of mustard seed, ye shall say unto this mountain, Remove hence to yonder place; and it shall remove; and nothing shall be impossible unto you* (Matthew 17:16–20).

When you live in oneness with Elohim, you will ask whatever you want and it will be given unto you. *If ye abide in me, and my words abide in you, ye shall ask what ye will, and it shall be done unto you* (John 15:7). *And whatsoever we ask, we receive of him, because we keep his commandments, and do those things that are pleasing in his sight* (1 John 3:22). I know this is mind-boggling, but this is the truth. You may say Yahusha had immovable faith simply because He was the Son of YHUH. This is not correct. His faith was not without substance or meaning. Yahusha suffered and overcame every temptation we have ever faced. *For we do not have a high priest who is unable to empathize with our weaknesses, but we have one who has been tempted in every way, just as we are—yet he did not sin* (Hebrews 4:15 NIV). Yahusha, just like us, had the freedom to choose. He chose to do His Father's will. Even Satan tried to tempt Him. All that was required was the smallest doubt, and Yahusha would have sinned against YHUH.

We can use fear to test the level of faith within us. If we are afraid of doing the right thing and instead choose to do the popular thing, we are allowing fear to lead us. If we are afraid or anxious about the future, then our faith is weak. If you pray and ask Elohim for something but immediately doubt that He heard you or that He will answer your prayer, your faith is flimsy. *Trust in the LORD with all thine heart: and lean not unto thine own understanding. In all thy ways acknowledge him, and he shall direct thy paths* (Proverbs 3:5–6).

If you would like to know what to do to have a closer walk with Elohim and be one of His own, all you have to do is the following:

- Confess your sins: *If we confess our sins, he is faithful and just to forgive us our sins, and to cleanse us from all unrighteousness* (1 John 1:9).
- Accept that Yahusha is the Son of YHUH (John 3:16) and He came and died for your sins and later rose from the dead: *That if thou shalt confess with thy mouth the Lord Jesus, and shalt believe in thine heart that God hath raised him from the dead, thou shalt be saved. For with the heart man believeth unto righteousness; and with the mouth confession is made unto salvation* (Romans 10:9–10).
- Accept in faith YHUH's gift of salvation: *For by grace are ye saved through faith; and that not of yourselves: it is the gift of God: Not of works, lest any man should boast* (Ephesians 2:8–9).
- Remember Galatians 2:16: *Knowing that a man is not justified by the works of the law, but by the faith of Jesus Christ, even we have believed in Jesus Christ, that we might be justified by the faith of Christ, and not by the works of the law: for by the works of the law shall no flesh be justified.*

None of these promises can be fully claimed without a measure of faith. For example, if we confess our sins but do not believe we're redeemable, we won't be eligible to receive His redemption.

You know, when we read about the prophets of the Old Testament and the mighty way YHUH used them to guide and warn His people, the many miracles the children of Israel witnessed and benefited from, when we consider the many dreams Joseph and Daniel interpreted and the battles fought and won because YHUH was with the Israelites, we have no choice but to confess that YHUH *is* Lord of all.

When we read about the birth, life, death, and resurrection of Yahusha or consider the great writings of the New Testament, concerning the gift of salvation by grace through faith, or the miraculous works recorded by those who believed and called upon the name of YHUH and His Son, Yahusha, or the great end-time events recorded in the book of Revelation, we need not marvel or question the existence, or authority of YHUH. *But ye, beloved, building up yourselves on your most holy faith, praying in the Holy Ghost, Keep yourselves in the love of God, looking for the mercy of our Lord Jesus Christ unto eternal life* (Jude 1:20–21).

After we accept Yahusha as our Saviour, we are commanded to live a life that is pleasing to Him by following His commandments. *If ye love me, keep my commandments* (John 14:15). We will mess up much of the time but His grace is sufficient. *And he said unto me, My grace is sufficient for thee: for my strength is made perfect in weakness. Most gladly therefore will I rather glory in my infirmities, that the power of Christ may rest upon me* (2 Corinthians 12:9). His mercies are renewed daily (Lamentations 3:22–23).

Keep trusting, keep pressing toward the mark. *I press toward the mark for the prize of the high calling of God in Christ Jesus. Let us therefore, as many as be perfect, be thus minded: and if in any thing ye be otherwise minded, God shall reveal even this unto you* (Philippians 3:14–15). His love will keep us covered and He will sustain us.

Above all, love each other deeply, because love covers over a multitude of sins (1 Peter 4:8 NIV). *Oh give thanks unto the LORD; for he is good; for his mercy endureth for ever* (1 Chronicles 16:34). *Oh that men would praise the LORD for his goodness, and for his wonderful works to the children of men! For he satisfieth the longing soul, and filleth the hungry soul with goodness* (Psalm 107:8–9).

When you pray and call upon the name of YHUH with unwavering faith, He will hear you and deliver you. *And if we know that he hear us, whatsoever we ask, we know that we have the petitions that we desired of him* (1 John 5:15). Your faith will sustain you, and YHUH's grace will carry you through. *Thou wilt keep him in perfect peace, whose mind is stayed on thee: because he trusteth in thee* (Isaiah 26:3). *Yet the LORD longs to be gracious to you; therefore he will rise up to show you compassion. For the LORD is a God of justice. Blessed are all who wait for him!* (30:18 NIV). The demons that torment you are powerless over your life when, in faith, you accept Elohim into your life. *Thou believest that there is one God; thou doest well: the devils also believe, and tremble* (James 2:19). *And unclean spirits, when they saw him, fell down before him, and cried, saying, Thou art the Son of God* (Mark 3:11).

You serve a mighty and living Elohim. YHUH is your heavenly Father. He zealously loves you and will enthusiastically protect you. If you believe this and claim this in faith, you will *never* walk in darkness again. Your life will be transformed, and people around you will begin to see the undeniable change in you. You'll become a shining example for others to see what's possible when we believe in YHUH and His Son, Yahusha Ha'Mashiach. *Therefore if any man be in Christ, he is a new creature: old things are passed away; behold, all things are become new* (2 Corinthians 5:17). Claim this today.

Remain faithful, pray without ceasing, and walk in the light of truth. Shalom.

Chapter 6
The Greatest Love of All

For God so loved the world, that he gave his only begotten Son, that whosoever believeth in him should not perish, but have everlasting life (John 3:16).

Greater love hath no man than this, that a man lay down his life for his friends (John 15:13).

I have thoroughly enjoyed writing every chapter of this book. However, I especially looked forward to writing this chapter. To write it, and for you to read it, by YHUH's grace, is remarkable. Admittedly, I became a bit intimidated after contemplating the enormity of His love and embarking upon the monumental task of capturing this complex and vast phenomenon. How can a love so wide, so deep, so infinite, be appropriately captured in these few measly pages?

We may feel Elohim's love within us and experience it along life's journey. Others see it all around, throughout nature. Because of how sweeping and incomprehensibly infinite His love is and the many emotions at play when we experience His love, it's sometimes very difficult to describe it in words alone.

As I began to contemplate the complexity and enormity of the all-encompassing characteristics of Elohim's love for us, I prayed constantly and waited for days to hear a word from Him on how to approach this extraordinarily delicate, yet most important topic. As I write this, at *this* very moment, I feel divinely impressed. Nevertheless, I'm fully mindful of how inadequately equipped I am, on my own, to pull back the veil and show you in molecular detail the power and greatness of His love and just how much we mean to Him. Before you begin to read this chapter, please welcome the Holy Spirit and ask for His leading upon your heart. Truly open your mind as you begin to read the most important chapter of this book. Hallelujah!

When we examine the meaning and concept of love, we quickly discover that love is probably one of the most complicated emotions to describe. Love is a phenomenon. It's a word used to convey our feelings toward people, places, or things that we have special and sometimes deep emotional attachment to. It's difficult to use words alone to adequately capture what "love" truly means. Love is a complex feeling, comprised of other emotions that, on their own, would never be confused as love but together, help to create the ambiance of love.

Love is not singular or one-dimensional. It cannot be confined to space, or to a moment in time, or even to a particular environmental condition or setting. For example, some people will love you deeply, but if you cross them, they will kill you and justify their action as a crime driven by *love* and dark passion. Love, mingled with deep pain and hurt, drove them to commit murder. At its very core, love is felt and not limited to mere words strung together to convey its meaning. It could be said that love is an intense symphony, crafted by a confluence of impressions, composed on a sheet of intricate emotion and played on the most delicate strings of your heart, mind, and soul.

Love is like air or water. They are perfect in construct and critically essential to life. Without them, we would die. In relation to love, we can identify its many parts and effects upon us, through a broad spectrum of emotions we feel and convey. Nevertheless, we find it difficult to adequately explain why love is symbiotic to life. We know it's vital because we have observed, felt, and seen its influence in our lives and the lives of countless others. Yet, because of what we've experienced and observed, we wholeheartedly concede that love can be exceedingly complex, multi-dimensional, and severely perplexing.

We roll the word *love* off of our tongues when we express how we feel about our spouses, partners, children, parents, siblings, extended family, pets, and dearest friends. When someone says "I love you," the meaning is varied depending on who is saying it, or to whom it is said. When your children tell you they love you, the *feeling* is different than when your spouse says the same three words. Similarly, you feel entirely different when your parents tell you that they love you.

It's immensely gratifying to hear your children affirm their love for you. It makes you feel like you did a good job, accomplishing your goals as a parent. You were able to adequately provide, protect, and care for them. You became their most trusted guide and life coach. By your deeds and actions, they have seen and experienced your love. When they say "I love you," it gives you a sense of achievement and a feeling of purpose. You feel that their love for you is born out of your love for them, the love you exhibited and poured into them. Their love for you, in essence, is the fruit from the tree of your heart.

Of course, some of us feel as though we could've and should've done more for our children. Perhaps we see some of their failures and shortcomings as failures and shortcomings on our part. Maybe if we'd been more present, spent more time teaching them, listened more, prayed more, hugged and kissed more, reassured or even admonished more, our children's lives could have been greater and more fulfilled. We may even conclude their mistakes and missteps, had we done more, could've been less painful and precipitous, their hopes and dreams, more attainable. Perhaps these feelings are justified. Notwithstanding, the love we have for our children persuades us to carry some of the weight of their setbacks and failures on our shoulders. That's our love for our children on display.

When we hear the words "I love you" from our spouses or significant others, different emotions come racing to the forefront of our minds. We feel privileged to have this exceptional someone in our lives. We think about all the things we've been through together. The love, joy, happiness; the tangible feeling of completeness and safety that surround and permeate us when we're with our special someone is amazing and incredibly euphoric. These three small words, *I love you*, at times seem so terribly inadequate when attempting to convey the depth of care, empathy, intimacy, protection, loyalty, generosity, thankfulness, joy and happiness we feel toward them.

We honestly desire our soulmates to experience exactly how we feel toward them. Often, a display of our deep and abiding love toward them can only be expressed through an affectionate embrace or a loving kiss. Holding and caressing our precious someone, while doling out sweet, soft, butterfly kisses and melodiously whispering in their ear our most sincere declarations of love, is perhaps one of the most effective ways of conveying our deepest, most solemn, intimate feelings.

Not even the most beautiful, elaborate floral arrangement, delectable chocolates, exquisite jewellery, or other thoughtful lavishments can adequately express and affirm your deepest feelings of love toward your significant other like a warm, *loving* embrace. The offering of gifts alone cannot, unreservedly, make your significant other *feel* the deep care, warm affection, profound passion, genuine sincerity, and ebullient emotion of your love toward them. However, an intensely abounding, heart penetrating embrace, or a long, passionate, dare I say, sensual kiss can immediately convey these powerful converging emotions. Yes, words alone are frequently, wholly inadequate when trying to express our love.

We hear it said repeatedly, "Don't tell me that you love me. Show me that you love me." Notice carefully the number of times you hear couples lament about being unable to spend enough quality time together. Seldom, a wife will complain about not receiving the flawless, seven-carat, princess cut diamond ring as a gift from her husband on their tenth wedding anniversary. She will however, vociferously protest not being able to spend their anniversary together.

Of course, we will also recall the days we felt deflated and defeated in our relationships. The days we felt derisory and the feelings of intimacy and oneness were all but gone. During those times, when we couldn't understand why anyone would want to be around us, our partners, because of their love for us, stood there, giving us their shoulders to cry on and being an emotional punching bag as we bitingly expressed our frustrations. Acting as a counsellor to guide us during times of ambivalence and chaos, a safe harbour to hide us from life's stormy seas, a rock to anchor us, and a pillar of love to hold and sustain us while reassuring us of how exceptional we are.

We remember the days of sickness, financial difficulty, and emotional turmoil. We recall all the times we stood by each other's side. Now, in a moment of quiet reflection, you hear the beautiful words, "I love you" from the love of your life, the keeper of your heart, the repository of your deepest thoughts and feelings. It gives you a moment of sweet victory, overwhelming joy, and true appreciation. *Live joyfully with the wife whom thou lovest all the days of the life of thy vanity, which he hath given thee under the sun, all the days of thy vanity: for that is thy portion in this life, and in thy labour which thou takest under the sun* (Ecclesiastes 9:9).

Though there were difficult periods and the road seemingly impassable at times, with love in the tank and one headlight of hope beaming through the darkness and fog of uncertainty, you were both able to drive past the great storms of life together, firmly holding on to each other. In this moment of flashback and sober reflection, you say and mean with every fibre of your being, and with true unbridled, visceral emotion, "I love you, too." The atmosphere is electrifying as you embrace and *experience* the love together.

After we have taken our anger and frustration out on our parents and they say, "I love you," we soften. The jagged edges of our sore feelings of frustration, failure, disappointment, and regret recede. We see the light of care and warmth in their eyes and feel their true, unwavering love in that moment. We recognise that their constructive criticism and balanced reproof were exactly what we needed to hear. After regaining control of our feelings, we realise there is no judgment in their observation, assessment, and counsel; just wisdom. No grave disappointment on their part; just insight. No rebuke, just admiration in seeing the strength of character we have displayed during our turbulent circumstances. We feel undeserving of their love, admiration, commitment, and unyielding patience toward us. Their belief in and love toward us forces us to look inward and seek their forgiveness for the way we lashed out. The love of a parent is truly an exceptionally remarkable kind of love.

YHUH's love for us comprises of all these scenarios and sentiments and so much more. He loves us dearly! Both as a parent and as a spouse. He longs for us to love Him as a child loves a parent. He yearns to establish a very intimate, uniquely personal relationship with us as a caring and loving spouse would. *Or do you think Scripture says without reason that he jealously longs for the spirit he has caused to dwell in us* (James 4:5 NIV)?

> *Love is patient, love is kind. It does not envy, it does not boast, it is not proud. It does not dishonour others, it is not self-seeking, it is not easily angered, it keeps no record of wrongs. Love does not delight in evil but rejoices with the truth. It always protects, always trusts, always hopes, always perseveres. Love never fails. But where there are prophecies, they will cease, where there are tongues, they will be stilled; where there is knowledge, it will pass away. And now these three remain: faith, hope and love. But the greatest of these is love* (1 Corinthians 13:4–8,13 NIV).

Ancient Geek philosophers identified five forms of love: familial love (*Storge*), friendly love or platonic love (*Philia*), romantic love

(*Eros*), guest love (*Xenia*), and divine love (*Agape*). Modern authors have distinguished further varieties of love: unrequited love, empty love, companionate love, consummate love, infatuated love, self-love, and courtly love.[xii]

1 John 4:16 says, *And we have known and believed the love that God hath to us. God is love; and he that dwelleth in love dwelleth in God and God in him.* This is powerful. YHUH *is* love. Carefully examine the characteristics of YHUH, while considering His universal power, His wisdom, and His overall presence. We will recognise YHUH's steadfast love at the very core of who He is. He is perfect love and everything from, of, and by Him operates within those parameters. What's particularly fascinating about this type of love, *Agape*, is it has no limitations.

When we contemplate the depth and complexity of YHUH's love (*What shall we then say to these things? If God be for us, who can be against us? He that spared not his own Son, but delivered him up for us all, how shall he not with him also freely give us all things?* [Romans 8:31-32]); while recognising the simplicity of receiving His love (*But Jesus called the children to him and said, "Let the little children come to me, and do not hinder them, for the kingdom of God belongs to such as these. Truly I tell you, anyone who will not receive the kingdom of God like a little child will never enter it"* [Luke 18:16-17 NIV]), we find it mind boggling when strictly tapping our limited, *human* intelligence.

Through this magnificent dichotomy, however, we're able to introspectively perceive and grasp the generosity (mercy) and greatness (faithfulness) of YHUH. *That Christ may dwell in your hearts by faith; that ye, being rooted and grounded in love, May be able to comprehend with all saints what is the breadth, and length, and depth, and height; And to know the love of Christ, which passeth knowledge, that ye might be filled with all the fulness of God* (Ephesians 3:17-19). YHUH's love isn't some contrived, trifling, one-dimensional, limited manifestation of His feelings toward us.

YHUH *is* love!

In His love, He allows us to exercise free will. Nevertheless, because of our predisposition to sin, we seldom choose His perfect will for our lives. Consequently, He scolds us according to the rules laid out against sin and in line with natural justice. He ensures the rules are adhered to. He never lies, never changes, is longsuffering, offers protection, and provides life, health, strength, and companionship. He extends His whole self to us even after we, His creation, have rebelled, disobeyed, and treated one another unfairly and unjustly. Again, through this entire display, we catch sight of the depth of YHUH's love, mercy, and grace toward us.

Some may ask, "If He loves us so much, why do we have to die?" The Bible tells us, the wages of sin is death (Romans 6:23). Perhaps a more appropriate question is, "Why did Adam and Eve sin and cause us to become fallen creatures to sin?" Wasn't the Garden of Eden perfect? Wasn't YHUH's love on full display? YHUH didn't give us death. He gave us life! When Adam and Eve disobeyed Him by embracing the spirit of ego, doubting His motives, and aspiring to become gods in their own right (they demonstrated this by attempting to walk in their own path and becoming self-absorbed), they rejected life in exchange for death.

If we observe the behaviour of people today, we see many pursuing wisdom and knowledge, including how to overcome death. Not even for a moment do they consider or acknowledge where the source of all life and knowledge comes from and why we're exposed to death. What's equally remarkable and worth highlighting is when tempting Eve, the devil asks her a question he knows the answer to. No doubt Satan knew the first couple was told not to eat from a certain tree. Yet he plays ignorant, while engaging Eve on a level she's comfortable with (see Genesis 3).

Satan does the same thing when tempting Yahusha in the wilderness. He asserts that if He's the Son of YHUH, He should turn the stones into bread. He knows precisely who Yahusha is. If He wasn't the Son of YHUH, the devil wouldn't have taken such fanatical interest in performing this elaborate scheme himself. He keenly monitored Yahusha in the wilderness for 40 days. When he felt Yahusha was at His weakest, he tempted Him. Remember, Yahusha was there to avail Himself to be tempted by the devil (Matthew 4:1). I suspect the devil and his entourage surveilled Yahusha while He was on Earth more than anyone else.

He tried to have Yahusha killed when He was a baby and throughout His entire life (Matthew 2:13-15; Luke 4:28-30; John 8:58-59). Yahusha's premature death would have circumvented YHUH's plan of salvation for us. YHUH ensured that Yahusha was protected until the allotted time of His crucifixion (remember the name alone, given to

Him by His Father, was a divine covering). Indeed, Satan would have witnessed the heavenly host boldly declaring the birth of Yahusha Ha'Mashiach. He would have certainly witnessed YHUH declaring that Yahusha was His Son immediately following His baptism. The demons knew who Yahusha was (Mark 1:23-26). Therefore Satan, their Chief Commander, most assuredly knew who Yahusha was and the important mission He was on. Hallelujah!

Dear friends, let's go back briefly and carefully observe how the father of lies deceived Eve. Through conversation and reasoning, he got her to become comfortable in his presence. He approached her and pretended to be her greatest advocate and friend. Even today, this is how he operates. When he casually engages us on the plane of congenial triviality, we let down our guard, becoming dangerously comfortable and extremely vulnerable. He presents himself as a strong alternative to YHUH, disguised as our friend, offering (deadly) solutions to our problems. He seductively suggests, through our thoughts, that YHUH expects too much from us. Because of our weakened state, due in part to the environmental conditions he himself has created, we wallow in self-pity and doubt. Satan's compelling, persuasive arguments cause us to feel like abandoned victims—hopeless and worthless failures, blowing in the harsh winds of circumstance.

We have all heard the saying, "Misery loves company." The devil is relentlessly looking for prey and insists on becoming our closest companion and dearest friend when we are awash in self-loathing and misery. However, it's all an elaborate scheme to ensnare and snatch us away from the love and protection of our Father. We are powerless against the wiles of the devil when we live a life of sin. Like a raging, pathetic drug fiend, we as sinners are strung-out on sin. Remember, Satan is the accuser of the brethren. He is cunning; he is wise. He is a thief and a vicious, diabolical murderer. *The thief comes only to steal and kill and destroy; I have come that they may have life, and have it to the full* (John 10:10 NIV).

Back to the story of Eve. Satan all but described YHUH as a liar and a dictator. Perhaps he came to Eve and tempted her because he saw a chink in her armour. Conceivably, he may have observed her contemplating what it meant to die, having heard YHUH say they would die if they ate from the "Tree of the Knowledge of Good and Evil." Clearly, she didn't know, and had no real appreciation for what death was. How could she? She had never seen anything die before.

The concept of death was alien to her. She was perfectly created and placed in a garden absent of chaos, suffering, disease, sickness, and death. The Garden of Eden was perfect. She was surrounded by pure love, which emanated pure life. In the same way that we cannot fully comprehend eternal life, or what living in total perfection is like, so too, was her lack of understanding of the consequences of sin. It's extremely sorrowful when we contemplate just how far we have fallen from YHUH's perfect love.

Eve may have wondered what it would be like to be less reliant on YHUH and be as gods (Genesis 3:5). Perhaps the devil saw her quickly glance at the tree from afar. Maybe she was standing in front of the tree and thinking about what YHUH had said to Adam concerning the tree and the consequences of eating its fruit. Whatever the circumstances, the devil presented himself as a wise serpent, willing to assist Eve in unravelling the great mystery occupying her thoughts.

We should be mindful, when we have doubt or question the plans YHUH has for our lives, we are inviting the devil to enter our hearts and minds (James 1:5–8; 2 Timothy 1:7). He presents himself as an angel of light (2 Corinthians 11:14), as a friend with our best interest at heart. Do not be deceived. Satan is a liar and a deceiver and a murderer (John 8:44–45).

Because of sin, we all have an appointment with death. However, this death is not permanent or final. For those who receive YHUH's gift of salvation, there is the reward of eternal life. For those who reject the gift of salvation, there will be a second death. *Marvel not at this: for the hour is coming, in the which all that are in the graves shall hear his voice, And shall come forth; they that have done good, unto the resurrection of life; and they that have done evil, unto the resurrection of damnation* (John 5:28–29).

And he said unto me, It is done. I am Alpha and Omega, the beginning and the end. I will give unto him that is athirst of the fountain of the water of life freely. He that overcometh shall inherit all things; and I will be his God, and he shall be my son. But the fearful, and unbelieving, and the abominable, and murderers, and whoremongers, and sorcerers, and idolaters, and all liars, shall have their part in the lake which burneth with fire and brimstone: which is the second death (Revelation 21:6–8).

YHUH is love (1 John 4:8). He knows everything (3:20; Psalm 139:4) and knew from the beginning that man would sin and fall short of His glory. *For all have sinned, and come short of the glory of God* (Romans 3:23). YHUH cannot change (Malachi 3:6); however, His mercy toward each of us is renewed daily (Lamentations 3:22–23). He sent His only Son (John 3:16) from Heaven to put on the sinful garment (flesh) of humanity and suffer and die for the sins of the world.

In your relationships with one another, have the same mindset as Christ Jesus: Who, being in very nature God, did not consider equality with God something to be used to his own advantage; rather, he made himself nothing by taking the very nature of a servant, being made in human likeness. And being found in appearance as a man, he humbled himself by becoming obedient to death — even death on a cross! (Philippians 2:5–8 NIV)

Through the death and resurrection of Yahusha Ha'Mashiach, we have free access to the gift of eternal life.

The story of redemption and the gift of salvation is contained throughout the New Testament. This is why the New Testament is referred to as the gospel. The word *gospel* comes from the Greek word ευαγγέλιο (evangélio) and means, "good news." The story of salvation is truly good news! YHUH's love, manifested through His gift of salvation to us, is the greatest love story of all. *For by grace are ye saved through faith; and that not of yourselves: it is the gift of God: Not of works, lest any man should boast* (Ephesians 2:8–9). *But because of his great love for us, God, who is rich in mercy, made us alive with Christ even when we were dead in transgressions — it is by grace you have been saved* (2:4–5 NIV).

Imagine the conversation between YHUH and Yahusha concerning the plan of salvation for humanity. In the conversation, the Father shares His deep disappointment regarding the fall of man. Although He knew what was going to transpire, it must have been deeply disappointing for YHUH to watch His perfect creation fall from righteousness. YHUH wouldn't have forcefully stopped humanity from sinning. He created us in His likeness, which means we have the freedom to choose. The devil knew if he could cause Adam and Eve to sin, it would greatly disappoint YHUH and, for all intents and purposes, humanity would be judged and condemned to death.

114

Nevertheless, the gift of salvation hadn't been comprehensively revealed to the heavenly host. Not even the angels fully understood it (1 Peter 1:10–12). When Adam sinned in the Garden of Eden, the devil thought he had won the battle against YHUH and humanity would be lost forever. When the plan of salvation was finally revealed, Satan realised he would have to once again deceive unfallen humanity. However, the only unfallen one was Yahusha, YHUH's Son. YHUH had to give Satan unfettered access to His Son to demonstrate He had free will and wasn't unfairly protected by YHUH. Yahusha was the unblemished Lamb. Only He could be the ransom for us.

And I saw a strong angel proclaiming with a loud voice, Who is worthy to open the book, and to loose the seals thereof? And no man in heaven, nor in earth, neither under the earth, was able to open the book, neither to look thereon. And I wept much, because no man was found worthy to open and to read the book, neither to look thereon. And one of the elders saith unto me, Weep not: behold, the Lion of the tribe of Judah, the Root of David, hath prevailed to open the book, and to loose the seven seals thereof. And I beheld, and, lo, in the midst of the throne and of the four beasts, and in the midst of the elders, stood a Lamb as it had been slain, having seven horns and seven eyes, which are the seven Spirits of God sent forth into all the earth. And he came and took the book out of the right hand of him that sat upon the throne. And when he had taken the book, the four beasts and four and twenty elders fell down before the Lamb, having every one of them harps, and golden vials full of odours, which are the prayers of saints. And they sung a new song, saying, Thou art worthy to take the book, and to open the seals thereof: for thou wast slain, and hast redeemed us to God by thy blood out of every kindred, and tongue, and people, and nation; And hast made us unto our God kings and priests and we shall reign on the earth (Revelation 5:2–10).

These were the stakes and both sides were playing for keeps. YHUH had the most to lose. He knew His Son was equipped to be the Saviour of the world. If Yahusha remained under YHUH's love and followed Him completely, all would be well. Satan would be defeated, and humanity would once again have access to the gift of eternal life.

Satan also knew if Yahusha sinned, YHUH would lose His Son to sin and humanity would be condemned to eternal death. Satan assumed that because YHUH sent His Son, clothed in the dirty rags of human fallibility, he would have a chance at capturing the Son of YHUH. What a prized possession that would have been.

Do not dare think for one moment that Satan didn't throw everything at Yahusha Ha'Mashiach when he tempted Him in the wilderness. Remember, both sides were playing for keeps and the stakes were high. So severe was the temptation, that when Satan finished tempting Yahusha in the wilderness, YHUH sent angels to minister to Him (Matthew 4:11). What's observed here is the devil testing the armour of Yahusha, tempting Him with what he's always used to tempt humanity:

- Planting feelings of entitlement and victimhood (if you are hungry, eat);
- Questioning YHUH's power, glory and love for us. In other words, to prove that YHUH is who He says He is and will do what He says He'll do, we should insist He perform signs and wonders (miracles) for our amusement. This mentality only erodes our faith and causes doubt to creep in, which ultimately separates us from the love of YHUH;
- Offering wealth and power in exchange for loyalty. If you worship me, I will give you the desires of your heart.

Yahusha didn't fall for any of Satan's deceptions, but instead, straightaway rebuked Him. *Then saith Jesus unto him, Get thee hence, Satan: for it is written, Thou shalt worship the Lord thy God, and him only shalt thou serve* (Matthew 4:10). We see keeping our rebuke short and simple is best (Jude 1:9). The entire plan of salvation was set with one goal in mind: to save a lost and perishing world (you and I) from eternal death and separation from YHUH.

YHUH's love knows no bounds. Sadly, we are happy, or at least unmolested, living in immorality because of our birth defect: sin. *Behold, I was shapen in iniquity; and in sin did my mother conceive me* (Psalm 51:5). While we were dabbling with and immersing ourselves in sin, totally ignorant of its consequences, YHUH was planning our escape.

At one time we too were foolish, disobedient, deceived and enslaved by all kinds of passions and pleasures. We lived in malice and envy, being hated and hating one another. But when the kindness and love of God our Savior appeared, he saved us, not because of righteous things we had done, but because of his mercy. He saved us through the washing of rebirth and renewal by the Holy Spirit, whom he poured out on us generously through Jesus Christ our Savior, so that, having been justified by his grace, we might become heirs having the hope of eternal life. This is a trustworthy saying. And I want you to stress these things, so that those who have trusted in God may be careful to devote themselves to doing what is good. These things are excellent and profitable for everyone (Titus 3:3–8 NIV).

Therefore, just as sin entered the world through one man, and death through sin, and in this way death came to all people, because all sinned — To be sure, sin was in the world before the law was given, but sin is not charged against anyone's account where there is no law. Nevertheless, death reigned from the time of Adam to the time of Moses, even over those who did not sin by breaking a command, as did Adam, who is a pattern of the one to come. But the gift is not like the trespass. For if the many died by the trespass of the one man, how much more did God's grace and the gift that came by the grace of the one man, Jesus Christ, overflow to the many! For if, by the trespass of the one man, death reigned through that one man, how much more will those who receive God's abundant provision of grace and of the gift of righteousness reign in life through the one man, Jesus Christ! Consequently, just as one trespass resulted in condemnation for all people, so also one righteous act resulted in justification and life for all people (Romans 5:12–15, 17-18 NIV).

The human race is constantly drawn to sin due to our sinful nature. As a result, we continually reject YHUH and His love for us. Nevertheless, YHUH overlooked all of this when He established His plan of salvation. *In this was manifested the love of God toward us, because that God sent his only begotten Son into the world, that we might live through him. Herein is love, not that we loved God, but that he loved us, and sent his Son to be the propitiation [atonement] for our sins* (1 John 4:9–10).

Imagine the love a doting father has for his only child. From as far back as the father can remember, his son, without even trying, captured his heart through his unwavering obedience, love, and respect for him. His intelligence, compassion, charisma, and overall disposition are equally worthy of high praise. The father is equally proud of his son's natural athletic abilities and striking academic prowess. In the father's eyes, his son is perfect and he will do anything to protect him and demonstrate his love for him.

One day, the son comes home and tells his father he was jumped and robbed by a street gang. Barely escaping with his life, he manages to get away and run home. The father is wrought with anger. Why would anyone want to do this to his son? He is filled with anguish about what could have happened. The thought of losing his only son, his perfect and precious boy, to unprovoked street violence moves the father to tears.

Years pass and the son grows up. Through hard work and commitment, he becomes a well-known, successful, criminal defence attorney. One day, he gets a call from someone in jail who's in desperate need of his legal services. When he gets to the jailhouse he sees, for the first time, the man who called for his assistance. He recognises him immediately. He was the ringleader of the gang that jumped him over a decade earlier. His first instinct is to rebuke the man sitting across from him and give him a piece of his mind—to remind him of what he did to him years earlier. He is certain the man has no idea who he is. This dude has been ripping and robbing for a very long time and has a trail of victims in his wake to prove it. The lawyer recognises that, decades earlier, he was just another faceless victim, simply prey for this criminal and his gang of hoodlums to pounce upon and brutalise. The lawyer feels like telling him he hopes the judge throws the book at him and gives him the maximum sentence allowed under the law.

However, his trained legal mind overrides his high emotions. He clears his throat and settles his mind. He asks the heavily restrained gentleman, under armed guard, to walk him through what happened. As the man begins to speak, the lawyer slowly recognises that this man is also a victim of domestic violence, a failed education system, drug addiction, poverty, discrimination, and the lack of opportunity. This criminal is a victim of the system, and the system is a victim of sin.

The lawyer realises this man is in desperate need of an advocate who can meticulously articulate his plight and vividly highlight the hellish circumstances that shaped him into the monster he is today. Although the man's crimes are inexcusable, it could be argued, they are justifiable. The *monster* before him is a felon the system, in large part, played an instrumental role in creating. The man sitting across from him, wearing the jailhouse jumpsuit and labelled a hardened criminal, was fed a rich diet of prejudice, injustice, violence, hate, and poverty. He was fashioned in an environment where survival by any means was not only encouraged, but necessary.

The system that is supposed to promote good governance, the rule of law, and equal opportunity for all is being run and controlled by individuals, governments, and corporations (agents of sin) who've cunningly commodified the misery of others. The entire system, even the parts that are supposed to assist "the least of these" and support a balanced environment to uphold order, fairness, and justice, while maintaining the rule of law, has been poisoned by narcissistic, sycophantic, sociopaths who hold vital, strategic roles within the system. These agents, and the government entities and private corporations they represent, are ultimately controlled by greed, power, world domination, and supremacy. The system, its handlers, and the agents are all being controlled *by* sin.

The lawyer decides to take the case. When he goes to court and represents his client, he shows the jurors the laundry list of circumstances where the system failed his client and others, living within the community and society at large. Although the law is bound to serve justice, it is compelled to exercise mercy. In closing arguments, the lawyer discloses that he, too, many years earlier, fell victim to his client. In order for justice to *truly* be served, he argues, it must be dispensed swiftly and impartially across the entire board. Hence, the environmental conditions that have allowed the system to thrive must also be placed before the bar and held to high scrutiny. All parties must pay the price and give a little sacrifice.

When the system fails, when the process is circumvented or manipulated, there are only losers. There are never any winners. You see, even the controlling participants, the agents of sin, will lose in the end. As the system continues to churn its wheels forward, eventually the protected and unreachable become unprotected and reachable. When it has devoured all the so-called unimportant and inconsequential individuals, it then turns its attention to its promoters and enablers with ferocious intent to devour them also. The system, poisoned by sin, sees mercy as weak, gratuitous, and even hazardous to its own survival. To consider *true* mercy would only distort and deconstruct the system. In the end, everyone is arrested, scarred, and traumatised by the failed system.

In a general sense, sin is the environment that creates the system of unfairness, upheld under the guise of justice. *And judgment is turned away backward, and justice standeth afar off: for truth is fallen in the street, and equity cannot enter* (Isaiah 59:14). The system of sin isn't really about justice but punishment (Romans 6:23). It's all about selecting winners from among losers (3:23). Sin is about injustice and oppression, not justice and liberty. *If you see the poor oppressed in a district, and justice and rights denied, do not be surprised at such things; for one official is eyed by a higher one, and over them both are others higher still* (Ecclesiastes 5:8 NIV). Sin is only concerned with accusation and punishment, never redemption and salvation. *No weapon that is formed against thee shall prosper; and every tongue that shall rise against thee in judgment thou shalt condemn. This is the heritage of the servants of the LORD, and their righteousness is of me, saith the LORD* (Isaiah 54:17).

Sin is guarded by narrow arguments and myopic reasoning. Thorough examination and truthful revelation begin to dismantle it. Sin doesn't hold itself accountable. It doesn't reveal the plot behind its elaborate and seemingly benign schemes. *Be not deceived; God is not mocked: for whatsoever a man soweth, that shall he also reap. For he that soweth to his flesh shall of the flesh reap corruption; but he that soweth to the Spirit shall of the Spirit reap life everlasting* (Galatians 6:7–8).

In the case of humanity before the bar in Heaven, Satan doesn't want a discussion about who he really is (John 8:44-45), nor does he want to discuss cause and effect. *And the great dragon was cast out, that old serpent, called the Devil, and Satan, which deceiveth the whole world: he was cast out into the earth, and his angels were cast out with him* (Revelation 12:9).

For if God spared not the angels that sinned, but cast them down to hell, and delivered them into chains of darkness, to be reserved unto judgment; And spared not the old world, but saved Noah the eighth person, a preacher of righteousness, bringing in the flood upon the world of the ungodly; And turning the cities of Sodom and Gomorrha into ashes condemned them with an overthrow, making them an ensample unto those that after should live ungodly; And delivered just Lot, vexed with the filthy conversation of the wicked: (For that righteous man dwelling among them, in seeing and hearing, vexed his righteous soul from day to day with their unlawful deeds;) The Lord knoweth how to deliver the godly out of temptations, and to reserve the unjust unto the day of judgment to be punished (2 Peter 2:4–9).

Yahusha comes before the judgment seat of YHUH and petitions on our behalf. *Who is he that condemneth? It is Christ that died, yea rather, that is risen again, who is even at the right hand of God, who also maketh intercession for us* (Romans 8:34).

Therefore, since we have a great high priest who has ascended into heaven, Jesus the Son of God, let us hold firmly to the faith we profess. For we do not have a high priest who is unable to empathize with our weaknesses, but we have one who has been tempted in every way, just as we are — yet he did not sin. Let us then approach God's throne of grace with confidence, so that we may receive mercy and find grace to help us in our time of need (Hebrews 4:14–16 NIV).

This is the same Yahusha who humanity unjustifiably killed. Satan is the prosecuting attorney, bringing accusations against Yahusha's redeemed before the heavenly court. *Who will bring any charge against those whom God has chosen? It is God who justifies* (Romans 8:33 NIV). Satan doesn't want the judge (YHUH) or jury (the saints) to consider the principal role sin has played.

Dare any of you, having a matter against another, go to law before the unjust, and not before the saints? Do ye not know that the saints shall judge the world? And if the world shall be judged by you, are ye unworthy to judge the smallest matters? Know ye not that we shall judge angels? how much more things that pertain to this life? If then ye have judgments of things pertaining to this life, set them to judge who are least esteemed in the church. I speak to your shame. Is it so, that there is not a wise man among you? no, not one that shall be able to judge between his brethren? (1 Corinthians 6:1–5)

Yahusha, in representing us, agrees there must be punishment, but the punishment must fit the crime.

For our offenses are many in your sight, and our sins testify against us. Our offenses are ever with us, and we acknowledge our iniquities: rebellion and treachery against the LORD, turning our backs on our God, inciting revolt and oppression, uttering lies our hearts have conceived. So justice is driven back, and righteousness stands at a distance; truth has stumbled in the streets, honesty cannot enter. Truth is nowhere to be found, and whoever shuns evil becomes a prey. The LORD looked and was displeased that there was no justice. He saw that there was no one, he was appalled that there was no one to intervene; so his own arm achieved salvation for him, and his own righteousness sustained him. He put on righteousness as his breastplate, and the helmet of salvation on his head; he put on the garments of vengeance and wrapped himself in zeal [Yahusha's name carries great zeal] as in a cloak. According to what they have done, so will he repay wrath to his enemies and retribution to his foes; he will repay the islands their due. From the west, people will fear the name of the LORD, and from the rising of the sun, they will revere his glory. For he will come like a pent-up flood that the breath of the LORD drives along. "The Redeemer will come to Zion, to those in Jacob who repent of their sins," declares the LORD (Isaiah 59:12–20 NIV).

Yahusha shed His blood for humanity. *For this is my blood of the new testament, which is shed for many for the remission of sins* (Matthew 26:28). This removes the punishment of death eternal but not the consequences of sin, which is physical death (Romans 6:23). The death that we must all die is not permanent (1 Thessalonians 4:13–18). It's not the end for those who are redeemed through Yahusha. We are all appointed to die once, but after that, there is a judgment. *For then must he often have suffered since the foundation of the world: but now once in the end of the world hath he appeared to put away sin by the sacrifice of himself. And as it is appointed unto men once to die but after this the judgment: So Christ was once offered to bear the sins of many; and unto them that look for him shall he appear the second time without sin unto salvation* (Hebrews 9:26–28).

Satan wants you to believe that because you are a sinner, you belong to him. He's a liar. *But God demonstrates his own love for us in this: While we were still sinners, Christ died for us* (Romans 5:8 NIV). ... *Ye are not your own. For ye are bought with a price: therefore glorify God in your body, and in your spirit, which are God's* (1 Corinthians 6:19-20). We belong to YHUH.

Be it known unto you all, and to all the people of Israel, that by the name of Jesus Christ of Nazareth, whom ye crucified, whom God raised from the dead, even by him doth this man stand here before you whole. This is the stone which was set at nought of you builders, which is become the head of the corner. Neither is there salvation in any other: for there is none other name under heaven given among men, whereby we must be saved. (Acts 4:10–12).

We have the gift of salvation through YHUH (Ephesians 2:8–9). Without a doubt, sin has created an imperfect existence for us. It interfered with YHUH's perfect plan for us, which was established before the foundation of the world. *For he chose us in him before the creation of the world to be holy and blameless in his sight. In love* (Ephesians 1:4 NIV).

Through YHUH's love, salvation is possible and available to *all* of us who, in faith, believe. The perfect governance and divine order by the true and living Elohim, the Master of the universe, is true and sure. *O LORD God of Israel, there is no God like thee in the heaven, nor in the earth; which keepest covenant, and shewest mercy unto thy servants, that walk before thee with all their hearts* (2 Chronicles 6:14). *Who is a God like you, who pardons sin and forgives the transgression of the remnant of his inheritance? You do not stay angry forever but delight to show mercy* (Micha 7:18 NIV).

If we entrust our lives to Elohim's care and allow Him to lead us, our lives will take on new meaning. We will begin to understand and truly experience the richness of life, which we receive through the indwelling of His Holy Spirit.

For if, by the trespass of the one man, death reigned through that one man, how much more will those who receive God's abundant provision of grace and of the gift of righteousness reign in life through the one man, Jesus Christ! Consequently, just as one trespass resulted in condemnation for all people, so also one righteous act resulted in justification and life for all people. For just as through the disobedience of the one man the many were made sinners, so also through the obedience of the one man the many will be made righteous. The law was brought in so that the trespass might increase. But where sin increased, grace increased all the more, so that, just as sin reigned in death, so also grace might reign through righteousness to bring eternal life through Jesus Christ our Lord (Romans 5:17-21 NIV).

For God so loved the world, that he gave his only begotten Son, that whosoever believeth in him should not perish, but have everlasting life (John 3:16). Allow Him to unreservedly take charge of your life (Romans 10:13). Wholeheartedly believe in the promises contained in His Word. *Your kingdom is an everlasting kingdom, and your dominion endures throughout all generations. [The LORD is faithful in all his words and kind in all his works.]* (Psalm 145:13 ESV).

By reading and listening to His Word, our belief and faith in Him will become strong, immoveable, and impenetrable (Romans 10:17). We will confidently defeat all doubt, intelligently defend the faith (Hebrews 11), which is anchored in His Word, and live a life that's pleasing to Him. *Study to shew thyself approved unto God, a workman that needeth not to be ashamed, rightly dividing the word of truth* (2 Timothy 2:15). Pursue wisdom, knowledge and understanding from Him (Proverbs 2:6; James 1:5). If we seek and follow after YHUH, He will prosper the plans for our lives (Deuteronomy 28, 30:19).

When you come to the knowledge of His love and discover the redeeming qualities His love extends, your life becomes illuminated and vibrant. *But God commendeth his love toward us, in that, while we were yet sinners, Christ died for us. Much more then, being now justified by his blood, we shall be saved from wrath through him. For if, when we were enemies, we were reconciled to God by the death of his Son, much more, being reconciled, we shall be saved by his life* (Romans 5:8–10). His love births hope in our lives! *Herein is love, not that we loved God, but that he loved us, and sent His Son to be the propitiation [atonement] for our sins* (1 John 4:10). *We love him, because he first loved us* (v.19).

> *Give thanks to the LORD, for he is good. His love endures forever. Give thanks to the God of gods. His love endures forever. Give thanks to the Lord of lords: His love endures forever. To him who alone does great wonders, His love endures forever. Who by his understanding made the heavens, His love endures forever. Who spread out the earth upon the waters, His love endures forever. Who made the great lights —His love endures forever. The sun to govern the day, His love endures forever. The moon and stars to govern the night; His love endures forever. To him who struck down the firstborn of Egypt, His love endures forever. And brought Israel out from among them His love endures forever. With a mighty hand and outstretched arm; His love endures forever. To him who divided the Red Sea asunder, His love endures forever. And brought Israel through the midst of it, His love endures forever. But swept Pharaoh and his army into the Red Sea; His love endures forever. To him who led his people through the wilderness; His love endures forever. To him who struck down great kings, His love endures forever. And killed mighty kings His love endures forever. Sihon king of the Amorites, His love endures forever. And Og king of Bashan His love endures forever. And gave their land as an inheritance, His love endures forever. An inheritance to his servant Israel. His love endures forever. He remembered us in our low estate, His love endures forever. And freed us from our enemies. His love endures forever. He gives food to every creature. His love endures forever. Give thanks to the God of heaven. His love endures forever* (Psalm 136 NIV).

Live and rejoice in the love of YHUH and bask in the rays of hope. For His love endures *forever.* Hallelujah!

Chapter 7
Living a Life of Purpose:
Our Gift to YHUH

Let us hear the conclusion of the whole matter: Fear God, and keep his commandments: for this is the whole duty of man. For God shall bring every work into judgment, with every secret thing, whether it be good, or whether it be evil (Ecclesiastes 12:13–14).

Have you ever wondered why it's so difficult to do the right thing? You know the risks associated with driving after having too much to drink. Yet, you take the chance. You know the potential consequences of engaging in reckless promiscuity. Nevertheless, you throw caution to the wind and engage in it. Imagine, there are entire television programmes dedicated to finding out who the fathers are of children born as a result of careless, promiscuous behaviour.

In 2020/21, as the world fought to survive the Coronavirus pandemic, according to the World Health Organisation (WHO), the National Institute of Allergy and Infectious Diseases (NIAID), and the National Health Service (NHS), wearing appropriate face masks, washing our hands often, wiping down public areas with disinfectant, practising social distancing and avoiding large gatherings was proven to be more effective in reducing the spread of the virus than even the vaccine and boosters. Yet, millions of people disregarded this advice and selfishly refused to follow these guidelines.

It was later discovered that many holding positions of significant influence and power within the upper echelons of the U.K. government flagrantly disregarded some of the very directives they had supported and championed. A good number of these mandates carried punitive damages, enforceable by law. The hypocritical behaviour that took place in the U.K. was exposed and publicly broadcasted across all major media news networks. In disgrace, members of the government's Cabinet resigned after it was revealed they hadn't socially distanced. Most shocking of all, some elected members hosted and attended private parties and social gatherings during the Christmas holidays. All this occurred while the government was compelling the rest of the country to remain indoors and isolate during this period. This fiasco was later termed "Partygate." So great was the debacle that it played a significant role in the Prime Minister later stepping down.

No matter what some conspiracy theorists suggest, it's a fact the virus is airborne and can be microscopically spread via bodily fluids. Yet millions continued to operate like normal and ignored simple recommendations. It is my opinion, based on personal observation, that selfishness and inconsideration contributed considerably to the spread of COVID-19.

A significant proportion of the prison population the world over is made up of individuals who engaged in larceny, bribery, fraud, and illegal gambling. Ponzi scheme organisers, money launderers, tax cheats, stock price manipulators, inside traders, and other white-collar criminals also occupy thousands of cells within the prison industrial complex. These offences, by and large, are classified as nonviolent crimes. I suspect more than half of these individuals had some idea of what the consequences would be if caught but, nevertheless, engaged in these crimes.

Perhaps the saddest and most disappointing to witness are the countless crimes being committed by persons who occupy positions of power, responsibility, and authority. Politicians taking bribes to enrich themselves or to secure another term, push to approve controversial projects or block the passage of much-needed legislation. Unfortunately, many of these decisions either damage the ecological environment or the lives of hundreds of thousands of people for generations, or both. How about judges taking bribes or being bent by powerful influencers to prejudicially rule? Thwarting justice, otherwise termed, "pimping out lady justice," is despicably egregious. Added to the list are ministers, priests, and leaders of religious movements engaging in affinity fraud, paedophilia, drug smuggling, and sex trafficking. Let's not forget medical doctors, who illegally write scripts for financial gain. In America and Europe, the abuse of prescription drugs has led to a serious health crisis, claiming the lives of tens of thousands annually.

We see across the world, but particularly in the United States, scores of police abusing their powers of search and arrest by regularly engaging in conduct unbecoming of law enforcement officers. The practice of racial profiling and the use of excessive force has led to the deaths of hundreds of people over the last decade. I could go on but I'm sure you get the point. Every one of these individuals in positions of power, responsibility, and authority knew what they were doing was wrong.

No doubt many tried to fight the temptation, but in the end, the urge to do wrong was stronger than the urge to do right. The Bible says in Matthew 26:41, *Watch and pray, that ye enter not into temptation: the spirit indeed is willing, but the flesh is weak.* Romans 7:18 says, *For I know that good itself does not dwell in me, that is, in my sinful nature. For I have the desire to do what is good, but I cannot carry it out* (NIV).

As stated previously, due to our sinful predisposition, we are inclined to sin. Only when we acknowledge our sinful ways (Romans 3:23; 1 John 1:9) and ask YHUH to give us the power to overcome (2 Thessalonians 3:3), will we succeed. *I have set the LORD always before me: because he is at my right hand, I shall not be moved* (Psalm 16:8). *But ye shall receive power, after that the Holy Ghost is come upon you: and ye shall be witnesses unto me both in Jerusalem, and in all Judaea, and in Samaria, and unto the uttermost part of the earth* (Acts 1:8). Only when, in faith, we believe He has heard our prayer and will deliver us (1 John 5:15), will we gain the victory over the temptation of sin. *Jesus answered and said unto them, Verily I say unto you, If ye have faith, and doubt not, ye shall not only do this which is done to the fig tree, but also if ye shall say unto this mountain, Be thou removed, and be thou cast into the sea; it shall be done. And all things, whatsoever ye shall ask in prayer, believing, ye shall receive* (Matthew 21:21–22).

When we trust and *know* that YHUH is the greatest and can never fail, His love will lead us to life eternal while providing supernatural covering. We will begin to live a life of true meaning and purpose. You may ask, "How do we live a life of purpose? How do we offer ourselves as a gift to YHUH?" For starters, we know we were never created to fail, to be defeated, to be weak and timid, to suffer and to die the death of eternal punishment and damnation. *And the LORD shall make thee the head, and not the tail; and thou shalt be above only, and thou shalt not be beneath; if that thou hearken unto the commandments of the LORD thy God, which I command thee this day, to observe and to do them* (Deuteronomy 28:13). Jeremiah 29:11 and Romans 8:37 assure us that we will overcome, no matter the obstacle, when we trust YHUH and allow Him to fight our battles. However, for this to happen, we need the Holy Spirit to dwell within us.

Remember, we *are* vessels. Vessels are made to hold and carry things.

> *But in a great house there are not only vessels of gold and of silver, but also of wood and of earth; and some to honour, and some to dishonour. If a man therefore purge himself from these, he shall be a vessel unto honour, sanctified, and meet for the master's use, and prepared unto every good work. Flee also youthful lusts: but follow righteousness, faith, charity, peace, with them that call on the Lord out of a pure heart.* (2 Timothy 2:20–22). *What? know ye not that your body is the temple of the Holy Ghost which is in you, which ye have of God, and ye are not your own? For ye are bought with a price: therefore glorify God in your body, and in your spirit, which are God's* (1 Corinthians 6:19–20).

We live a life of purpose by doing what we were created to do. As vessels, if we carry Elohim's Spirit, His purpose for our lives will become manifest. We decide what spirit to carry within us. We can carry strife, dishonesty, anger, fear, greed, self-loathing, hate, jealousy, selfishness, etc. By default, due to our sinful nature, we effortlessly carry many of these tainted attributes within us. It requires transformation by the Holy Spirit along with a contrite heart, diligent prayer, conscious effort, and consistent practice to purge our minds (our vessels) of these traits and replace them with a different set of qualities and behaviours. *But the fruit of the Spirit is love, joy, peace, forbearance, kindness, goodness, faithfulness, gentleness and self-control. Against such things there is no law* (Galatians 5:22–23 NIV).

Imagine the qualities we carry within us, as plants in our garden. All of these plants were just seeds when we were being formed in the womb. As infants, we learnt that whenever we cried, we received the attention of our parents or guardians. Therefore, in order to get what we wanted or needed, we insistently cried and that seeded characteristic

130

sprouted. As we got older, we realised if we threw a tantrum, we could get even more. So, we threw tantrums to get what we wanted, and those manipulative sprouts grew taller and stronger.

As we blossomed into teenagers, we saw that our parents could be easily swayed by our persistent misbehaviour. To persuade, we masterfully used the art of manipulation. Crying, temper tantrums, one-sided arguments, cheap psychological games, and other forms of persuasion are all methods of manipulation. Over time, we developed this behaviour and became exceptionally efficient and effective at it. This plant in our garden matured and flourished. By practising the art of manipulation, we watered and nurtured emotions and characteristics that ultimately formed part (branches) of this overall trait (plant).

Generally, people don't become superb liars, cheats, thieves, or worse, overnight. Our environment, circumstances, perceptions, emotional, and psychological proclivities all play a crucial role in our mental and social development. As we grow and mature, we observe how others get ahead and get what they want, even at the expense of doing what's right. I'm sure most of us have heard the saying, "Monkey see, monkey do." More accurately, the Bible says, *Train up a child in the way he should go: and when he is old, he will not depart from it* (Proverbs 22:6). We're influenced by what we see, but become what we practice. When we abuse someone's kindness and exploit their feelings, we become manipulators, attempting to bend their will to suit our desires. For a time, we feel untouchable, emotionally intelligent and supreme. However, the longer we engage in this practice, the more proficient and toxic we become.

It takes incredible fortitude, unyielding maturity, a generous measure of introspection and divine leading to endeavour to do what is right *all* of the time. Of course, because all mentally sound and stable individuals are born with seeds of goodness as well, we will, from time to time, do the right thing. We usually find doing good easy when it's to our advantage. *And if you do good to those who are good to you, what credit is that to you? Even sinners do that* (Luke 6:33 NIV).

The traits we use to guide our decisions and actions become the principal plants in our garden. If we practice the art of lying, eventually, we will become proficient fabricators, effortlessly spinning the tallest tales. Ultimately, we'll lie for absolutely no reason. Equally, if we rarely allow peace to fill our lives, we will find it difficult to lead a life of peace. Our "peace plant" will remain weak, delicate, and malnourished. We will blame everything and everyone for disrupting our peace instead of acknowledging that we, through the power of the Holy Spirit, are responsible for our state of mind. *Thou wilt keep him in perfect peace, whose mind is stayed on thee: because he trusteth in thee* (Isaiah 26:3).

When we feed and nurture the seeds and plantlets of love, joy, peace, forbearance, kindness, goodness, faithfulness, gentleness, and self-control, we will pay less attention to the mature plants of fear, misery, conflict, impatience, unkindness, wickedness, betrayal, brutality, and indiscipline. In time, our garden will transform from a patchwork of shambolic, overgrown, repulsive, achromatic, stubborn, poisonous weeds and thistles to a beautifully organised, cultivated, attractive, colourful, acquiescent, innocuous, diverse garden, showcasing stunning designs, protected by a strong and impenetrable bulwark.

As vessels carrying a beautifully balanced, organised garden of behavioural traits (which influence emotions that shape and guide decisions and actions), we showcase what we were primarily created for: worship.

> *Make a joyful noise unto the LORD, all ye lands. Serve the LORD with gladness: come before his presence with singing. Know ye that the LORD he is God: it is he that hath made us, and not we ourselves; we are his people, and the sheep of his pasture. Enter into his gates with thanksgiving, and into his courts with praise: be thankful unto him, and bless his name. For the LORD is good; his mercy is everlasting; and his truth endureth to all generations* (Psalm 100).

When we worship YHUH, we fight and overcome by the power of the Holy Spirit. When we worship, we're actively serving as warriors in the battle against evil (2 Chronicles 20:15–24). We enthusiastically worship our Creator and His Son when we are basking in the light of His glory. This light nourishes the fruit of the Holy Spirit within us. *But the hour cometh, and now is, when the true worshippers shall worship the Father in spirit and in truth: for the Father seeketh such to worship him. God is a Spirit: and they that worship him must worship him in spirit and in truth* (John 4:23–24). When we worship in spirit and in truth, we are cultivating and pruning our spiritual gardens.

Be aware, however, that true worship cannot come from a double-minded person. *But let him ask in faith, nothing wavering. For he that wavereth is like a wave of the sea driven with the wind and tossed. For let not that man think that he shall receive any thing of the Lord. A double minded man is unstable in all his ways* (James 1:6–8). Worship is so important that it ultimately caused war to break out in Heaven. *And war broke out in heaven: Michael and his angels fought with the dragon; and the dragon and his angels fought* (Revelation 12:7).

Satan wanted to be equal to YHUH so he, too, could receive worship. Can you imagine how potent the self-absorbed pride and inexplicable ego of Lucifer had to have been to think that he, the created, was worthy to be like the Creator and share in His worship? *How art thou fallen from heaven, O Lucifer, son of the morning! how art thou cut down to the ground, which didst weaken the nations! For thou hast said in thine heart, I will ascend into heaven, I will exalt my throne above the stars of God: I will sit also upon the mount of the congregation, in the sides of the north: I will ascend above the heights of the clouds; I will be like the most High* (Isaiah 14:12–14).

Total, undivided worship to YHUH cannot come from us when we are broken with fear and despair or plotting against one another. When we are double-minded, Satan is sharing in the worship intended for YHUH. It is, after all, Satan's influence over our lives that's causing us to feel overwhelmed and dispirited. Our dishevelled and depressed lives, being played out in real time, keeps our suffering in sharp relief. For as long as we focus on our dreadful predicaments, we keep the bane of our frustrations and pains at the forefront of our minds. Consequently, YHUH is placed in the background. We cannot worry and worship. We cannot complain and still be glad. *Be careful for nothing; but in every thing by prayer and supplication with thanksgiving let your requests be made known unto God* (Philippians 4:6).

Am I saying, when we are stressed and feeling down, we cannot worship? Not at all! What I *am* saying is genuine, complete worship isolates our souls and causes us to concentrate on YHUH alone. Unadulterated worship removes all distractions and clears our minds of all doubt and anxiety. It restores the mind and induces total reliance on YHUH. Worship encourages self-examination through the right lens and under perfect lighting conditions. It places everything into proper perspective. It's akin to defragmenting our computer's hard drive, removing viruses, erasing large unnecessary files, and emptying the cache. Worship is our perfect, factory reset program.

Here are a few Bible verses you may want to remember the next time you prepare to worship:

- *Sing unto the LORD, praise ye the LORD: for he hath delivered the soul of the poor from the hand of evildoers* (Jeremiah 20:13).

- *Wherefore we receiving a kingdom which cannot be moved, let us have grace, whereby we may serve God acceptably with reverence and godly fear: For our God is a consuming fire* (Hebrews 12:28-29).

- *And the Levites—Jeshua, Kadmiel, Bani, Hashabneiah, Sherebiah, Hodiah, Shebaniah and Pethahiah—said: "Stand up and praise the LORD your God, who is from everlasting to everlasting." "Blessed be your glorious name, and may it be exalted above all blessing and praise. You alone are the LORD. You made the heavens, even the highest heavens, and all their starry host, the earth and all that is on it, the seas and all that is in them. You give life to everything, and the multitudes of heaven worship you"* (Nehemiah 9:5-6 NIV).

- *Thou art worthy, O Lord, to receive glory and honour and power: for thou hast created all things, and for thy pleasure they are and were created* (Revelation 4:11).

- *The LORD reigns, let the nations tremble; he sits enthroned between the cherubim, let the earth shake. Great is the LORD in Zion; he is exalted over all the nations. Let them praise your great and awesome name—he is holy. The King is mighty, he loves justice—you have established equity; in Jacob you have done what is just and right. Exalt the LORD our God and worship at his footstool; he is holy. Moses and Aaron were among his priests, Samuel was among those who called on his name; they called on the LORD and he answered them. He spoke to them from the pillar of cloud; they kept his statutes and the decrees he gave them. LORD our God, you answered them; you were to Israel a forgiving God, though you punished their misdeeds. Exalt the LORD our God and worship at his holy mountain, for the LORD our God is holy* (Psalm 99 NIV).

We have *nothing* to worry about when we serve and worship YHUH. Unpretentiously, we must surrender all of our suffering and malice to Him in steadfast faith. We must believe that He will heal our broken hearts and set us (the captives) free from the bondage of sin. *The Spirit of the Sovereign LORD is on me, because the LORD has anointed me to proclaim good news to the poor. He has sent me to bind up the brokenhearted, to proclaim freedom for the captives and release from darkness for the prisoners* (Isaiah 61:1 NIV).

What causes fights and quarrels among you? Don't they come from your desires that battle within you? You desire but do not have, so you kill. You covet but you cannot get what you want, so you quarrel and fight. You do not have because you do not ask God. When you ask, you do not receive, because you ask with wrong motives, that you may spend what you get on your pleasures. You adulterous people, don't you know that friendship with the world means enmity against God? Therefore, anyone who chooses to be a friend of the world becomes an enemy of God. Or do you think Scripture says without reason that he jealously longs for the spirit he has caused to dwell in us? But he gives us more grace. That is why Scripture says: "God opposes the proud but shows favour to the humble." Submit yourselves, then, to God. Resist the devil, and he will flee from you. Come near to God and he will come near to you. Wash your hands, you sinners, and purify your hearts, you double-minded. Grieve, mourn and wail. Change your laughter to mourning and your joy to gloom. Humble yourselves before the Lord, and he will lift you up. Brothers and sisters, do not slander one another. Anyone who speaks against a brother or sister or judges them speaks against the law and judges it. When you judge the law, you are not keeping it, but sitting in judgment on it. There is only one Lawgiver and Judge, the one who is able to save and destroy. But you who are you to judge your neighbour? (James 4:1–12 NIV)

How can we give our full attention to worshipping YHUH when we are preoccupied with fear or plotting retribution against those who have wronged us? These are the fruit of darkness. The fruit from the garden of Satan. Fear and disappointment maim us. It directs our attention away from YHUH and instead places the focus on our immediate circumstances. We begin to live by sight and not by faith.

We become overwhelmed by seemingly insurmountable challenges and doubt the power of YHUH. We say, nothing is impossible with Him; yet, we fret and worry when we lose our jobs or don't have the money for an unexpected bill. The slightest unexpected challenge or disappointment robs us of our faith, and fear sets in.

Remember what happened to Peter when he was walking on the water to Yahusha and he took his eyes off of Him (Matthew 14:22–33)? *For God hath not given us the spirit of fear; but of power, and of love, and of a sound mind* (2 Timothy 1:7). *But the fearful, and unbelieving, and the abominable, and murderers, and whoremongers, and sorcerers, and idolaters, and all liars, shall have their part in the lake which burneth with fire and brimstone: which is the second death* (Revelation 21:8). Only the unbelieving fear.

When we worship YHUH, we create an attitude of gratitude within our hearts. We become confident, not timid, joyful, not remorseful or bitter. When we worship undistracted, we place YHUH at the *centre* of our worship and our lives. We assiduously consider and thoughtfully examine the many blessings that have occurred in our lives. We reflect upon His unmerited favour (grace) toward us. When we worship, the attitude of thankfulness creates sincere appreciation. Through indescribable joy and love springing up from within, it feels volitional, not contrived, to give YHUH unrestrained thanks and offer Him all the worship and all the high praise He so justly deserves. *The LORD is my light and my salvation; whom shall I fear? the LORD is the strength of my life; of whom shall I be afraid?* (Psalm 27:1).

Praise ye the LORD. Praise God in his sanctuary: praise him in the firmament of his power. Praise him for his mighty acts: praise him according to his excellent greatness. Praise him with the sound of the trumpet: praise him with the psaltery and harp. Praise him with the timbrel and dance: praise him with stringed instruments and organs. Praise him upon the loud cymbals: praise him upon the high sounding cymbals. Let every thing that hath breath praise the LORD. Praise ye the LORD (Psalm 150).

The fruit of the Holy Spirit flourishes in abundant showers of blessings, not rain contaminated by the acidity of hopelessness. In this environment, the spiritual Tree of Life, rooted in Yahusha and planted within us, blooms. The fruit of the Holy Spirit ripens and becomes savoury, nutritious food to our souls. As we praise and worship, the Master restores our spirits, speaks to our hearts and minds, and covers us with His love, mercy and grace. Hallelujah!

That he would grant you, according to the riches of his glory, to be strengthened with might by his Spirit in the inner man; That Christ may dwell in your hearts by faith; that ye, being rooted and grounded in love, may be able to comprehend with all saints what is the breadth, and length, and depth, and height; and to know the love of Christ, which passeth knowledge, that ye might be filled with all the fulness of God (Ephesians 3:16–19).

YHUH is the potter; we are the clay. He'll restore us to perfection through His grace, which is manifested through His love for us. We experience this transformation when we worship Him in spirit and in truth.

Make me to hear joy and gladness; that the bones which thou hast broken may rejoice. Hide thy face from my sins, and blot out all mine iniquities. Create in me a clean heart, O God; and renew a right spirit within me. Cast me not away from thy presence; and take not thy holy spirit from me. Restore unto me the joy of thy salvation; and uphold me with thy free spirit (Psalm 51:8–12).

The book of Psalms, written in part by King David, the second king of Israel, contains psalms that were to be performed as songs or poems dedicated to the worship of YHUH.

O come, let us sing unto the LORD: let us make a joyful noise to the rock of our salvation. Let us come before his presence with thanksgiving, and make a joyful noise unto him with psalms. For the LORD is a great God, and a great King above all gods. In his hand are the deep places of the earth: the strength of the hills is his also. The sea is his, and he made it: and his hands formed the dry land. O come, let us worship and bow down: let us kneel before the LORD our maker. For he is our God; and we are the people of his pasture, and the sheep of his hand. To day if ye will hear his voice, Harden not your heart, as in the provocation, and as in the day of temptation in the wilderness (95:1–8).

As vessels, we're also created for a life of service for YHUH's purpose. *But be sure to fear the LORD and serve him faithfully with all your heart; consider what great things he has done for you* (1 Samuel 12:24 NIV). *Each of you should use whatever gift you have received to serve others, as faithful stewards of God's grace in its various forms* (1 Peter 4:10 NIV).

We are more than servants when we faithfully follow YHUH all the way.

This is my commandment, That ye love one another, as I have loved you. Greater love hath no man than this, that a man lay down his life for his friends. Ye are my friends, if ye do whatsoever I command you. Henceforth I call you not servants; for the servant knoweth not what his lord doeth: but I have called you friends; for all things that I have heard of my Father I have made known unto you. Ye have not chosen me, but I have chosen you, and ordained you, that ye should go and bring forth fruit, and that your fruit should remain: that whatsoever ye shall ask of the Father in my name, he may give it you. These things I command you, that ye love one another (John 15:12–17).

When the Holy Spirit dwells within you, you'll experience a profound, personal change in your life. You'll exhibit new behaviours. *I beseech you therefore, brethren, by the mercies of God, that ye present your bodies a living sacrifice, holy, acceptable unto God, which is your reasonable service. And be not conformed to this world: but be ye transformed by the renewing of your mind, that ye may prove what is that good, and acceptable, and perfect, will of God* (Romans 12:1–2). You will become less agitated and anxious and more grateful. *But seek first his kingdom and his righteousness, and all these things will be given to you as well. Therefore do not worry about tomorrow, for tomorrow will worry about itself. Each day has enough trouble of its own* (Matthew 6:33–34 NIV).

You will experience new and unspeakable joy in your life. *That the trial of your faith, being much more precious than of gold that perisheth, though it be tried with fire, might be found unto praise and honour and glory at the appearing of Jesus Christ: Whom having not seen, ye love; in whom, though now ye see him not, yet believing, ye rejoice with joy unspeakable and full of glory: Receiving the end of your faith, even the salvation of your souls* (1 Peter 1:7–9).

Although you will go through trials and tribulations, your attitude will demonstrate that you know, in the end, you'll be victorious. *For whatsoever is born of God overcometh the world: and this is the victory that overcometh the world, even our faith* (1 John 5:4). Through the indwelling of the Holy Spirit, you will overcome every great temptation. *There hath no temptation taken you but such as is common to man: but God is faithful, who will not suffer you to be tempted above that ye are able; but will with the temptation also make a way to escape, that ye may be able to bear it* (1 Corinthians 10:13).

You will accept the hardships of life with a spirit of forbearance, understanding these are just challenges to strengthen and grow your faith in the Creator of the universe (Psalm 23:4; Proverbs 3:5–6). These trials will refine and purify the spirit within you.

Through whom we have gained access by faith into this grace in which we now stand. And we boast in the hope of the glory of God. Not only so, but we also glory in our sufferings, because we know that suffering produces perseverance; perseverance, character; and character, hope. And hope does not put us to shame, because God's love has been poured out into our hearts through the Holy Spirit, who has been given to us (Romans 5:2-5 NIV).

And it shall come to pass, that in all the land, saith the LORD, two parts therein shall be cut off and die; but the third shall be left therein. And I will bring the third part through the fire, and will refine them as silver is refined, and will try them as gold is tried: they shall call on my name, and I will hear them: I will say, It is my people: and they shall say, The LORD is my God (Zechariah 13:8–9).

Often, we live in the storm of life. However, YHUH can place you in the *eye* of the storm, where there is steadfast peace. Even though everything around is being violently tossed, twisted, and destroyed, you are assured that as long as you remain in the eye of the storm and abiding under His shadow (protection), all will be well (Psalm 91). *The Lord will rescue me from every evil attack and will bring me safely to his heavenly kingdom. To him be glory for ever and ever. Amen* (2 Timothy 4:18 NIV). *Beloved, think it not strange concerning the fiery trial which is to try you, as though some strange thing happened unto you: But rejoice, inasmuch as ye are partakers of Christ's sufferings; that, when his glory shall be revealed, ye may be glad also with exceeding joy* (1 Peter 4:12–13).

> *My brethren, count it all joy when ye fall into divers temptations; Knowing this, that the trying of your faith worketh patience. But let patience have her perfect work, that ye may be perfect and entire, wanting nothing. If any of you lack wisdom, let him ask of God, that giveth to all men liberally, and upbraideth not; and it shall be given him. But let him ask in faith, nothing wavering. For he that wavereth is like a wave of the sea driven with the wind and tossed. For let not that man think that he shall receive any thing of the Lord. A double minded man is unstable in all his ways* (James 1:2–8).

As you undergo this spiritual metamorphosis, the Holy Spirit will enrich your life. Those around you will see a difference in your attitude and in the way you conduct yourself. Your friends, family, and associates will want to know what has brought about this change. *Ye are of God, little children, and have overcome them: because greater is he that is in you, than he that is in the world* (1 John 4:4).

You are constantly presented with choices to do right or to do wrong. *I call heaven and earth to record this day against you, that I have set before you life and death, blessing and cursing: therefore choose life, that both thou and thy seed may live* (Deuteronomy 30:19). When you do the right thing, like tell the truth, be kind and generous, give a positive word to your friends and family, or help someone in need, you get a tremendous feeling of joy within your spirit. You are also walking in your purpose. *Is it not to deal thy bread to the hungry, and that thou bring the poor that are cast out to thy house? when thou seest the naked, that thou cover him; and that thou hide not thyself from thine own flesh?* (Isaiah 58:7). *And if thou draw out thy soul to the hungry, and satisfy the afflicted soul; then shall thy light rise in obscurity, and thy darkness be as the noon day* (v.10).

140

Then shall the King say unto them on his right hand, Come, ye blessed of my Father, inherit the kingdom prepared for you from the foundation of the world: For I was an hungred, and ye gave me meat: I was thirsty, and ye gave me drink: I was a stranger, and ye took me in: Naked, and ye clothed me: I was sick, and ye visited me: I was in prison, and ye came unto me. Then shall the righteous answer him, saying, Lord, when saw we thee an hungred, and fed thee? or thirsty, and gave thee drink? When saw we thee a stranger, and took thee in? or naked, and clothed thee? Or when saw we thee sick, or in prison, and came unto thee? And the King shall answer and say unto them, Verily I say unto you, Inasmuchas ye have done it unto one of the least of these my brethren, ye have done it unto me (Matthew 25:34–40).

On the other hand, when you choose to do wrong, you may experience guilt, anxiety, or deep disappointment. Maybe you become petrified at being found out and try to cover up what you have done. Often times, you have to lie and cheat to cover up the original wrong. It becomes a never-ending, burdensome cycle. Eventually, your deeds are exposed, and you feel embarrassed and remorseful. *For nothing is secret, that shall not be made manifest; neither any thing hid, that shall not be known and come abroad* (Luke 8:17). Feeling embarrassed, ashamed and afraid of facing the consequences that are sure to follow, many people choose to double down, resorting to desperate and unspeakable acts in an attempt to mitigate the fallout.

No amount of lying or evasiveness can conceal the truth forever or make a bad thing right. In the end, we all pay for our mistakes and misdeeds. Some call it karma. I prefer to call it consequences for our actions. *Be not deceived; God is not mocked: for whatsoever a man soweth, that shall he also reap* (Galatians 6:7); *Even as I have seen, they that plow iniquity, and sow wickedness, reap the same* (Job 4:8). We cannot dig our way out of a situation by lying and covering up.

Admitting our wrongs and facing the consequences is the only way to avoid the destructive, spiralling fallout. Only after we acknowledge the wrong committed and make restitution, starting by asking YHUH for forgiveness and surrendering the entire ordeal over to Him, will restoration begin. Most of us have never investigated the extent to which bad decisions bring about great suffering, mostly self-inflicted wounds. *This is the verdict: Light has come into the world, but people loved darkness instead of light because their deeds were evil. Everyone who does evil hates the light, and will not come into the light for fear that their deeds will be exposed. But whoever lives by the truth comes into the light, so that it may be seen plainly that what they have done has been done in the sight of God* (John 3:19–21 NIV). We fall prey to the deceptive lie that we can do as we please for as long as we like.

We also fall victim to the idea that our lives are inconsequential and have no connection or impact on the wider world around us. *Keeping mercy for thousands, forgiving iniquity and transgression and sin, and that will by no means clear the guilty; visiting the iniquity of the fathers upon the children, and upon the children's children, unto the third and to the fourth generation* (Exodus 34:7). It would behoove us to do the right thing.

Once we realise *what* we are created for (light bearers for YHUH), what our life's purpose is (worship, praise and glorify YHUH), and *how* best to carry out His plan for our lives (in faith, sharing the good news of salvation and being doers of the Word, while constantly trusting and believing), we will begin to live a life of unimaginable meaning, joy and peace. We will discover just how wrong we were for believing that our lives didn't matter, that we just randomly appeared on Earth to wander about aimlessly, living a life of insignificance. **YOU** matter a great deal to YHUH!

> *But even the very hairs of your head are all numbered. Fear not therefore: ye are of more value than many sparrows. Also I say unto you, Whosoever shall confess me before men, him shall the Son of man also confess before the angels of God* (Luke 12:7-8). *This people have I formed for myself; they shall shew forth my praise* (Isaiah 43:21). *For we are his workmanship, created in Christ Jesus unto good works, which God hath before ordained that we should walk in them* (Ephesians 2:10).

When we welcome Elohim into our lives, we become living vessels of light, illuminating in a world of darkness. *You are the light of the world. A town built on a hill cannot be hidden. Neither do people light a lamp and put it under a bowl. Instead they put it on its stand, and it gives light to everyone in the house. In the same way, let your light shine before others, that they may see your good deeds and glorify your Father in heaven* (Matthew 5:14–16 NIV). Yes, when we are restored by our Creator, we illuminate. *And God said, Let there be light: and there was light* (Genesis 1:3). *Then spake Jesus again unto them, saying, I am the light of the world: he that followeth me shall not walk in darkness, but shall have the light of life* (John 8:12).

The light of life will bring hope to those who are living in the darkness of mendacity and wickedness. It will restore all who have been broken by disappointment, tragedy, shame, and despair. The light from (the Holy Spirit) within provides the perfect environment for the fruit of the Holy Spirit to bloom and grow inside us. The Holy Spirit will strengthen us to overcome our iniquitous circumstances.

Let no man deceive you with vain words: for because of these things cometh the wrath of God upon the children of disobedience. Be not ye therefore partakers with them. For ye were sometimes darkness, but now are ye light in the Lord: walk as children of light: (For the fruit of the Spirit is in all goodness and righteousness and truth;) Proving what is acceptable unto the Lord. And have no fellowship with the unfruitful works of darkness, but rather reprove them. For it is a shame even to speak of those things which are done of them in secret (Ephesians 5:6–12).

The light of life that now dwells within will sanitise our vessels from the impurities of sin. Light and darkness cannot coexist. *You are not the same as those who don't believe. So don't join yourselves to them. Good and evil don't belong together. Light and darkness cannot share the same room* (2 Corinthians 6:14 ERV). Can we switch on our bedroom light at night and the room remain dark? *This then is the message which we have heard of him, and declare unto you, that God is light, and in him is no darkness at all* (1 John 1:5).

Contemplate this: YHUH is the powerplant. The Holy Spirit is the electricity. You are the lightbulb. The electricity is responsible for providing the energy needed to illuminate the filament at the core of the lightbulb. The electricity is generated by the powerplant. The bulb's filament, in this instance, represent our souls. The filament is designed to receive the electrical charge and immediately light up. That is its *only* purpose. Notice, we rarely consider the powerplant. We also never see the electricity. Instead, we see the effect of the electricity on the bulb, i.e., illumination. The powerplant generates the electricity that energises the bulb, causing illumination. The light extinguishes the darkness. As previously mentioned, darkness is simply the absence of light.

This is exactly how the Holy Spirit impacts us when we fully commit to YHUH and live the life He intended for us. *For this is what the Lord has commanded us: "'I have made you a light for the Gentiles, that you may bring salvation to the ends of the earth'"* (Acts 13:47 NIV). *For you were once darkness, but now you are light in the Lord. Live as children of light* (Ephesians 5:8 NIV). When we live according to His purpose, we present ourselves to Him as a most sacred gift (Romans 12:1–2).

When we are in Him and His Holy Spirit abides in us, we become ambassadors of the Heavenly Kingdom.

Therefore, from now on, we regard no one according to the flesh. Even though we have known Christ according to the flesh, yet now we know Him thus no longer. Therefore, if anyone is in Christ, he is a new creation; old things have passed away; behold, all things have become new. Now all things are of God, who has reconciled us to Himself through Jesus Christ, and has given us the ministry of reconciliation, that is, that God was in Christ reconciling the world to Himself, not imputing their trespasses to them, and has committed to us the word of reconciliation. Now then, we are ambassadors for Christ, as though God were pleading through us: we implore you on Christ's behalf, be reconciled to God. For He made Him who knew no sin to be sin for us, that we might become the righteousness of God in Him (2 Corinthians 5:16-21 NKJV).

As ambassadors, we are to be about YHUH's work, just as Yahusha Ha'Mashiach was. *Abide in me, and I in you. As the branch cannot bear fruit of itself, except it abide in the vine; no more can ye, except ye abide in me. I am the vine, ye are the branches: He that abideth in me, and I in him, the same bringeth forth much fruit: for without me ye can do nothing* (John 15:4–5). *But ye are a chosen generation, a royal priesthood, an holy nation, a peculiar people; that ye should shew forth the praises of him who hath called you out of darkness into his marvellous light* (1 Peter 2:9).

Every year Jesus' parents went to Jerusalem for the Festival of the Passover. When he was twelve years old, they went up to the festival, according to the custom. After the festival was over, while his parents were returning home, the boy Jesus stayed behind in Jerusalem, but they were unaware of it. Thinking he was in their company, they travelled on for a day. Then they began looking for him among their relatives and friends. When they did not find him, they went back to Jerusalem to look for him. After three days they found him in the temple courts, sitting among the teachers, listening to them and asking them questions. Everyone who heard him was amazed at his understanding and his answers. When his parents saw him, they were astonished. His mother said to him, "Son, why have you treated us like this? Your father and I have been anxiously searching for you." "Why were you searching for me?" he asked. "Didn't you know I had to be in my Father's house?" (Luke 2:41–49 NIV)

When living according to the fruit of the Holy Spirit, your life is centred around the love of Elohim. This is evident as you demonstrate patience, thoughtfulness, forgiveness, and care. For example, forgiving those who have wronged you is an example of the Holy Spirit living within you. Forgiving people is surprisingly easier when you perceive them as a vessel (a container). Just imagine how ridiculous it would be to animus a container carrying poison. Instead, focus your energy on the poison and methodically work to neutralise what's in the container and then dispose of it safely. You can then wash out the container and fill it with something else more pleasing and useful, like medicine or food.

Yahusha Ha'Mashiach, while hanging on the cross, asked His Father to forgive the people for the sin they were committing against Him. *Then said Jesus, Father, forgive them; for they know not what they do. And they parted his raiment, and cast lots* (Luke 23:34). Notice that Yahusha was asking YHUH to forgive the *human* participants because they didn't know what they were doing. Their ignorance granted them a reprieve. However, the demonic forces that were occupying their vessels and influencing their actions will never be forgiven. They knew precisely what they were doing. Satan and his forces will never be forgiven. However, the earthen vessels that were unsuspectedly used were forgiven. *Now when the centurion, and they that were with him, watching Jesus, saw the earthquake, and those things that were done, they feared greatly, saying, Truly this was the Son of God* (Matthew 27:54).

When people do us wrong, they are participating in the work of Satan. *For they sleep not, except they have done mischief; and their sleep is taken away, unless they cause some to fall. For they eat the bread of wickedness, and drink the wine of violence. But the path of the just is as the shining light, that shineth more and more unto the perfect day* (Proverbs 4:16–18). The Bible says that we should pray for people who are being used by the devil to do us wrong.

Ye have heard that it hath been said, Thou shalt love thy neighbour, and hate thine enemy. But I say unto you, Love your enemies, bless them that curse you, do good to them that hate you, and pray for them which despitefully use you, and persecute you; That ye may be the children of your Father which is in heaven: for he maketh his sun to rise on the evil and on the good, and sendeth rain on the just and on the unjust. For if ye love them which love you, what reward have ye? do not even the publicans the same? And if ye salute your brethren only, what do ye more than others? do not even the publicans so? Be ye therefore perfect, even as your Father which is in heaven is perfect (Matthew 5:43–48).

Now, friend, to be clear, this is not easily achieved, and without the Holy Spirit within us, it can be brutally difficult, if not altogether impossible. *A brother offended is harder to be won than a strong city: and their contentions are like the bars of a castle* (Proverbs 18:19). The Bible also warns that if we do not forgive, YHUH will not forgive us of our transgressions. *For if ye forgive men their trespasses, your heavenly Father will also forgive you: But if ye forgive not men their trespasses, neither will your Father forgive your trespasses* (Matthew 6:14–15).

Where the Holy Spirit abides, there is love. Where there's love, there's light and life everlasting. The spiritual Tree of Life, grounded in Yahusha, will abundantly feed your soul and cause you to experience a new life in Him. You'll be full of unspeakable joy for all that YHUH has done for you. Count your blessings, for they are many!

Practice peace and contentment. Why worry when we can pray?

We will be patient when we know and fully believe that YHUH works out everything for our good. Paul reminds us, *…All things work for good to them who love the Lord and are called according to his purpose* (Romans 8:28).

A life of peace, joy, forbearance, and gratefulness adjusts our frame of mind and allows us to see the condition of others. We move and act on their behalf, feeling compelled to address their needs in whatever way we can. Practising kindness opens opportunities to minister to the spiritual needs of others. We cannot be judgmental. If it wasn't for YHUH's saving grace, we would be in the same predicament.

Instead, we are to demonstrate empathy and exhibit gentleness and sensitivity to the needs of others. *But in your hearts revere Christ as Lord. Always be prepared to give an answer to everyone who asks you to give the reason for the hope that you have. But do this with gentleness and respect* (1 Peter 3:15 NIV). Because of our genuine concern and call to action, the minds of unbelievers will become more receptive to hearing and receiving the good news of salvation. We should refrain from preaching religious dogma or the principles of becoming a good member of particular denominations.

You are still worldly. For since there is jealousy and quarreling among you, are you not worldly? Are you not acting like mere humans? For when one says, "I follow Paul," and another, "I follow Apollos," are you not mere human beings? What, after all, is Apollos? And what is Paul? Only servants, through whom you came to believe—as the Lord has assigned to each his task. I planted the seed, Apollos watered it, but God has been making it grow. So neither the one who plants nor the one who waters is anything, but only God, who makes things grow. The one who plants and the one who waters have one purpose, and they will each be rewarded according to their own labor. For we are co-workers in God's service; you are God's field, God's building (1 Corinthians 3:3-9 NIV).

Our singular mission should be to introduce people to the Creator of the universe, the Redeemer of the world, through the Word of Truth. Remember, when Yahusha ministered to the people of His day, He fed the poor, healed the sick, and rid many of demons. He didn't preach before He did these things and when He did preach, He spoke mostly of YHUH and His character, not what it meant to be a good Jew. *Come to me, all you who are weary and burdened, and I will give you rest. Take my yoke upon you and learn from me, for I am gentle and humble in heart, and you will find rest for your souls. For my yoke is easy and my burden is light* (Matthew 11:28–30 NIV).

Self-control will be on display when the Holy Spirit dwells within you. When you place Elohim at the centre of your life, fully trusting Him and consecrating all to Him, the physical wants and desires of your heart become less alluring. The desire to be wealthy or to accumulate assets is no longer the focus and impetus for living. The energy exerted to acquire more than is necessary to provide food, clothing, shelter, and other necessities of life for you and your loved ones, shifts. Instead, your energy is redirected to improve the quality of life for others. *And thou shalt love the Lord thy God with all thy heart, and with all thy soul, and with all thy mind, and with all thy strength: this is the first commandment. And the second is like, namely this, Thou shalt love thy neighbour as thyself. There is none other commandment greater than these* (Mark 12:30-31). Need, not greed, is the new driving force. The need to share light with a world in utter darkness becomes your top priority. *For what shall it profit a man, if he shall gain the whole world, and lose his own soul? Or what shall a man give in exchange for his soul?* (8:36–37).

Receiving accolades and praise for doing the right thing will become increasingly uncomfortable to accept because it's Elohim and His Holy Spirit operating within you that's directing you. All the praise is due to Him! When the Holy Spirit is in control of your life, doing the right thing becomes especially appealing and rewarding. The more you practice it, the easier it becomes and over time, you will think twice before you lie, cheat, steal, hurt, or exploit others for any reason. When you repress your carnal desires and live thoughtfully, you will experience a new life that is rich and fulfilling.

Every good and perfect gift is from above, coming down from the Father of the heavenly lights, who does not change like shifting shadows. He chose to give us birth through the word of truth, that we might be a kind of first-fruits of all he created. My dear brothers and sisters, take note of this: Everyone should be quick to listen, slow to speak and slow to become angry, because human anger does not produce the righteousness that

God desires. Therefore, get rid of all moral filth and the evil that is so prevalent and humbly accept the word planted in you, which can save you. Do not merely listen to the word, and so deceive yourselves. Do what it says (James 1:17–22 NIV).

Sometimes we may feel nervous and unqualified to speak about YHUH or share the good news of salvation. Maybe we see ourselves as unworthy, because we know our own struggles intimately and feel hypocritical to speak to others about His love. Perhaps we don't have a theology degree, cannot recall Scripture verses well, or find public speaking intimidating. Whatever it is, it's an excuse planted by the father of lies to dim the lifesaving light within us. It's an accusation, deployed to lead us away from performing what we are created to do. We are the light of the world. We are to shine the light of truth throughout the world!

Being a redeemed sinner doesn't disqualify you from sharing the good news of salvation. Does suffering from former addictions disqualify you to speak on the subject of addiction? Truly, you are highly qualified to speak on this topic. We are all born in sin and shaped in iniquity. Which of Yahusha Ha'Mashiach's followers and disciples were without sin? Was Paul not a sinner? Which of the prophets and chosen men of YHUH were perfect? Abraham, Isaac, Jacob, Joseph, Moses, Samuel, Elijah, Isaiah, Jeremiah, Daniel ...all were sinners. King David and King Solomon were sinners. Yet YHUH used all of these people to speak of Him and His glory. *Do not offer any part of yourself to sin as an instrument of wickedness, but rather offer yourselves to God as those who have been brought from death to life; and offer every part of yourself to him as an instrument of righteousness* (Romans 6:13 NIV). YHUH used them all to bring light to a world in darkness.

And so, somehow, attaining to the resurrection from the dead. Not that I have already obtained all this, or have already arrived at my goal, but I press on to take hold of that for which Christ Jesus took hold of me. Brothers and sisters, I do not consider myself yet to have taken hold of it. But one thing I do: Forgetting what is behind and straining toward what is ahead, I press on toward the goal to win the prize for which God has called me heavenward in Christ Jesus (Philippians 3:11–14 NIV).

The Holy Spirit empowers us to live a more perfect life in accordance with Elohim's will for us. You and I *must* share the good news of salvation. This is a part of our purpose. Don't be reluctant. We are speaking in the name of Yahusha Ha'Mashiach, and we have been given power and authority to do so. *For we are to God the pleasing aroma of Christ among those who are being saved and those who are perishing. To the one we are an aroma that brings death; to the other, an aroma that brings life. And who is equal to such a task? Unlike so many, we do not peddle the word of God for profit. On the contrary, in Christ we speak before God with sincerity, as those sent from God* (2 Corinthians 2:15-17 NIV).

> *You know the message God sent to the people of Israel, announcing the good news of peace through Jesus Christ, who is Lord of all. You know what has happened throughout the province of Judea, beginning in Galilee after the baptism that John preached—how God anointed Jesus of Nazareth with the Holy Spirit and power, and how he went around doing good and healing all who were under the power of the devil, because God was with him. "We are witnesses of everything he did in the country of the Jews and in Jerusalem. They killed him by hanging him on a cross, but God raised him from the dead on the third day and caused him to be seen. He was not seen by all the people, but by witnesses whom God had already chosen— by us who ate and drank with him after he rose from the dead. He commanded us to preach to the people and to testify that he is the one whom God appointed as judge of the living and the dead. All the prophets testify about him that everyone who believes in him receives forgiveness of sins through his name."* (Acts 10:36-43 NIV)

When speaking of YHUH to others, you are not boasting in yourself. Rather, you are admitting you would be nothing without Him. You are broken but He has restored you.

I can assure you, I messed up my life in many ways. If it wasn't for YHUH's steadfast love, generous grace and unrelenting mercy, who knows where I would be today. He carried me when I couldn't go any further on my own. He used others to minister to me, to provide for me. I remember on numerous occasions receiving a word of encouragement or a Bible verse from someone who had no idea what I was going through. That word fed my spirit with great encouragement when I was utterly broken and washed up.

I am living proof that YHUH is real, that He loves us and is willing and able to save us. He saved me! If He can save me, there's nothing He cannot do for you. Hallelujah! YHUH's grace *is* sufficient for you and His strength *is* perfected in our weakness (2 Corinthians 12:9).

Moses, who led the Israelites out of Egyptian bondage, didn't feel like he was best suited for the job. He was quick to give YHUH excuses. He brought up the speech impediment he suffered from as a legitimate defence. Yet, YHUH chose him to lead His people out of Egypt to the Promised Land. *And the LORD said unto Moses, See, I have made thee a god to Pharaoh and Aaron thy brother shall be thy prophet* (Exodus 7:1).

Most of the people used by YHUH in Bible times were not highly educated. All of Yahusha's disciples were blue-collar workers. At least four of them were fishermen. Nevertheless, when you submit yourself to Him and allow His Holy Spirit to guide and direct you, He will inspire you to say and do what's necessary.

And ye shall be brought before governors and kings for my sake, for a testimony against them and the Gentiles. But when they deliver you up, take no thought how or what ye shall speak: for it shall be given you in that same hour what ye shall speak (Matthew 10:18–19). *And it [kings and rulers] shall turn to you for a testimony. Settle it therefore in your hearts, not to meditate before what ye shall answer: For I will give you a mouth and wisdom, which all your adversaries shall not be able to gainsay nor resist* (Luke 21:13–15).

When we live a life of purpose, YHUH *chooses* us as His ambassadors to make an impact in the world. We are also commanded to be our brothers' and sisters' keepers. *Brethren, if a man be overtaken in a fault, ye which are spiritual, restore such an one in the spirit of meekness; considering thyself, lest thou also be tempted. Bear ye one another's burdens, and so fulfil the law of Christ* (Galatians 6:1–2).

A life of purpose is a life of discipleship. We should be so overwhelmed with gratitude and joy after finding this new truth and living in the light, that we are ecstatic about sharing what we have discovered with others. We're to be kingdom workers, wanting our friends, families, co-workers, and even our enemies to be redeemed to life eternal. *The Lord is not slack concerning his promise, as some men count slackness; but is longsuffering to us-ward, not willing that any should perish, but that all should come to repentance* (2 Peter 3:9).

As mentioned earlier, a battle is raging in the spiritual world for our souls. Yahusha wants us to choose life and live with Him forever. *Let not your heart be troubled: ye believe in God, believe also in me. In my Father's house are many mansions: if it were not so, I would have told you. I go to prepare a place for you. And if I go and prepare a place for you, I will come again, and receive you unto myself; that where I am, there ye may be also. And whither I go ye know, and the way ye know* (John 14:1–4).

Living a life of purpose is our gift to YHUH. He, who provided the way of salvation through grace, wants us to serve as lights, carrying the Holy Spirit and sharing the good news of salvation with others. Our spiritual walk will create greater illumination in a world bombarded by darkness. *And we know that we are of God, and the whole world lieth in wickedness* (1 John 5:19). I am here today, living a more perfect life because someone thought it important to share this good news with me. I am now sharing this good news with you, because you, too, are worth saving and experiencing a life of purpose in the light and love of YHUH.

Now unto him [YHUH] that is able to do exceeding abundantly above all that we ask or think, according to the power [Holy Spirit] that worketh in us, unto him be glory in the church by Christ Jesus throughout all ages, world without end. Amen (Ephesians 3:20-21).

Chapter 8
Remaining Thankful

Wherein ye greatly rejoice, though now for a season, if need be, ye are in heaviness through manifold temptations: That the trial of your faith, being much more precious than of gold that perisheth, though it be tried with fire, might be found unto praise and honour and glory at the appearing of Jesus Christ: Whom having not seen, ye love; in whom, though now ye see him not, yet believing, ye rejoice with joy unspeakable and full of glory: Receiving the end of your faith, even the salvation of your souls (1 Peter 1:6–9).

It is easy to lose sight of the fact that we are exceedingly special to our Creator and He desires nothing more than for us to prosper and enjoy all the good things *He* has to offer. *Blessed is the man that walketh not in the counsel of the ungodly, nor standeth in the way of sinners, nor sitteth in the seat of the scornful. But his delight is in the law of the LORD; and in his law doth he meditate day and night. And he shall be like a tree planted by the rivers of water, that bringeth forth his fruit in his season; his leaf also shall not wither; and whatsoever he doeth shall prosper* (Psalm 1:1–3). We seldom remember that Elohim is always with us, protecting and delivering us.

God is our refuge and strength, a very present help in trouble. Therefore will not we fear, though the earth be removed, and though the mountains be carried into the midst of the sea; Though the waters thereof roar and be troubled, though the mountains shake with the swelling thereof. Selah. There is a river, the streams whereof shall make glad the city of God, the holy place of the tabernacles of the most High. God is in the midst of her; she shall not be moved: God shall help her, and that right early. The heathen raged, the kingdoms were moved: he uttered his voice, the earth melted. The LORD of hosts is with us; the God of Jacob is our refuge. Selah. Come, behold the works of the LORD, what desolations he hath made in the earth. He maketh wars to cease unto the end of the earth; he breaketh the bow, and cutteth the spear in sunder; he burneth the chariot in the fire. Be still, and know that I am God: I will be exalted among the heathen, I will be exalted in the earth. The LORD of hosts is with us; the God of Jacob is our refuge. Selah (46).

Life happens! It's a meandering journey of ups and downs, peaks and valleys. Profound loss, deep disappointment, nagging frustration, and absolute uncertainty are guaranteed. When life comes at us from all angles, we become anxious and overwhelmed. We attempt to fight and overcome on our own. We often feel alone and desperate, forgetting that Elohim is *always* with us. *Know ye not that your bodies are the members of Christ? shall I then take the members of Christ, and make them the members of an harlot? God forbid. What? know ye not that he which is joined to an harlot is one body? for two, saith he, shall be one flesh. But he that is joined unto the Lord is one spirit* (1 Corinthians 6:15–17).

If only we remembered that it's in the struggle that our faith is enlarged and strengthened (2 Corinthians 12:9), we wouldn't forget Elohim's promise to always be with us: to never leave us nor forsake us. *Teaching them to observe all things whatsoever I have commanded you: and, lo, I am with you always, even unto the end of the world. Amen* (Matthew 28:20). Unfortunately, there are those whose faith collapses under the pressures of life. They forget that He will send His angels to protect them, that no harm will come to them if they call on His name, trust in Him, and worship Him.

And call upon me in the day of trouble: I will deliver thee, and thou shalt glorify me (Psalm 50:15). *The angel of the LORD encampeth round about them that fear him, and delivereth them. O taste and see that the LORD is good: blessed is the man that trusteth in him. O fear the LORD, ye his saints: for there is no want to them that fear him* (34:7–9). *The LORD is my strength and my shield; my heart trusted in him, and I am helped: therefore my heart greatly rejoiceth; and with my song will I praise him* (28:7).

We should always remember that the name of YHUH's Son, Yahusha, whom He sent into this world so that we might be saved, means, "YHUH saves." *And she shall bring forth a son, and thou shalt call his name JESUS: for he shall save his people from their sins* (Matthew 1:21). Remember the name *JESUS* replaces the true name of YHUH's Son (Chapter two went into detail about this).

As a teenager, I studied martial arts and for several years was a student of Shotokan karate. I went to the dojo (practice hall) and spent thousands of hours throwing punches, kicks, blocks, and mastering fight combinations while also perfecting numerous stances. I spent countless hours practicing katas (elaborate, choreographed martial arts routines, depicting an imaginary fight). Endless hours were spent learning about the anatomy and physiology of the human body and working assiduously to perfect dozens of locks and grips. This made me very proficient in the art of self-defence. I became skilled at exploiting hundreds of pressure points to gain control over an opponent or aggressor.

There was a particular class my sensei (teacher) called, "A thousand hours." In this class, we would stand in a very low front (horse) stance or different fighting stances for hours, while throwing thousands of punches, kicks, blocks, and combinations. Sometimes, students would collapse from sheer exhaustion. Others would get severe muscle cramps during these feats of endurance. For those of us who survived, it gave us a sense of confidence and belief in our abilities to defend and protect ourselves and our loved ones.

These classes not only improved our physical stamina but also our mental toughness. It taught us that pain and fatigue should not impact our ability to think and act. The mind *must* control the body. We practiced and endured many other things to build our bodies and strengthen our minds. We were taught that every battle is first won or lost in the mind. If we can see it and believe it, we can achieve it.

We practised in the dojo because it was a safe, controlled environment. Our sensei would first demonstrate the manoeuvre or routine we were to learn. He would show us at normal application speed, then in slow motion, and finally, break it down step by step, explaining why each move was important.

Shotokan is an efficient form of martial arts that teaches *Ikken Hissatsu*, which means, "one blow, one kill." Sensei oversaw what we did and was quick to correct mistakes and quash mediocre performances. Sensei constantly reminded us that perfect execution wasn't an accident, so it was imperative to take training seriously. These fighting moves could be the deciding factor in a life-or-death situation.

Sensei kept a close watch on us and instructed us on every aspect of our training to ensure proper technique and safety. You see, in a controlled environment like the dojo, parameters for every routine or challenge are prearranged and maintained to ensure the highest safety and efficacy standards. For example, sensei would set the scenario of unarming an attacker with a knife or a gun. The attacker was not real, the weapons were not real, and so, the threat wasn't real. Nevertheless, the scenario created the necessary environment to proficiently learn the self-defence moves safely and effectively. We did these self-defence routines over and over and over. Even after perfecting the moves, the repetition never ceased.

At home, I continued practicing, in front of a mirror and outside, for hours. Eventually, I tried the moves out on my friends and siblings. Practice makes perfect but practice also makes permanent. Doing something repeatedly develops a behaviour. When new habits form, we no longer have to contemplate choices or plan out scenarios in our minds. Instead, we act without conscious thought.

I have not practised martial arts for over 30 years but I can still execute some of these moves today without a second thought. I can still count to ten in Japanese and I remember words and phrases in the traditional language of the art form. I can also attest that the discipline I received from practising martial arts helped me tremendously throughout my adolescent and early adult life. I still practice a few things today as a result of my former training. Additionally, Shotokan is partially responsible for my practicing a degree of circumspect. At crucial points in my life, I was able to successfully make the right choices, thanks to the discipline developed through Shotokan karate.

The same is true as it relates to having an attitude of thankfulness. It's particularly strenuous to practice thankfulness when the storms of life are pounding you. The practice must come *before* the trial so that you're prepared when faced with the real deal. Whenever worry and doubt interfere with your peace and joy, recite the promises of YHUH (Isaiah 54:17). Whenever you feel weak and diminished from the weight of the world, remember Elohim is with you to carry your burden. *In a desert land he found him, in a barren and howling waste. He shielded him and cared for him; he guarded him as the apple of his eye, like an eagle that stirs up its nest and hovers over its young, that spreads its wings to catch them and carries them aloft* (Deuteronomy 32:10-11 NIV). *For I the LORD thy God will hold thy right hand, saying unto thee, Fear not; I will help thee* (Isaiah 41:13).

Practice the punches of faith (*In whom we have boldness and access with confidence by the faith of him* [Ephesians 3:12]), the kicks of patience (*Rest in the LORD, and wait patiently for him: fret not thyself because of him who prospereth in his way, because of the man who bringeth wicked devices to pass. Cease from anger, and forsake wrath: fret not thyself in any wise to do evil. For evildoers shall be cut off: but those that wait upon the LORD, they shall inherit the earth* [Psalm 37:7–9]), the blocks of wisdom and the pressure points of knowledge (*And though the LORD give you the bread of adversity, and the water of affliction, yet shall not thy teachers be removed into a corner any more, but thine eyes shall see thy teachers: And thine ears shall hear a word behind thee, saying, This is the way, walk ye in it, when ye turn to the right hand, and when ye turn to the left* [Isaiah 30:20–21]), in the controlled environment of prayer and with the mindset of thankfulness (*Pray without ceasing. In everything give thanks: for this is the will of God in Christ Jesus concerning you* [1 Thessalonians 5:17–18]).

Have you ever watched martial artists perform group kata routines? Group kata is similar to a dance troupe performing complex, choreographed moves. It's amazing to watch them perform in perfect, synchronised fashion. The stances, punches, kicks, flips and blocks are all meticulously executed with impeccable timing. Everyone is moving with the same energy, same intensity and purpose. You're witnessing, but probably not fully appreciating, the results from hundreds of hours of training, countless mistakes made and corrected, sore muscles, blistered hands and feet, and lots of blood, sweat and tears.

Perhaps, if you observed that same kata being performed by a single practitioner, you'd probably not appreciate the complexity or beauty quite so much. You might even find it boring and unappealing. Small mistakes would be easily overlooked. In a group performance, however, everything, the good and the bad, is magnified and exposed for everyone to see. Individual mistakes within the group are recognised more easily as they are juxtaposed with the majority, who are perfectly executing the routine.

Like kata, so too is the amplification of the power of our faith when we practice together (fellowship). *Therefore encourage one another and build each other up, just as in fact you are doing* (1 Thessalonians 5:11 NIV). *And let us consider how we may spur one another on toward love and good deeds, not giving up meeting together, as some are in the habit of doing, but encouraging one another and all the more as you see the Day approaching* (Hebrews 10:24–25 NIV).

Besides learning from the sensei, students also benefit from one another. Fellow students share information in different ways, making it easier for peers to understand and relate. The same is true when working on our spiritual transformation in small, intimate group settings, like Bible study groups. *Iron sharpeneth iron; so a man sharpeneth the countenance of his friend* (Proverbs 27:17). *I appeal to you, brothers and sisters, in the name of our Lord Jesus Christ, that all of you agree with one another in what you say and that there be no divisions among you, but that you be perfectly united in mind and thought* (1 Corinthians 1:10 NIV).

Gradually, martial artists forge strong, fraternal, lifelong bonds. When students train together, trust and camaraderie develop naturally over time. The same can be said about the armed forces. Camaraderie among the rank and file is strong and, indeed, vital. So too are the bonds forged when we study the Word of Truth together and carry one another's burdens.

Let the peace of Christ rule in your hearts, since as members of one body you were called to peace. And be thankful. Let the message of Christ dwell among you richly as you teach and admonish one another with all wisdom through psalms, hymns, and songs from the Spirit, singing to God with gratitude in your hearts. And whatever you do, whether in word or deed, do it all in the name of the Lord Jesus, giving thanks to God the Father through him (Colossians 3:15-17 NIV). *Bear ye one another's burdens, and so fulfil the law of Christ* (Galatians 6:2).

As warriors in YHUH's army of truth, we should practice our faith constantly. Not only in the controlled environment of worship and prayer but also as we go about in the wider world. We should also zealously admonish and discourage lackadaisical behaviour among fellow believers. If necessary, we must separate ourselves from those who are compromising in their relationship with YHUH or fail to take the mission and, therefore, the threat, seriously. By remaining in the company of such individuals, while preparing for battle, we run the risk of being ill-prepared and sustaining severe and catastrophic casualties on the battlefield, even to the extent of losing our own souls.

Follow God's example, therefore, as dearly loved children and walk in the way of love, just as Christ loved us and gave himself up for us as a fragrant offering and sacrifice to God. But among you there must not be even a hint of sexual immorality, or of any kind of impurity, or of greed, because these are improper for God's holy people. Nor should there be obscenity, foolish talk or coarse joking, which are out of place, but rather thanksgiving. For of this you can be sure: No immoral, impure or greedy person—such a person is an idolater—has any inheritance in the kingdom of Christ and of God. Let no one deceive you with empty words, for because of such things God's wrath comes on those who are disobedient. Therefore do not be partners with them. For you were once darkness, but now you are light in the Lord. Live as children of light (for the fruit of the light consists in all goodness, righteousness and truth) and find out what pleases the Lord. Have nothing to do with the fruitless deeds of darkness, but rather expose them. It is shameful even to mention what the disobedient do in secret. But everything exposed by the light becomes visible—and everything that is illuminated becomes a light (Ephesians 5:1-13 NIV).

It is actually reported that there is sexual immorality among you, and of a kind that even pagans do not tolerate: A man is sleeping with his father's wife. And you are proud! Shouldn't you rather have gone into mourning and have put out of your fellowship the man who has been doing this? For my part, even though I am not physically present, I am with you in spirit. As one who is present with you in this way, I have already passed

159

judgment in the name of our Lord Jesus on the one who has been doing this. So when you are assembled and I am with you in spirit, and the power of our Lord Jesus is present, hand this man over to Satan for the destruction of the flesh, so that his spirit may be saved on the day of the Lord. Your boasting is not good. Don't you know that a little yeast leavens the whole batch of dough? Get rid of the old yeast, so that you may be a new unleavened batch—as you really are. For Christ, our Passover lamb, has been sacrificed (1 Corinthians 5:1-7 NIV).

Remember, the battle is raging and the fight is for our souls! *And fear not them which kill the body, but are not able to kill the soul: but rather fear him [YHUH] which is able to destroy both soul and body in hell* (Matthew 10:28). When practising Shotokan, students are often reminded that karate is a way of life, not just a sport. Likewise, if we continually practice our faith in Elohim, it will become more than just a goaded behaviour. It will become our *new* way of life. In turn, we will remain eternally thankful for all of the protection and strength it provides.

For the grace of God that bringeth salvation hath appeared to all men, Teaching us that, denying ungodliness and worldly lusts, we should live soberly, righteously, and godly, in this present world; Looking for that blessed hope, and the glorious appearing of the great God and our Saviour Jesus Christ; Who gave himself for us, that he might redeem us from all iniquity, and purify unto himself a peculiar people, zealous of good works (Titus 2:11–14).

As you put your faith into practice, over time, you will come to rely upon its strength and the power of YHUH to deliver you out of all your troubles. *Yes, and from ancient days I am he. No one can deliver out of my hand. When I act, who can reverse it* (Isaiah 43:13 NIV)? *My brethren, count it all joy when ye fall into divers temptations; Knowing this, that the trying of your faith worketh patience. But let patience have her perfect work, that ye may be perfect and entire, wanting nothing* (James 1:2–4). When you're going through turbulent times and realise your faith is being heavily tested, build it up by recalling stories from the Bible while simultaneously remembering the marvellous work

He has already done in your life. Do not surrender to the mayhem. Instead, cry out to Him for strength and deliverance.

You may recall the time you didn't have the money to keep the lights on or to buy groceries, but Elohim sent someone, a raven, to provide. You will shout for joy when you recollect the time you were very ill and didn't have the means to go to the doctor. Before going to bed, you prayed, asking Elohim to heal you and when you arose the next morning, Hallelujah, you were healed! No matter the situation or circumstances of your life, Elohim will see you through. His promises are guaranteed and He has never, ever failed. He sees what you are going through, and He knows your heart. His deliverance is always on time, and when His help arrives, you know it could've only come from Him.

I sought the LORD, and he heard me, and delivered me from all my fears (Psalm 34:4); *Then they cried unto the LORD in their trouble, and he delivered them out of their distresses* (107:6); *Remember ye not the former things, neither consider the things of old. Behold, I will do a new thing; now it shall spring forth; shall ye not know it? I will even make a way in the wilderness, and rivers in the desert* (Isaiah 43:18–19).

Recalling the many miracles and blessings *you* have experienced strengthens your faith. So does giving thanks at all times. The most difficult times in our lives challenge us, but also build us up in the Holy Spirit. *Rooted and built up in him, strengthened in the faith as you were taught, and overflowing with thankfulness* (Colossians 2:7 NIV). Remember, YHUH will never give us more than we can bear. *There hath no temptation taken you but such as is common to man: but God is faithful, who will not suffer you to be tempted above that ye are able; but will with the temptation also make a way to escape, that ye may be able to bear it* (1 Corinthians 10:13). He gives the greatest challenges to His greatest warriors. You're in a battle, so put on the whole armour of YHUH.

Put on the full armour of God, so that you can take your stand against the devil's schemes. For our struggle is not against flesh and blood, but against the rulers, against the authorities, against the powers of this dark world and against the spiritual forces of evil in the heavenly realms. Therefore put on the full armour of God, so that when the day of evil comes, you may be able to stand your ground, and after you have done everything, to stand. Stand firm then, with the belt of truth buckled around your waist, with the breastplate of righteousness in place, and with your feet fitted with the readiness that comes from the gospel of peace. In addition to all this, take up the shield of faith, with which you can extinguish all the flaming arrows of the evil one. Take the helmet of salvation and the sword of the Spirit, which is the word of God. And pray in the Spirit on all occasions with all kinds of prayers and requests. With this in mind, be alert and always keep on praying for all the Lord's people (Ephesians 6:11–18 NIV).

Regular civilians do not wear full-body armour or drive armoured vehicles. They don't go to work wearing bulletproof vests, military-grade helmets, or government-issued, assault rifles. Only persons engaged in warfare or serving on the frontlines of law enforcement, or elite private security contractors are required to dress and operate like this. However, as light-bearing, YHUH-worshipping vessels, we are instructed to put on the full *armour* of YHUH because we're engaged in spiritual warfare and operate in hostile environments.

Soldiers returning from combat to base are relieved when they and their comrades arrive back safely. Having witnessed death and carnage, a soldier has a heightened appreciation for life and the heavy cost of war. Maybe you have experienced similar circumstances. As light-bearing, YHUH-worshipping vessels, we too are extremely thankful and sing Hallelujah when we're victorious in spiritual warfare!

Perhaps you've sustained injuries that can only be described as wounds from the battlefield of life: fleeing from your war-torn country, health and financial struggles, loss of dear loved ones, destroyed relationships and reputation, drug and alcohol addiction. Yet you survived! Thankful to have been rescued from the heat of battle, fully restored by YHUH's mercy and grace. The cost was steep and defeat would have been certain had it not been for the protection and deliverance of Elohim. Having switched sides and now fully aware of who you are fighting, you battle with supernatural, military-grade armour and equipment. Still, there are times when you are shaken and severely tested. Sometimes the only way to test your armour and the attributes of your armour is through live battlefield experiences (theatre of war).

In the battle against the forces of evil, we sometimes encounter setbacks. I am sure many of us can attest to this. When we fight in YHUH's army and unveil redeeming, life-saving truth to the world, distresses are occasionally sustained. However, in the end, He will restore us. *Whom resist stedfast in the faith, knowing that the same afflictions are accomplished in your brethren that are in the world. But the God of all grace, who hath called us unto his eternal glory by Christ Jesus, after that ye have suffered a while, make you perfect, stablish, strengthen, settle you* (1 Peter 5:9-10).

He will not give us anything that will compromise our life's purpose, and He will certainly not withhold any good thing from us. But the devil will, if we bare ourselves to him. We must always strive to remain under the protective care of Elohim. Not every disappointment is a misfortune. Remember, *all* things work together for good, to those who love YHUH and are called according to His purpose (Romans 8:28). This is why sometimes, when we ask for certain things, He denies us. He wants our lights to fully shine for *His* kingdom while perfecting our faith. *Not only so, but we also glory in our sufferings, because we know that suffering produces perseverance; perseverance, character; and character, hope. And hope does not put us to shame, because God's love has been poured out into our hearts through the Holy Spirit, who has been given to us* (5:3-5 NIV).

The LORD will guide you always; he will satisfy your needs in a sun-scorched land and will strengthen your frame. You will be like a well-watered garden, like a spring whose waters never fail. Your people will rebuild the ancient ruins and will raise up the age-old foundations; you will be called Repairer of Broken Walls, Restorer of Streets with Dwellings. "If you keep your feet from breaking the Sabbath and from doing as you please on my holy day, if you call the Sabbath a delight and the LORD's holy day honourable, and if you honour it by not going your own way and not doing as you please or speaking idle words, then you will find your joy in the LORD, and I will cause you to ride in triumph on the heights of the land and to feast on the inheritance of your father Jacob." For the mouth of the LORD has spoken (Isaiah 58:11–14 NIV).

163

His everlasting love is reason enough to remain thankful. Even before challenges arise, thank YHUH for His protection and mercies, which are renewed daily (Lamentations 3:22–23). Give Him thanks for life, health, food, clothing, shelter, employment, family, friends, freedom, joy, peace, contentment, etc. Millions of people lose these blessings daily. Millions more don't know what it's like to live with basic freedoms that we enjoy and, frankly, take for granted. This acknowledgement and attitude of thankfulness bring us into a deeper worship communion with our Heavenly Father. Equally, we'll come to appreciate just how real the battle raging in the spiritual world is and how significant, and potentially permanent, the stakes are.

Transforming our bodies into living temples for the Holy Spirit to dwell within (1 Corinthians 6:19–20; Hebrews 3:6; 2 Timothy 1:14; 1 Peter 2:5) quickens us in our spirits to hold fast and fight the good fight for the Master.

For though we walk in the flesh, we do not war after the flesh: (For the weapons of our warfare are not carnal, but mighty through God to the pulling down of strongholds;) Casting down imaginations, and every high thing that exalteth itself against the knowledge of God, and bringing into captivity every thought to the obedience of Christ; And having in a readiness to revenge all disobedience, when your obedience is fulfilled (2 Corinthians 10:3–6).

Remaining thankful keeps us humble and neutralises our egos. Allowing our egos to become inflated and behaving arrogantly when considering the wonderful, supernatural transformation occurring in our lives does create the very serious risk of losing our relationship with YHUH. *Do not keep talking so proudly or let your mouth speak such arrogance, for the LORD is a God who knows, and by him deeds are weighed* (1 Samuel 2:3 NIV). We may be tempted to claim the victory over sin as our own, rather than acknowledge the Holy Spirit within us deserves *all* the credit, *all* the praise, and *all* the glory. *No man can come to me, except the Father which hath sent me draw him: and I will raise him up at the last day* (John 6:44). *When the Spirit of truth comes, he will guide you into all the truth, for he will not speak on his own authority, but whatever he hears he will speak, and he will declare to you the things that are to come. He will glorify me, for he will take what is mine and declare it to you* (16:13-14 ESV).

164

We should never forget, without YHUH, we are nothing. ... *'God opposes the proud but shows favour to the humble.' Submit yourselves, then, to God. Resist the devil, and he will flee from you* (James 4:6–7 NIV). Pride is of Satan.

How could we ever bring ourselves to salvation? After all, we are flesh and sinful. *For there is not a just man upon earth, that doeth good, and sinneth not* (Ecclesiastes 7:20). We cannot redeem ourselves. We should also note, we don't sin against one another. Many times, by committing sins we harm and hurt one another. Nevertheless, sin is simply the transgression against YHUH's divine law. Therefore, we sin *only* against YHUH, the Lawmaker. It's only He who can redeem us of our sins (1 John 1:9). Graciously, YHUH imputed our sins to Yahusha (2 Corinthians 5:21).

Some may question the validity of this claim by referring to Matthew 18:15-17 and similar Bible verses. These verses simply highlight how to reconcile with our fellow man after being aggrieved. When we have wronged someone, we should do everything in our power, starting with seeking forgiveness, to right the wrong. Sin isn't just a moral aberration; it's also a spiritual departure from what we know to be right. Each of us *knows* that it's wrong to commit murder, long before we ever read the penal code or familiarised ourselves with YHUH's commandments. Receiving forgiveness from an aggrieved party doesn't remove the *consequences* of our sins (Hebrews 9:27-28).

Because we sin only against YHUH and sin separates us from Him, and He is the life-giver (the way, the truth, and the life), death isn't *just* the penalty for sin. Death is the *result* of being separated from eternal life, which comes only from Him. Only YHUH could decide what the perfect atonement sacrifice would be for the remission of our sins (Isaiah 59:16; John 3:16).

Only the blood of the Lamb can change our collision course with eternal death (Revelation 12:10-11). Only the Lawmaker whom we have sinned against has the power to extend His grace (Romans 6:23) through the washing away of our sins.

But if we walk in the light, as he is in the light, we have fellowship with one another, and the blood of Jesus, his Son, purifies us from all sin (1 John 1:7 NIV). *Have mercy upon me, O God, according to thy lovingkindness: according unto the multitude of thy tender mercies blot out my transgressions. For*

165

I acknowledge my transgressions: and my sin is ever before me. Against thee, thee only, have I sinned, and done this evil in thy sight: that thou mightest be justified when thou speakest, and be clear when thou judgest (Psalm 51:1, 3–4).

Our habitual, carnal behaviour and strong proclivity toward sin, while also being hardwired to worship, will urge us to worship the wrong things. We need to constantly remind ourselves not to worship anything but the One who created us for His glory and, through righteousness, restores us. *I, John, am the one who heard and saw these things. And when I had heard and seen them, I fell down to worship at the feet of the angel who had been showing them to me. But he said to me, "Don't do that! I am a fellow servant with you and with your fellow prophets and with all who keep the words of this scroll. Worship God!"* (Revelation 22:8-9 NIV).

Remaining thankful maintains an attitude of peace. Counting our blessings and contemplating how far we have come, we worship YHUH. Rather than absorbing worship, we project worship. Instead of wanting to *be* worshipped, we long *to* worship. Once again, this attitude quells self-importance and brings into stark focus who YHUH is. *And be renewed in the spirit of your mind; And that ye put on the new man, which after God is created in righteousness and true holiness* (Ephesians 4:23–24). We must carefully avoid wanting to be worshipped and exclusively acknowledged for things we didn't do by ourselves.

If we're unable to keep our egos in check, we will begin to see very disturbing similarities between our behaviour and that of Lucifer just before he was expelled from Heaven. *Pride goeth before destruction, and an haughty spirit before a fall* (Proverbs 16:18). Just like the angelic host, we are created to worship. For this reason, we find ourselves constantly worshipping.

The question is, what or whom do we worship? Many people worship money, fame and power. Others worship their homes, cars, careers, children, spouses, celebrities, and royals. Some may, out of tremendous pride, worship themselves. Anything we worship, including ourselves, becomes the centre of our lives. It becomes our god. We must not fall into the deadly trap of worshipping anything other than the Creator of the universe.

We are not to worship images of dead saints, ancestors, animals, charms, beads, and jewellery that have been prayed over for our protection. These objects are not alive and do not possess any form of power, whatsoever.

"Of what value is an idol carved by a craftsman? Or an image that teaches lies? For the one who makes it trusts in his own creation; he makes idols that cannot speak. Woe to him who says to wood, 'Come to life!' Or to lifeless stone, 'Wake up!' Can it give guidance? It is covered with gold and silver; there is no breath in it." The LORD is in his holy temple; let all the earth be silent before him (Habakkuk 2:18-20 NIV).

Their idols are silver and gold, the work of men's hands. They have mouths, but they speak not: eyes have they, but they see not: They have ears, but they hear not: noses have they, but they smell not: They have hands, but they handle not: feet have they, but they walk not: neither speak they through their throat. They that make them are like unto them; so is every one that trusteth in them (Psalm 115:4-8).

Faithful believers must not mix this most profane practice with the sacred worship and holy communion we ought to have with YHUH. *Little children, keep yourselves from idols. Amen* (1 John 5:21).

The cup of blessing that we give thanks for is a sharing [communion] in the blood sacrifice of Christ, isn't it? And the bread that we break is a sharing [communion] in the body of Christ, isn't it? There is one loaf of bread, so we who are many are one body, because we all share in that one loaf. And think about what the people of Israel do. When they eat the sacrifices, they are united by sharing what was offered on the altar. So, am I saying that sacrifices to idols are the same as those Jewish sacrifices? No, because an idol is nothing, and the things offered to idols are worth nothing. But I am saying that when food is sacrificed to idols, it is an offering to demons, not to God. And I don't want you to share anything with demons. You cannot drink the cup of the Lord and then go drink a cup that honors demons. You cannot share a meal at the Lord's table and then go share a meal that honors demons. Doing that would make the Lord jealous. Do you really want to do that? Do you think we are stronger than he is? (1 Corinthians 10:16-22 ERV)

Coming to the knowledge of worshipping our Creator alone is so important that it was the first commandment YHUH gave to the children of Israel. *Thou shalt have no other gods before me* (Exodus 20:3). To avoid worshipping false gods and idols, we should seek a genuine, intimate relationship with YHUH and serve, worship, and praise Him only.

Money is perhaps the most worshipped idol. Having money is not a bad thing. On the other hand, loving money and becoming obsessed with money and money matters is horrific. *No one can serve two masters. Either you will hate the one and love the other, or you will be devoted to the one and despise the other. You cannot serve both God and money* (Matthew 6:24 NIV). If you ask YHUH to bless you with financial wealth, believing the only blessing in life is money and wealth, He becomes nothing more than your genie.

When you skip prayer, Bible study, fellowship with believers, or even quality time with the family to close a business deal, simply to earn superfluous money, you are placing money ahead of everything, including YHUH. When you sit quietly to protect your job while a co-worker is wrongfully accused and dismissed, you have chosen financial security over defending the truth. *If you falter in a time of trouble, how small is your strength! Rescue those being led away to death; hold back those staggering toward slaughter. If you say, "But we knew nothing about this," does not he who weighs the heart perceive it? Does not he who guards your life know it? Will he not repay everyone according to what they have done* (Proverbs 24:10-12 NIV)?

When you find excuses not to assist the less fortunate but instead, use your surplus money to build more wealth via greedy investment deals, you are making money your god. *And if thou draw out thy soul to the hungry, and satisfy the afflicted soul; then shall thy light rise in obscurity, and thy darkness be as the noon day* (Isaiah 58:10). *Lay not up for yourselves treasures upon earth, where moth and rust doth corrupt, and where thieves break through and steal: But lay up for yourselves treasures in heaven, where neither moth nor rust doth corrupt, and where thieves do not break through nor steal: For where your treasure is, there will your heart be also* (Matthew 6:19-21).

When you believe that without money nothing is possible, you are relying on money for your strength and protection, not YHUH. *Command those who are rich in this present world not to be arrogant nor to put their hope in wealth, which is so uncertain, but to put their hope in God, who richly provides us with everything for our enjoyment* (1 Timothy 6:17 NIV). When you operate in this manner, the love of money *does* become the root of *all* evil. *Love not the world, neither the things that are in the world. If any man love the world, the love of the Father is not in him. For all that is in the world, the lust of the flesh, and the lust of the eyes, and the pride of life, is not of the Father, but is of the world* (1 John 2:15-16). You will lie, cheat, steal, and exploit others for money. You will kill and destroy for money. These thoughts will prime your mind to sell your soul to the Prince of Darkness. *Blessed is the man that trusteth in the LORD, and whose hope the LORD is. For he shall be as a tree planted by the waters, and that spreadeth out her roots by the river, and shall not see when heat cometh, but her leaf shall be green; and shall not be careful in the year of drought, neither shall cease from yielding fruit* (Jeremiah 17:7–8). *Some trust in chariots, and some in horses: but we will remember the name of the LORD our God* (Psalm 20:7).

> *And having food and raiment [clothing] let us be therewith content. But they that will be rich fall into temptation and a snare, and into many foolish and hurtful lusts, which drown men in destruction and perdition [hell/eternal damnation]. For the love of money is the root of all evil: which while some coveted after, they have erred from the faith, and pierced themselves through with many sorrows. But thou, O man of God, flee these things; and follow after righteousness, godliness, faith, love, patience, meekness. Fight the good fight of faith, lay hold on eternal life, whereunto thou art also called, and hast professed a good profession before many witnesses* (1 Timothy 6:8–12).

If you want true success, follow this formula: *But seek ye first the kingdom of God, and his righteousness; and all these things shall be added unto you* (Matthew 6:33). Nothing on Earth deserves our worship. Nothing on Earth can cover us and protect us from the plans of the evil one. Nothing on Earth can restore us and save us.

When you remain under the shadow of the Almighty (Psalm 91:1), you remain thankful. When you decree and declare that no weapon formed against you shall prosper (Isaiah 54:17), you remain thankful. When you remember that YHUH declared He would make you the head and not the tail (Deuteronomy 28:13), you remain thankful. When you *know* He wants you to prosper (Jeremiah 29:11), you remain thankful. When you recall that, no matter where you are, even in Hell (Psalm 139:7–8), He will be with you, He will never leave you nor forsake you (Deuteronomy 31:6), you remain thankful. When you have tasted the goodness of YHUH (Psalm 34:8), you remain thankful.

When you know it's His mercy that allowed you to walk away from that near-fatal accident, you remain thankful. When you're able to leave that toxic relationship and experience peace and joy, you remain thankful. When you experience healing, whether miraculously or medically, you remain thankful. When your child is delivered from destructive behaviours and is now feasting on the Word of YHUH, you remain thankful. When, during financial turmoil, you are able to make the mortgage payments and put food on the table, you remain thankful.

When you cried out to Him to save you from your depression and deep despair, He found you and saved you! He placed you on a high hill (Isaiah 57:7). He prepared a table of enormous blessings in the presence of your enemies (Psalm 23:5). He has been with you, even, as you walk through the valley of the shadow of death (v.4). Who can do this? What power on Earth can do this? What god of stone, wood, iron, or clay can do this? What manmade structure on Earth could contain a god as powerful and majestic as the God of all creation (Acts 17:24–28)?

O give thanks unto the LORD; for he is good: because his mercy endureth for ever. Let Israel now say, that his mercy endureth for ever. Let the house of Aaron now say, that his mercy endureth for ever. Let them now that fear the LORD say, that his mercy endureth for ever. I called upon the LORD in distress: the LORD answered me, and set me in a large place. The LORD is on my side; I will not fear: what can man do unto me? The LORD taketh my part with them that help me: therefore shall I see my desire upon them that hate me. It is better to trust in the LORD than to put confidence in man. It is better to trust in the LORD than to put confidence in princes. All nations compassed me about: but in the name of the LORD will I destroy them. They compassed me about; yea, they compassed me about: but in the name of the LORD I will destroy them. They compassed me about like bees: they are quenched as the fire of thorns: for in the name of the LORD I will destroy them. Thou hast thrust sore at me that I might fall: but the LORD helped me. The LORD is my strength and song, and is become my salvation. The voice of rejoicing and salvation is in the tabernacles of the righteous: the right hand of the LORD doeth valiantly. The right hand of the LORD is exalted: the right hand of the LORD doeth valiantly. I shall not die, but live, and declare the works of the LORD. The LORD hath chastened me sore: but he hath not given me over unto death. Open to me the gates of righteousness: I will go into them, and I will praise the LORD: This gate of the LORD, into which the righteous shall enter. I will praise thee: for thou hast heard me, and art become my salvation. The stone which the builders refused is become the head stone of the corner. This is the LORD'S doing; it is marvellous in our eyes. This is the day which the LORD hath made; we will rejoice and be glad in it. Save now, I beseech thee, O LORD: O LORD, I beseech thee, send now prosperity. Blessed be he that cometh in the name of the LORD: we have blessed you out of the house of the LORD. God is the LORD, which hath shewed us light: bind the sacrifice with cords, even unto the horns of the altar. Thou art my God, and I will praise thee: thou art my God, I will exalt thee. O give thanks unto the LORD; for he is good: for his mercy endureth for ever (Psalm 118).

No matter the situation or circumstance, remain thankful! YHUH is the God of gods and Lord of lords (Deuteronomy 10:17). There is no God like Him!

There is none holy as the LORD: for there is none beside thee: neither is there any rock like our God (1 Samuel 2:2); *Forasmuch as there is none like unto thee, O LORD; thou art great, and thy name is great in might* (Jeremiah 10:6); *Which in his times he shall shew, who is the blessed and only Potentate, the King of kings, and Lord of lords; Who only hath immortality, dwelling in the light which no man can approach unto; whom no man hath seen, nor can see: to whom be honour and power everlasting. Amen* (1 Timothy 6:15–16).

Remaining thankful creates an insatiable hunger to want to learn more about our heavenly Father, the Most High God. *As newborn babes, desire the sincere milk of the word, that ye may grow thereby*

(1 Peter 2:2). You will want to investigate who He is by reading His Word, the Holy Bible.

Ask, and it shall be given you; seek, and ye shall find; knock, and it shall be opened unto you: For every one that asketh receiveth; and he that seeketh findeth; and to him that knocketh it shall be opened. Or what man is there of you, whom if his son ask bread, will he give him a stone? Or if he ask a fish, will he give him a serpent? If ye then, being evil, know how to give good gifts unto your children, how much more shall your Father which is in heaven give good things to them that ask him? (Matthew 7:7–11)

You will want to search for the answers to life's many questions. *If any of you lack wisdom, let him ask of God, that giveth to all men liberally, and upbraideth not; and it shall be given him. But let him ask in faith, nothing wavering. For he that wavereth is like a wave of the sea driven with the wind and tossed* (James 1:5–6). He doesn't want your blind obedience or sacrifice. He wants a personal, intimate relationship with you.

And it shall come to pass, that before they call, I will answer; and while they are yet speaking, I will hear (Isaiah 65:24); *Seek ye the LORD while he may be found, call ye upon him while he is near* (55:6). *The LORD hath appeared of old unto me, saying, Yea, I have loved thee with an everlasting love: therefore with lovingkindness have I drawn thee* (Jeremiah 31:3); *Call unto me, and I will answer thee, and show thee great and mighty things, which thou knowest not* (33:3). *The angel of the LORD encampeth round about them that fear him, and delivereth them. O taste and see that the LORD is good: blessed is the man that trusteth in him. O fear the LORD, ye his saints: for there is no want to them that fear him* (Psalm 34:7–9).

He wants to protect and care for you, and He wants you to get to know Him. Only when you seek after Him with all of your heart will you find Him. *But if from thence thou shalt seek the LORD thy God, thou shalt find him, if thou seek him with all thy heart and with all thy soul* (Deuteronomy 4:29).

To what purpose is the multitude of your sacrifices unto me? saith the LORD: I am full of the burnt offerings of rams, and the fat of fed beasts; and I delight not in the blood of bullocks, or of lambs, or of he goats. Bring no more vain oblations; incense is an abomination unto me; the new moons and sabbaths, the calling of assemblies, I cannot away with; it is iniquity, even the solemn meeting. Learn to do well; seek judgment, relieve the oppressed, judge the fatherless, plead for the widow. Come now, and let us reason together, saith the LORD: though your sins be as scarlet, they shall be as white as snow; though they be red like crimson, they shall be as wool. If ye be willing and obedient, ye shall eat the good of the land (Isaiah 1:11, 13, 17–19).

We're *all* His children, but unfortunately, not all of us want to build a personal and meaningful relationship with Him. Because He is merciful and His love covers an abundance of sins, He will not forsake us. *For God sent not his Son into the world to condemn the world; but that the world through him might be saved* (John 3:17). We *all* belong to Him. All nations and peoples of the world are His. Here are some passages of Scripture to support this point:

- *I saw in the night visions, and, behold, one like the Son of man came with the clouds of heaven, and came to the Ancient of days, and they brought him near before him. And there was given him dominion, and glory, and a kingdom, that all people, nations, and languages, should serve him: his dominion is an everlasting dominion, which shall not pass away, and his kingdom that which shall not be destroyed* (Daniel 7:13-14).
- *There is neither Jew nor Greek, there is neither bond nor free, there is neither male nor female: for ye are all one in Christ Jesus* (Galatians 3:28).
- *Simon Peter has told us how God showed his love for the non-Jewish people. For the first time, God accepted them and made them his people. The words of the prophets agree with this too: 'I will return after this. I will build David's house again. It has fallen down. I will build again the parts of his house that have been pulled down. I will make his house new. Then the rest of the world will look for the Lord God—all those of other nations who are my people too. The Lord said this. And he is the one who does all these things.' 'All this has*

been known from the beginning of time' (Acts 15:14-18 ERV).

- *And he said, It is a light thing that thou shouldest be my servant to raise up the tribes of Jacob, and to restore the preserved of Israel: I will also give thee for a light to the Gentiles, that thou mayest be my salvation unto the end of the earth* (Isaiah 49:6).

- *Also the sons of the stranger, that join themselves to the LORD, to serve him, and to love the name of the LORD, to be his servants, every one that keepeth the sabbath from polluting it, and taketh hold of my covenant; Even them will I bring to my holy mountain, and make them joyful in my house of prayer: their burnt offerings and their sacrifices shall be accepted upon mine altar; for mine house shall be called an house of prayer for all people. The Lord GOD, which gathereth the outcasts of Israel saith, Yet will I gather others to him, beside those that are gathered unto him* (56:6-8).

- *That the Gentiles should be fellowheirs, and of the same body, and partakers of his promise in Christ by the gospel: Whereof I was made a minister, according to the gift of the grace of God given unto me by the effectual working of his power. Unto me, who am less than the least of all saints, is this grace given, that I should preach among the Gentiles the unsearchable riches of Christ; And to make all men see what is the fellowship of the mystery, which from the beginning of the world hath been hid in God, who created all things by Jesus Christ* (Ephesians 3:6-9).

If you would like to experience a much richer life while walking in the light and covering of YHUH, search for Him (Jeremiah 29:13). *Draw nigh to God, and he will draw nigh to you. Cleanse your hands, ye sinners; and purify your hearts, ye double minded* (James 4:8).

He will light your dark path. *And I will bring the blind by a way that they knew not; I will lead them in paths that they have not known: I will make darkness light before them, and crooked things straight. These things will I do unto them, and not forsake them* (Isaiah 42:16). He will be your enduring, sustaining hand. *Cast thy burden upon the LORD, and he shall sustain thee: he shall never suffer the righteous to be moved* (Psalm 55:22).

Live in thankfulness today! Don't wait for the perfect moment to arrive before you begin your journey to discovering real joy and in *whom* to worship and praise. Don't wait for your life to become perfect. It never will. Don't wait until you become clean and sober, or until you stop lying, cheating, and stealing. He will transform your life and put you back together. You will come to Him broken and miserable, lost and confused, but you won't remain that way. *Restore unto me the joy of thy salvation; and uphold me with thy free spirit* (51:12). He is our Creator; He is our Restorer!

He will do a great work in you! *Being confident of this very thing, that he which hath begun a good work in you will perform it until the day of Jesus Christ* (Philippians 1:6). Remember, YHUH sent His Son, Yahusha Ha'Mashiach, into the world to save and restore the lost. *When Jesus heard it, he saith unto them, They that are whole have no need of the physician, but they that are sick: I came not to call the righteous, but sinners to repentance* (Mark 2:17). Don't wait for the perfect job to come along or the perfect soulmate to step into your life before discovering the *gift* of life and the love of YHUH. Don't wait until you move into your dream home before you seek Him.

You cannot sustain yourself, by yourself. You cannot save yourself from this life, and you certainly cannot save yourself from yourself. Until you give your life completely over to Him, your happiness and joy will be brief and fleeting. Only in the presence of YHUH can you remain thankful and joyful.

Make a joyful noise unto the LORD, all ye lands. Serve the LORD with gladness: come before his presence with singing. Know ye that the LORD he is God: it is he that hath made us, and not we ourselves; we are his people, and the sheep of his pasture. Enter into his gates with thanksgiving, and into his courts with praise: be thankful unto him, and bless his name. For the LORD is good; his mercy is everlasting; and his truth endureth to all generations (Psalm 100).

I AM THAT I AM, divinely inspired me to write this book, for **YOU***!* He desires You!

I have tried life in almost every way. I have done mostly all I have ever wanted to do. I have travelled a road and gone down paths many seldom come back from. I have the scars and stories to prove it. I have deliberately refrained from telling my story to avoid it from becoming a distraction while telling you about YHUH and His Son, Yahusha, who died on Calvary for you and for me. My story is for another time.

YHUH's light *is* power. His light *is* truth. Spiritual darkness *is* deceptive. The deceptions and illusions rooted in darkness have been spawned by the Prince of Darkness. I know what it is like to look in the face of evil, to feel the presence of darkness. I know what it's like to hear that still, small voice urging me to flee from the presence of iniquity. I have counted the cost and paid the price of rebellion and sinning against YHUH. I can assure you, *There is a way that seems right to a man, but its end is the way of death* (Proverbs 14:12 ESV). I encourage you to try Him, today. Follow Him, without delay, right now. *As God's co-workers we urge you not to receive God's grace in vain. For he says, "In the time of my favour I heard you, and in the day of salvation I helped you." I tell you, now is the time of God's favour, now is the day of salvation* (2 Corinthians 6:1–2 NIV).

> *I will lift up mine eyes unto the hills, from whence cometh my help. My help cometh from the LORD, which made heaven and earth. He will not suffer thy foot to be moved: he that keepeth thee will not slumber. Behold, he that keepeth Israel shall neither slumber nor sleep. The LORD is thy keeper: the LORD is thy shade upon thy right hand. The sun shall not smite thee by day, nor the moon by night. The LORD shall preserve thee from all evil: he shall preserve thy soul. The LORD shall preserve thy going out and thy coming in from this time forth, and even for evermore* (Psalm 121).

Remain thankful at all times is my most solemn wish and prayer for you. *As He says also in Hosea: I will call them My people, who were not My people, And her beloved, who was not beloved." "And it shall come to pass in the place where it was said to them, 'You are not My people,' There they shall be called sons of the living God"* (Romans 9:25-26 NKJV).

> *Behold what manner of love the Father has bestowed on us, that we should be called children of God! Therefore the world does not know us, because it did not know Him. Beloved, now we are children of God; and it has not yet been revealed what we shall be, but we know that when He is revealed, we shall be like Him, for we shall see Him as He is. And everyone who has this hope in Him purifies himself, just as He is pure* (1 John 3:1-3 NKJV).

May the indescribable peace and joy of YHUH fill you up abundantly as His love covers, restores, and illuminates your life!

About the Author

Jonathan Piercy is a Bible follower who loves God with all of his heart and works daily on his salvation with fear and trembling. He claims his redemption through the precious blood of the Lamb, the Son of God, Yahusha Ha'Mashiach (Jesus the Messiah).

Jonathan desires to share the good news of salvation with all who are willing to listen. He believes the gift of eternal life is just that–a gift from the Most High God to all humanity. It cannot be obtained through good and noble deeds.

Although born and raised in the beautiful Cayman Islands, he considers himself a citizen of the world and an ambassador for the Kingdom of God.

His background is in finance and banking. In the past, he stood as a candidate for political office in the Cayman Islands. Always passionate about the condition of his fellow men and women and deeply concerned about justice and fairness throughout the world, he's now on a different mission, seeing this new undertaking as a higher and more noble calling. Jonathan wants to be a light in this world and lead people out of the darkness of sin and into the marvellous light of truth through the inspiration of the Holy Spirit.

He can be contacted at jonathanpiercy.author@gmail.com.

Endnotes

Chapter One

i   Ethan Siegel, "Can Science Prove the Existence of God?" Forbes, January 20, 2017, https://www.forbes.com/sites/startswithabang/2017/01/20/can-science-prove-the-existence-of-god/#2f95fc295ada.

ii   Natalie Wolchover, "What Makes Pi Special?" Live Science, August 09, 2012, https://www.livescience.com/34132-what-makes-pi-special.html.

iii   Justin Kuepper, "Fibonacci and the Golden Ratio," Investopedia, November 3, 2020, https://www.investopedia.com/articles/technical/04/033104.asp.

iv   Carl Zimmer, "The Surprising Origins of Life's Complexity," Quanta magazine, July 16, 2013, https://www.quantamagazine.org/the-surprising-origins-of-lifes-complexity-20130716/.

v   "Letter 12041—Darwin, C. R. to Fordyce, John, 7 May 1879," University of Cambridge, Darwin Correspondence Project, Retrieved 24 January 2011.

Chapter Two

vi   "Meet The Man Responsible for the Letter 'J'," Dictionary.com, https://www.dictionary.com/e/j/#:~:text=It%20wasn't%20until%201524,distinction%20between%20the%20two%20sounds.

vii   "Why is LORD spelled with all capital letters in the Old Testament but never all caps in the New Testament?" Quora.com, https://www.quora.com/Why-is-LORD-spelled-with-all-capital-letters-in-the-Old-Testament-but-never-all-caps-in-the-New-Testament#:~:text=has%20been%20customary-The%20capitalized%20LORD%20in%20the%20Hebrew%20Bible%20is%20a%20silent,never%20to%20pronounce%20that%20word.

viii   Wayne Jackson, "LORD and Lord: What's the Difference?" Christian Courier, https://www.christiancourier.com/articles/305-lord-and-lord-whats-the-difference.

ix   "Yahshua," Wikipedia, February 2, 2021, https://en.wikipedia.org/wiki/Yahshua#:~:text=Yahshua%20is%20a%20proposed%20transliteration,)%20is%20salvation%20(Shua).

x   "YAHUSHA☐ How Is the Name of the Saviour Transliterated?" Cepher Publishing Group, https://www.cepher.net/how-is-the-name-of-the-savior-transliterated.aspx.

Chapter Three

xi "yin and yang," Def. #1, Dictionary.com, https://www.dictionary.com/browse/yin-and-yang.

Chapter Six

xii   "Love, Wikipedia, March 11, 2021, https://en.wikipedia.org/wiki/Love#:~:text=Ancient%20Greek%20philosophers%20identified%20five,and%20divine%20love%20(Agape).

www.ingramcontent.com/pod-product-compliance
Ingram Content Group UK Ltd.
Pitfield, Milton Keynes, MK11 3LW, UK
UKHW031915080525
458351UK00010B/233